The Roots of Modern Social Psychology
1872–1954

To the memory of my parents who, among many other
things, helped to ensure that I went to university

The Roots of Modern Social Psychology 1872–1954

Robert M. Farr

First published 1996
2 4 6 8 10 9 7 5 3 1

Blackwell Publishers Ltd
108 Cowley Road
Oxford OX4 1JF
UK

Blackwell Publishers Inc
238 Main Street
Cambridge, Massachusetts 02142,
USA

British Library Cataloguing in Publication Data

A CIP catalogue record for this book is available from the British Library.

Library of Congress Cataloging-in-Publication Data
Farr, Robert M.
The roots of modern social psychology, 1872–1954 /
Robert M. Farr
p. cm.
Includes bibliographical references and index.
ISBN 0–631–15251–2 (hc: alk. paper)—0–631–19447–9 (pbk.: alk. paper)
Social psychology – History.
HM251. F355 1996
302/ .09 20
95046084

Typeset in 10 on 12 pt Sabon by Pure Tech India Ltd, Pondicherry, India

This book is printed on acid-free paper

While the roots of social psychology lie in the intellectual soil of the whole Western tradition its present flowering is recognized to be characteristically an American phenomenon.

G. W. Allport, 'The historical background of modern social psychology'

The history of social psychology, as a critical examination of the past leading to a better understanding of the present, still remains to be written.

F. Samelson, 'History, origin myth and ideology'

Social psychology more than any other branch of science, with the possible exception of anthropology, requires a breadth of perspective that can only be achieved by a truly international community of scholars.

D. Cartwright, 'Contemporary social psychology in historical perspective'

Constructing a history of the human sciences is quite different from recapturing the history of the natural sciences, for consensus on basics is lacking both in the past and in the present.

D. Joravsky, *Russian Psychology*

Contents

Illustrations

Preface

This book comprises, apart from the final chapter which was published previously, a series of original essays. I need, first, to explain and, then, to justify why I have chosen this particular literary form as my principal mode of communication.

The Perspective Explained

The essay, as a literary genre, neatly captures the tentative and experimental nature of the task I have set myself. It is, however, an unusual mode of communication, at least within the community of *psychological* social psychologists to whom I belong in terms of disciplinary identity. Within that particular community, the reports of experiments still carry much greater prestige than essays. Just why this is so is part of the story. The essay, however, is a far more common form of scholarship among *sociological* social psychologists and this book is intended for them as well as for their more numerous psychological cousins. Goffman, for example, was an accomplished essayist. Indeed, it is part of my purpose in writing this book to explain how it came about that there are so many different forms of social psychology, many of which have developed within the context of social sciences other than psychology. The essay is also a perfectly acceptable form of scholarship among philosophers and historians. I dare to hope that some of the essays in the present collection will be of interest to such scholars, especially to philosophers and historians of science. I derive some comfort from the knowledge that I am not a literary pariah within my own community. Social psychologists of the eminence of Milgram (1977) and Brown (1965, 1986) were and are, respectively, highly accomplished essayists. I wish only that I could match their literary style.

The task I have set myself is tentative because, at present, no one, in my opinion, is in a position to write even a brief history of social psychology, never mind attempting to write the definitive history of the subject. I wish, instead, to identify the issues that anyone who sets out to write such a history will need to address. The considerations I raise are antecedent to the writing of a history of the discipline. I seek, merely, to draw up an agenda, rather than to provide definitive answers. An agenda is a list of things to be done and of decisions to be taken. I believe that the writing of history is both a collective and a collaborative enterprise. At present, there are just not enough people working in this field to generate the sort of infrastructure necessary for the writing of good history. This book is an open invitation to others to become directly involved in the development of this field of scholarship.

I have attempted, wherever possible, to be provocative. I believe that this is the best strategy, in the present circumstances, for making progress. I found it helpful, myself, that others had stated their ideas in the form of a thesis that could be tested. In chapter 6, for example, I make use of Manicas's thesis concerning the Americanization of the social sciences (Manicas, 1987). I seek to show how it might apply in the specific case of social psychology. In the same chapter, I consider the truthfulness of Graumann's provocative thesis that the individualization of the social is equivalent to the desocialization of the individual (Graumann, 1986). Particularly seminal, in my opinion, has been Danziger's thesis concerning the positivist repudiation of Wundt (Danziger, 1979). I have sought, in my concluding chapter, to apply this thesis, which concerns psychology in general, to the field of social psychology in particular. Certain other aspects of Danziger's thesis appear in chapters 1 and 8.

A set of essays also reflects, appropriately, the fragmented, yet diverse, nature of the field. I do not claim that my treatment of the topic is comprehensive. The work, necessarily, is incomplete. I am happy for others to correct my errors, to repair my omissions and to counteract the excesses of my interpretation by their critiques. The book is in no sense final. If it succeeds in provoking others to respond then it will have served its purpose. Any coherence it may have is due to the fact that all of the essays were written by the same author and at the same time. My point of entry into the historical process is 1954. My opening and concluding essays are concerned with what I call modern social psychology. The eight essays in between are arranged in rough chronological order of the events to which they relate.

Current State of the Literature

It would be premature, in my opinion, to write a history of social psychology. Good histories of psychology, however, are beginning to emerge (Ash, 1982; Boakes, 1984; O'Donnell, 1985). What is exciting, today, about the history of psychology is the increasing number of young historians, like Ash and O'Donnell, who are now writing about it. They are not so susceptible to the sources of error and bias that characterize 'internal' histories of the discipline. Histories, whether they are 'internal' or 'external', can now cover, quite legitimately, more than a century of the institutionalized practice of psychology. In the case of social psychology, however, the period is less than half a century. From an institutional perspective, the formative period for social psychology is the period immediately following the end of the Second World War. This is true both in America and in Europe.

We are still too close to the beginnings of modern social psychology to be able to set it in a proper historical perspective. It is appropriate, therefore, to be more tentative about the history of social psychology than we need be about the history of psychology in general. Cartwright noted, a decade and a half ago, that 'The entire history of social psychology as a field of empirical research extends over a period of only approximately eighty years. And since most of its growth has occurred within the past four decades, it is largely the product of scholars who are still active in the field' (Cartwright, 1979, p. 82). Now is a good time for collecting 'oral histories' of the discipline that may be of use to future historians. Indeed, quite a few such 'histories' have already appeared in print (Cohen, 1977; Cartwright, 1979; Evans, 1980; Festinger, 1980; Patnoe, 1988).

There are some excellent histories, now, of behaviourism (Boakes, 1984; O'Donnell, 1985) and many pseudo-histories of psychology as a cognitive science. Behaviourism is the form that positivism assumed in the historical development of psychology. Now that behaviourism is no longer the dominant paradigm it once was, at least in American psychology, it is much easier for the would-be historian to be 'objective' about its historical importance. It is, however, much more difficult to be objective if one is leading a crusade to establish a new paradigm like cognitive science. Once a field of study enters the positive phase of its development there is an assumption that progress will then be inevitable. New knowledge is prized more highly than old knowledge. This set of values undermines the work of the historian and affects his or her career if that should lie in academic departments of psychology. It is claimed that the historian is dealing with what is known already and that this is not research in any sense that a scientist would recognize, i.e. it is not producing anything new. Needless to say, this is not my view.

While behaviourism is no longer the driving force behind new developments in modern psychology, it is by no means a spent force. Indeed, one of my intentions in writing this book is to demonstrate how positivism, as a philosophy of science, continues to influence the historiography both of psychology and of social psychology. It is important, I believe, to recognize its residual role in this respect. Danziger (1979) was directly concerned with positivism as an important historical phenomenon in the development of experimental psychology. I am more directly concerned with it in relation to the development of social psychology. We are both interested, however, in positivism as a fertile source of error and bias in the writing of historical accounts. Its pernicious influence on the historiography of the discipline is spelled out in several of the essays that follow, most notably in chapters 1 and 10.

There would be no point in developing the groundwork for a history of social psychology if existing accounts were perfectly adequate. It is part of my task, in clearing the ground, to demonstrate the inadequacies of the currently available histories of the discipline. The classic account is Allport's chapter on the historical background of modern social psychology (Allport, 1954). It was written very much within the history of ideas tradition of historical scholarship. I shall demonstrate how the whole structure of that chapter, and not just the offending section in which he identifies Comte as the 'founding father' of social psychology, is informed by a positivist philosophy of science. When it was reprinted, with only minor amendments and additions, in the second edition of *The Handbook of Social Psychology* (Lindzey and Aronson, 1968–9), Allport was attacked by Samelson (1974) for creating a false origin myth for the discipline. I thought the article by Samelson was a cogent critique of Allport's history. I was dismayed, therefore, to find the Allport article appearing, for the third time, in the 1985 edition of *The Handbook of Social Psychology* (Lindzey and Aronson, 1985).

The publication of the 1985 *Handbook* was the immediate stimulus to my setting out to write the present book. Admittedly, the new edition of the *Handbook* contained an additional historical chapter. This was a chapter by Jones (1985) on 'Major developments in social psychology during the past five decades'. I develop my own critique of this chapter and discuss the nature of the relationship between it and Allport's *Handbook* chapter in my final chapter on 'The long past and the short history of social psychology'. If the Allport chapter is omitted from the next edition of the *Handbook*, then I shall not have written this book in vain!

Some Thoughts on the History and Philosophy of Science

In his book on *The Structure of Scientific Revolutions*, Kuhn (1962) stressed the importance, in the context of the history and philosophy of science, of both the temporal and the societal dimensions of scientific research. Within the history and philosophy of science community, his book helped to redress the balance in favour of the history of science. He also introduced an important sociological dimension into the study of science. His book is, itself, a seminal contribution to the sociology of knowledge. I hope, in the essays that follow, to make sociological forms of social psychology more salient within the history of social psychology than they otherwise would be if the history were to be written by a mere psychologist.

With regard to the history and philosophy of social psychology, I treat the former more extensively than I do the latter. Issues of a philosophical nature, I hope, are not entirely neglected. I devote a whole essay to the work of George Herbert Mead who was both a philosopher and a social psychologist. His philosophy of history (Mead, 1932) pervades several other essays and informs my whole approach to the history of science. A theme common to a number of the other essays concerns the influence of the philosophy of science on the historiography of science.

A related issue, of a philosophical nature, concerns the sort of science that psychology, legitimately, can claim to be. I consider the whole of psychology to be a social science and not just those parts of it currently labelled 'social psychology'. In chapter 2, for example, I discuss the controversy within the German academic community concerning whether psychology is a branch of the *Geisteswissenschaften* or of the *Naturwissenschaften*. I accept the opposition, in the history of Western thought, noted by Marková (1982), between the philosophies of Descartes and of Hegel. I think she is correct to refer to these rival systems of philosophy as paradigms. I hope to demonstrate how the Cartesian paradigm has been inimical, historically, to the development of social science, especially to the development of social psychology. A number of important traditions of social psychology, however, derive from the Hegelian paradigm. These tend to be European rather than American traditions of social psychology and, if they are American, then they tend to be sociological rather than psychological forms of social psychology.

Some Hopes for the Future

My principal hope is that social psychologists will become more historically conscious of the development of their discipline. It is argued that those who are ignorant of history are doomed to repeat its mistakes. This applies to science as well as to politics and to war. When I first set out, several years ago, to discover why Wundt chose to separate his experimental psychology from his social psychology, I thought I had before me a summer's reading. Tackling such an apparently discrete task, I thought, would be simple. It turned out, however, to be rather like opening Pandora's box. Things turn out to be rather different from your expectations. This applies as much to our knowledge of the past as it does to the future.

The main reason for critically examining the past is to understand the present better. I hope my readers will be able to understand modern social psychology better as a result of my critical examination of some of its roots. In my final chapter I give an account of how this might work. I hope also that it is possible to achieve a *rapprochement* between psychological and sociological forms of social psychology. I offer some suggestions of possible ways forward in this respect in chapter 7.

My point of entry into and exit from the historical process is 1954. One reason for this choice of date is that Allport (1954), in his article of that year, provides me with the title for my book. The date is almost a decade into the modern era in social psychology. This provides me with the second reason for my choice of date. I accept that modern social psychology began with the end of the Second World War. I do not accept, however, that there is a sharp divide between its history since then and its long past as a part of the whole Western tradition of thought. The sharp divide is a product of a positivist historiography. I prefer to finish my account from just inside the modern era, rather than teetering on its threshold.

Some of the key dates in the emergence of psychology as an experimental and social science can be found in appendix 1. This appendix is intended to be of general use to the reader throughout the book.

Acknowledgements

I have exchanged papers during the past 15 years with Kurt Danziger, whose seminal and pioneering work in the history of psychology I so very much admire. I have also enjoyed our conversations when international congresses and other events have provided us with a common platform. Over a longer period of time, I have discussed with Serge Moscovici a common interest in the discipline of social psychology. My attempt in what follows to describe the differences, in the modern era, between sociological and psychological forms of social psychology is a direct consequence of those discussions. I have learned from Ivana Marková that it is not possible to write about the history of a science without also discussing the philosophy of that science. I have found her distinction between Cartesian and Hegelian paradigms in psychology highly germane to an understanding of the individualistic nature of much so-called social psychology. I am indebted to Gustav Jahoda, who used to be a neighbour when we lived in Scotland, for drawing my attention to the importance of culture in the study of mind. The interface between psychology and anthropology, which was important historically, is now, once again, a lively topic of debate.

I am deeply indebted to Fiona Paton, the administrative secretary in the Department of Social Psychology at the School, for overseeing the electronic transformation of my manuscript and for liaising with my publishers in relation to such matters. Without her expert help the book would have taken even longer to produce. I appreciate the meticulous copy-editing of Sue Ashton, most of whose queries I was able to answer. I should like to thank Nathalie Manners of Blackwell for the crucial role she played in editing the book. A special word of thanks is due to Alison Mudditt, the commissioning editor at

Blackwell, for her patience and her continuing faith that, eventually, I would produce the manuscript.

In connection with the research reported in chapter 6 on 'The Individualization of Social Psychology in North America', I wish to acknowledge support from the Economic and Social Research Council of the UK (Research grant R000234766 on 'Individualism in a Period of Rapid Political and Economic Change'). I also wish to acknowledge, over the years, support from the Laboratoire de Psychologie Sociale of the Maison des Sciences de l'Homme in Paris and of the Werner Reimer Stiftung in Bad Homburg, Germany. Many of the ideas reported here first took shape in one or other of these two highly congenial settings.

1

Modern Social Psychology: a Characteristically American Phenomenon

The Flower and its Roots

'While the roots of social psychology lie in the intellectual soil of the whole Western tradition its present flowering is recognized to be characteristically an American phenomenon.' This is how Gordon Allport (1954, pp. 3–4) introduced the discipline to a new generation of graduate students in America at the start of what I call, here, the modern era in social psychology. This era began at the end of the Second World War.

Interdisciplinary collaboration during the war

The Second World War provided the sort of boost to the development of social psychology that the First World War had provided for psychometric testing. Social scientists collaborated in conducting social surveys on the adjustment of soldiers to life in the army (Stouffer, Suchman et al., 1949), and their participation in combat and its aftermath (Stouffer, Lumsdaine et al., 1949); in assessing the efficacy of different ways of briefing military personnel (Hovland et al., 1949); and in solving technical problems relating to the measurement of attitudes and the prediction of behaviour (Stouffer et al., 1950). These were the subjects of *The American Soldier* series of volumes published, after the war, under the general editorship of the sociologist, Stouffer.

This wartime programme of collaborative research was important for a number of reasons. It will suffice, here, to mention two. It provided a model for the development of interdisciplinary doctoral programmes in social psychology in the period following the end of the war. These were usually joint programmes between psychology and sociology, though they sometimes also involved anthropology. Interdisciplinary programmes were established at Harvard, Yale and Michigan. At a later stage, an interdisciplinary programme in social psychology was established at Columbia. None of these joint programmes exists today. They all eventually fractured along disciplinary lines (Jackson, 1988; Collier et al., 1991). This in itself is very revealing about the development of social psychology in the modern era. Why this occurred can best be understood in terms of developments that began in the period between the two world wars. This is a theme that is taken up and developed in chapter 6, on the individualization of social psychology in America, and in chapter 7, on sociological and psychological forms of social psychology.

The other reason for the importance of *The American Soldier* series of volumes is that some of the wartime research teams continued their collaboration well beyond the end of the war. The most important of these teams was the one under the direction of Hovland (who had edited volume 3 of *The American Soldier* series) which formed the nucleus of the postwar programme of research at Yale on communication and attitude change. This resulted in a further series of volumes which are important in the history of experimental social psychology in America in the modern era. This wartime collaboration was concerned with the experimental study of mass communication. The continuity between this and the postwar programme of research at Yale is provided by a common model of the mass media of communication and of the effects of those media, together with the adoption of the experiment as the preferred strategy for research. Also, a high degree of control is possible over both the form and the content of communication both during wartime and in a laboratory context. The other volumes in the series, those edited by Stouffer, were concerned with social surveys and the measurement of attitudes.

The postwar generation of graduate students in social psychology

In social psychology, as in a number of other academic disciplines, the immediate postwar generation of graduate students was particularly talented. This was especially true of that cohort of doctoral students whom Lewin attracted to the Massachusetts Institute of Technology (MIT) where he had established the Research Center for Group Dynamics in 1945. Much has been written already about that particular cohort of graduate students in social psychology, either by others who interviewed them (e.g. Patnoe, 1988) or by themselves by way of retrospection (Festinger, 1980). They helped to establish social psychology, in the course of the modern era, as distinctively an American phenomenon. Their role was vital to the development of a cognitive social psychology. They reflected the influence, in America, of Gestalt psychology. The roots here were European, though the flower was characteristically American.

The older generation of academics in Europe and America, who have now retired from university life, often recall, nostalgically, the cohort of students (both undergraduate and graduate) who enrolled in universities immediately following the end of the war. They were mature students, and there was frequently little to separate them, in terms of age and qualifications, from the faculty who taught them. Often, particularly in America, they had interrupted their studies and their university careers for the duration of the war. The interruption was less severe in America than it was in Europe where the consequences of the war were much more devastating. In the social sciences, more generally, this postwar generation of students was important. Dahrendorf (1995) identifies this as one of the great periods in the history of the London School of Economics and Political Science.

We have an interesting snapshot of this particular generation of engineering student at MIT. It is provided by Festinger et al. (1950) in their classic study *Social Pressures in Informal Groups: a study of human factors in housing*. Here we have the social scientists at MIT studying the engineers. They show how the informal networks of friends on a housing estate develop as a function of the physical layout of the estate. They are careful to point out, however, that their findings may be specific to that particular generation of mature students. They were, in the main, ex-GIs with young families, all of whom were studying engineering. Given such a high degree of homogeneity in terms of common values and their recent shared experience of service in the armed forces, it may not be altogether surprising that proximity played an important role in determining the formation of friendships. At the time of the study, Schachter and Back were themselves graduate students at MIT, while Festinger was a young faculty member.

There were other important postwar centres of research in social psychology besides the one at MIT, though this was the most innovative in terms of both its theory and its methods of research. Shortly after Lewin's untimely death in 1947 the Research Center for Group Dynamics, under the direction of Cartwright, moved from MIT to the University of Michigan where it became part of the Institute for Social Research. Also at the Institute for Social Research at Michigan was Rensis Likert who was in charge of survey research. He brought with him to Ann Arbor some of the researchers who had worked with him during the war on survey research. The broad range of research methods actively used by researchers at the Institute for Social Research is reflected in the volume edited by Festinger and Katz (1953), *Research Methods in the Behavioral Sciences*. The Institute attracted many distinguished social scientists to Ann Arbor. They were drawn by the prospect of holding, simultaneously, a chair of one of the social sciences in the University and a directorship of research within the Institute.

The postwar programme of research at Yale on communication and attitude change, under the direction of Hovland, brought together an impressive group of researchers, many of whom had collaborated previously in a wartime context. It also attracted to Yale a talented cohort of graduate students in social psychology, many of whom went on to become leaders in their field during the modern era. This new generation played an important role in establishing social psychology as an experimental science. The experimental social psychology which they helped to fashion was indeed a characteristically American phenomenon.

The programme of experimental research at Yale was more orthodox than the one at MIT. Researchers at Yale relied heavily on analysis of variance (ANOVA) designs in their experimental studies. Their main independent variables were the forms and content of communications and the sources from which they appeared to come. Hovland and his collaborators tried to turn rhetoric into an exact science (Billig, 1987). They sought to establish a few general principles of persuasion that would be universally true, independently of the issue involved or the medium employed for the delivery of the message. Initially, it was a purely empirical programme of research. What happens if we vary the credibility of the source from which a message emanates? Is it more effective to present both sides of an issue or only the side which the communicator wishes the target audience to accept? If the former is more effective (which it was), does the order of presentation of the two sides make any difference? Some argued that people are more influenced by what they hear first concerning an issue (i.e. a primacy effect); others argued that people are more influenced by what they have heard most recently concerning the issue (i.e. a recency effect).

Most of the data from the Yale programme favoured recency effects in persuasion.

If there was a broad theoretical orientation at the outset in the Yale programme of studies, it was, appropriately enough, that of Hull/Spence behaviour theory. By the end of the programme, however, the main theoretical orientation was cognitive. It was easy at the beginning to manipulate the main independent variables, since they related to the form and content of messages in various media. It was not until volume 3 of the Yale series (Rosenberg et al., 1960), which was published some 15 years into the postwar programme, that the focus of interest switched to understanding how information was organized in the minds of individuals exposed to the various experimentally constructed communications. The concern here was with cognitive consistency models of attitude change. The Yale series of studies was not cognitive in its orientation ab initio. Unlike the rival programme at MIT (and then later at Michigan), it did not reflect the influence of Gestalt psychology. It became a cognitive programme of research rather than setting out as one.

Many of the influential researchers in social psychology during the modern era served their apprenticeships in one or other of these two programmes. A few, like Kelley, even managed to serve an apprenticeship in both programmes. The original faculty of both programmes, and their immediate postwar cohorts of doctoral students, have recently retired from active research or are now dead. In some ways it is, currently, the end of an era. This makes the present an opportune moment for appraising the significance of their achievements. This, however, is not my intention in this book. Here, I am concerned not with the flowering of social psychology in America during the modern era but with its roots. Cartwright, a prominent member of the generation of social psychologists with whom I am concerned, expressed it thus in his 1978 Katz–Newcomb lecture at the University of Michigan: 'The entire history of social psychology as a field of empirical research extends over a period of only approximately 80 years. And since most of its growth has occurred within the past four decades, it is largely the product of scholars who are still active in the field' (Cartwright, 1979, p. 82). Now, over a decade and a half later, many of those scholars are no longer active.

The European dimension

Cartwright (1979) is somewhat diffident concerning his own credentials to be a historian of modern social psychology. In the lecture referred to above he described himself, modestly, as a participant observer. As a historian of social psychology, he has the advantage over both Allport (1954) and Jones (1985) of not subscribing to a positivist philosophy of science which could distort his historical account (see below). His account, admittedly, is sketchy and impressionistic as befits that of a participant observer.

Cartwright is acutely aware of the many contingencies that have shaped the historical development of social psychology in America in the modern era. Unlike the much fuller accounts provided by Allport (1954) and by Jones (1985), Cartwright (1979), in his brief sketch, does not adopt a narrowly internalist perspective. He is prepared to consider a much wider cast of characters than either Allport or Jones did in their accounts as influencing the historical development of social psychology: 'If I were required to name the one person who has had the greatest impact upon the field, it would have to be Adolf Hitler' (Cartwright, 1979, p. 84).

Events in the real world can have a dramatic influence on the historical development of academic disciplines. In chapter 9 I trace the impact of war on the development of social psychology. This includes the effect of the Great War of 1914–18 as well as the Second World War. It also includes an assessment of the consequences of the recent Cold War on the historical development of social psychology in America. Cartwright (1979), in common with Allport, Jones and myself, believes that social psychology, in the modern era, is characteristically an American phenomenon. He displays a better appreciation than Jones (1985) does, however, of the European contribution to the peculiar flowering of social psychology in America in the postwar period:

> The rise of Nazism in Germany, with its accompanying anti-intellectualism and vicious anti-Semitism, resulted as we all know in the migration to America of many of Europe's leading scholars, scientists and artists . . . One can hardly imagine what the field would be like to-day if such people as Lewin, Heider, Kohler, Werthheimer, Katona, Lazarsfeld, and the Brunswiks had not come to the United States when they did. (Cartwright, 1979, p. 85)

Of particular importance, I argue in chapter 6, was the migration of the Gestalt psychologists from Austria and Germany to America. This began as early as 1927 but accelerated with Hitler's rise to power in 1933 and with the Anschluss of 1938. While the migration occurred before the Second World War, its full effects were not detectable until after the war. Some of the key events in this migration are included in the list of important historical dates reproduced in appendix 1.

If one draws an over-sharp distinction between the long past of social psychology as part of the whole Western intellectual tradition and its short history as an experimental science in America, then it is easy to lose sight of the significance of a movement that occurred during the earlier of these two periods, the full effect of which (i.e. a cognitive social psychology) did not become apparent until the latter period. Lindzey and Aronson (1985) do this in the latest edition of the *Handbook of Social Psychology* by devoting separate chapters to the long past (Allport, 1985) and the short history (Jones, 1985) of social psychology. Such an oversight can also lead to a more ethnocentric account of modern social psychology than is strictly warranted by the historical facts: the roots are seen as European and the flower as peculiarly American. The movement of people between cultures is at least as significant as what happens within any one culture. This is as true in Europe as it is in America.

The migration of the Gestalt psychologists from Austria and Germany to America was the principal source of inspiration for the cognitive social psychology which is such a distinctive feature of social psychology throughout the modern era. Its roots are to be found in phenomenology. This was a quite different form of philosophy from the positivism that had become established in America in the form of behaviourism during the period between the two world wars. The Gestalt psychologists had not previously encountered behaviourism until they arrived in the New World. It was out of the conflict between these two rival, but incompatible, philosophies (i.e. phenomenology and positivism) that social psychology emerged in America in the distinctive form in which it did right at the start of the modern period. I shall argue that Gestalt psychology was the crucial ingredient in this transformation. The conflict occurred on American soil and so the outcome – a strongly cognitive social psychology – was clearly an American product. Modern social psychology may indeed be characteristically an American phenomenon, but at least the phenomenology was European.

Cognitive social psychology and cognitive science

Social psychologists in America were cognitive theorists at a time when it was not fashionable to be so, i.e. in the heyday of behaviourism. This was mainly due to the influence of the Gestalt psychologists. The cognitive tradition within American social psychology was not only

change as social psychology becomes better established in Europe and the hegemony of English as the language of publication in social psychology is challenged by a burgeoning literature in social psychology in the languages of Latin America.

Positivism in the History and Historiography of Social Psychology

Social psychology is usually transmitted from one generation of students to the next through the medium of a doctoral programme. Handbooks play a key role in the graduate education of most social psychologists. The series of *Handbooks of Social Psychology*, edited by Lindzey (1954) or by Lindzey and Aronson (1968-9, 1985) throughout the period of modern social psychology, has been important in transmitting the dominant psychological forms of social psychology. This is true whether the graduate programme in which the handbooks are used is offered in the United States of America or elsewhere in the world. This is the period in which social psychology emerged as an experimental science, mainly in America. Positivism played a vital role in this process. This is part of the story that unfolds in the pages that follow. I also hope to make explicit the role of positivism in shaping the historical accounts we currently have available of modern social psychology. The evidence for this latter claim will be presented more fully in chapter 10. By then, I hope, the reader will be in a better position to judge the truth of the claim and to assess its historical significance. It is also the warrant I need for presenting an alternative historical account of the roots of modern social psychology.

Allport's account of the historical background of modern social psychology forms the opening chapter of the *Handbook of Social Psychology* edited by Lindzey (1954). This was the first in the series of three *Handbooks* edited by Lindzey (1954) or by Lindzey and Aronson (1968-9, 1985) which, collectively, comprise modern social psychology. Allport's account has now appeared in all three editions of the *Handbook*. It has appeared in its original, in a revised and in an amended format (Allport, 1954, 1968 and 1985 respectively). Handbooks are important in the history of a discipline (see chapter 5) since they comprise a formative influence in the socialization of successive generations of graduate students. They are an important source of the professional identity of students enrolled in doctoral programmes in social psychology. They are a more reliable guide to the historical

development of a discipline than, for example, are textbooks which tend to reflect the popularity of a subject among undergraduates.

The focus of my interest in this book is modern social psychology, though I shall have more to say about its roots than about its flowering. To appreciate the flower, it is first of all necessary, in my opinion, to understand its roots and the relationship between those roots and the flower. It is also necessary, I would argue, to understand the varieties of the genus that are extant today. These will include varieties to be found only in Europe and others to be found only in neighbouring disciplines such as sociology. A history specifically of modern social psychology, as distinct from an account of the background to that history (Allport, 1954), does not appear in the modern series of *Handbooks* until the most recent edition (Jones, 1985). In his account, Jones outlined major developments in the discipline during the course of the previous five decades (i.e. 1935 to 1985). His account is a history of institutions, of joint doctoral programmes between social psychology and other social sciences, of textbooks and of major programmes of research. It is an account of research and of progress in research rather than a history of thought. In this respect it differs quite markedly from the neighbouring chapter by Allport (1985) which is more a history of ideas than a history of institutions.

Jones confined his account to the history of social psychology in America. This, in itself, is a significant contribution to modern scholarship. In the opinion of Allport (1954), with which I concur, modern social psychology is characteristically an American phenomenon. Jones provides us with a historical account of that phenomenon. His account, however, is seriously incomplete, even with regard to the American scene. This is because his primary concern, quite explicitly, is to trace the development of social psychology as a subdiscipline of psychology. This ignores the traditions of social psychology that have developed in the context of sociology and of other social sciences. I hope, in the present volume, to include sociological as well as psychological forms of social psychology. Jones feels justified in ignoring sociological forms of the discipline because, as he demonstrates in his analysis of textbooks for example, they are a minority tradition in the modern era. The failure of joint doctoral programmes between social psychology and other social sciences is a further piece of empirical evidence that Jones cites in support of his position. More controversially, he believes that sociological forms of social psychology are less scientific than the American tradition of social psychology as a subdiscipline of psychology. It is the history of the latter that he traces.

I have reservations about the wisdom of separating the history of thought (Allport, 1954) from the history of research (Jones, 1985). This, however, reflects more on the judgement of the editors than it does on the judgement of Jones in relation to the nature of his own contribution to that volume. The coexistence of these two chapters in the latest edition of the *Handbook* (Allport, 1985; Jones, 1985) fails to provide social psychologists, worldwide, with a useful framework for evaluating the historical development of their discipline. This is because the roots of modern social psychology are treated separately from its flower. The roots are predominantly European while the flower, typically, is American. The division of responsibility between Allport and Jones with regard to their coverage of the history of social psychology reflects, I suspect, on the part of the editors, a positivist philosophy of science. Allport covers the metaphysical past of social psychology, while Jones covers its short history since it became an experimental science, mainly in America. This is a theme to which I shall return in more detail in the final chapter of this book. Jackson (1988) provides a better account of both the past and the present of modern social psychology without creating such a damaging split between metaphysics and science.

There is no point in writing the history of a discipline if an adequate account already exists. I have indicated above some of my reasons for being dissatisfied with the account provided by Jones (1985). My objectives in the present work are more comprehensive than those of Jones since I wish to include European, as well as American, traditions of thought and of research. I also wish to include sociological as well as psychological forms of social psychology (chapter 7). This is especially important for me since the roots of modern social psychology lie in the intellectual soil of this whole Western tradition.

I differ from Jones in yet another respect. He accepts, but I would reject, Allport's account of the historical background of modern social psychology. I am not alone in challenging the validity of that account (e.g. Samelson, 1974). When it was first published (Allport, 1954), it was a valuable contribution to knowledge. It is less so now, over 40 years on. It has been re-issued twice (Allport, 1968, 1985) with only minor revisions or amendments. This may reflect a belief on the part of the editors of the *Handbook* (i.e. Lindzey and Aronson) that, since the long past of social psychology is now long past, there is no need to revise one's account of it. It is unwise, in my view, to separate the past of a discipline from its present in this manner. As Mead (1932) demonstrated, in his philosophy of history, the past is always being reconstructed from the perspective of the present. There is no end to this process.

The problem with the history of ideas approach to the writing of history, which Allport adopted, is that the criteria for deciding what to include and what to exclude are often far from clear and only rarely made explicit. Smith (1988) raised this issue with respect to histories of psychology. Of what, he asks, is the history of psychology the history? There are many possible historical backgrounds to modern social psychology of which the one written by Allport is but one. In its day it was important and now it is itself part of the history of the discipline to which, initially, it was but an introduction.

Samelson (1974) accused Allport of creating a false origin myth for social psychology by nominating Comte as its founder. He identified the secondary, English language, source from which Allport obtained his knowledge of Comte. Samelson regarded Allport's article as an instance of what Butterfield (1951), the English historian, called the Whig fallacy in the interpretation of history. This is the 'tendency in many historians to write on the side of Protestants and Whigs, to praise revolutions provided they have been successful, to emphasize certain principles of progress in the past and to produce a story which is the ratification if not the glorification of the present' (Butterfield, 1951, p. v).

By identifying Comte as its founder, Allport was claiming that social psychology was now a science. For Allport (1954) it is a social science. For Jones (1985) it is an experimental science. Both authors, however, frame their historical accounts in terms of a positivist philosophy of science. It is the same broad philosophy of science subscribed to by the editors of the volume in which their work appears. I shall treat at greater length in chapter 8 the hazards involved in naming ancestors and in identifying founders and, in chapter 10, the influence of positivism on the writing of histories and on the editing of handbooks.

The issues identified in the previous paragraph relate to the historiography, rather than to the history, of social psychology. Positivism is an important force both in and on the history of social psychology. Behaviourism is the form it assumed in the history of social psychology. Here Floyd Allport, the brother of Gordon, played an important role (see chapter 6). The creation of a false origin myth for social psychology is but one of the forms that positivism has assumed in the historiography of the discipline. Here Gordon Allport, the brother of Floyd, played an important role. Gordon thus compliments and complements the work of his brother Floyd. The one creates the revolution which the other celebrates. The Whig fallacy is here a purely family affair.

Postscript

I share the belief of Allport (1954) and of Jones (1985) that the modern era of social psychology began at the end of the Second World War. My belief, unlike theirs, is not rooted in any particular philosophy of science. My account is much closer to the history provided by Jones than it is to that provided by Allport. This is because my concern is with the history of institutions rather than with the history of ideas. The historical period I cover, however, in the book as a whole is that of Allport rather than that of Jones. This is because I am concerned with the historical background of modern social psychology. I have no difficulty in accepting, along with both Allport and Jones, that the flowering of social psychology in the modern era is characteristically an American phenomenon.

2

The Emergence in Germany of Psychology as a Natural and Social Science

Since the dominant form of modern social psychology developed in America as a subdiscipline of psychology rather than of sociology, it is necessary to trace its roots in the context of the former discipline. Psychology emerged as a distinct discipline in Germany in the second half of the nineteenth century. Wundt is widely credited (by, for example, Boring, 1929) with being the founder of psychology as an experimental science. The first edition of Wundt's textbook *Grundzüge der physiologische Psychologie* was published in 1873–4; he established a psychological laboratory at Leipzig in 1879 and he launched a research journal *Philosophische Studien* in 1881. It is less widely known, especially among psychologists, that Wundt also wrote ten volumes of social psychology (his *Völkerpsychologie*) between 1900 and 1920. It is highly germane to the theme of this volume to understand why Wundt chose to separate his social psychology from his experimental psychology. Before turning to tackle this quite precise question, it is, first of all, desirable to understand something of the wider context in which these developments took place.

Wissenschaft: the Birth of the Modern Research University

The medieval university trained its students for the ancient professions of medicine, law and the Church. Humboldt created the modern university when he re-established the University of Berlin in 1809. The novel element in the modern university was research or *wissenschaft*. Humboldt's own field of research was comparative linguistics. It now became possible for the first time to obtain degrees by research alone. The degree of Doctor of Philosophy attracted many scholars from abroad. The historian Sokal (1981) estimates that around 10,000 Americans studied at German universities between 1865 and 1914. They were attracted not only by the prospects of graduate study but also by the emergence, within the German university system, of wholly novel fields of study. Psychology was one such field. Others included linguistics, physiology, botany and chemistry. It was the faculty of arts, in the main, that gave birth to these new disciplines. This is reflected in the fact that, even today, the main degree by research in most faculties of science and of social science around the world is still a doctorate in philosophy.

Boring (1929) felt that the predominantly American readers of his *History of Experimental Psychology* would be unable to follow the text of his account without a more detailed knowledge of the German university system. He (or his publishers) conveniently provided a double-page map of these ancient universities (together with the dates of their foundation). The map, which is reproduced as figure 2.1, is taken from the second edition of the book (Boring, 1950).

In both editions the map is reproduced twice: inside both the front and back covers of the volume. This location expresses its importance in relation to the volume as a whole. It seems to convey a double message. It accurately enough identifies the university system within which psychology was born as a natural and social science. The university system itself is ancient. Many of the universities on the map were established during the pre-colonial and colonial periods in American history. As a subject, psychology is thus both ancient and modern. As a science, it is modern; as a field of speculation within philosophy, it is ancient.

When Boring (1929) wrote his *History of Experimental Psychology*, psychology at Harvard was still part of philosophy. Indeed, one of his motives in writing the book was to convince his colleagues at Harvard that psychology should now be funded separately from philosophy and be recognized as an experimental science (O'Donnell, 1979). It was part of his case that psychology had a respectable pedigree as a field of study but that it had emerged, in recent times, as a modern science. About 20 years earlier, Ebbinghaus (1908) had expressed it more succinctly: 'Psychology has a long past, but only a short history.' History, here, is the history of a science. What went before, i.e.

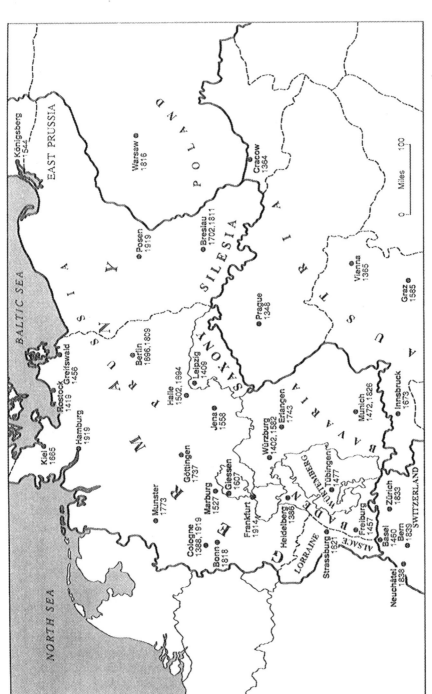

Figure 2.1 Universities of Central Europe, showing political divisions before the First World War (1914). Political divisions agreed upon at the Potsdam Conference after the Second World War are shown by broken lines. The dates when the universities were founded or re-established are given below the city names (from Boring, 1950).

metaphysics, is now part of the prehistory of the new science. This manner of distinguishing between the past and the present of a science reflects the operation of a positivist philosophy of science.

Rival forms of Wissenschaft: Naturwissenschaft *and* Geisteswissenschaft

While the *wissenschaft* tradition marks off the modern from the medieval university, there was much debate within academic circles in Germany concerning rival forms of *wissenschaft*. The most widely accepted distinction was between the *Naturwissenschaften* and the *Geisteswissenschaften*. This roughly corresponds, in the English-speaking world, to the distinction between the natural sciences, on the one hand, and the human and social sciences, on the other hand. In England and Wales, for example, it corresponds to the distinction between the Royal Society of London and the British Academy. The distinction is an important one in the present context since it led Wundt to separate his experimental psychology (part of the *Naturwissenschaften*) from his social psychology (part of the *Geisteswissenschaften*). Psychology, for Wundt, was only in part a branch of the natural sciences. He felt it was possible to resolve experimentally certain discrete problems within philosophy. This strictly limited project, however, needed, in his opinion, to be supplemented by a form of *Geisteswissenshaft*.

Wundt's belief that the experimental science which he had established at Leipzig was a limited project led to his repudiation by the younger generation of experimental psychologists many of whom he had himself trained. This is what Danziger (1979) refers to as the 'positivist repudiation of Wundt'. The main issue in dispute between the two generations of experimentalists, as Danziger (1979, 1990) has so amply demonstrated, was whether psychology was wholly, or only in part, a branch of the natural sciences. The younger generation could not forgive the founder of their discipline for claiming that psychology was only in part a branch of the natural sciences. Wundt claimed it was not possible to study higher mental processes experimentally. The younger generation set out almost immediately to prove him wrong: Külpe at Würzburg by studying imageless thought and Ebbinghaus at Berlin by studying memory.

In the thinking of the younger generation of experimentalists, especially Külpe and Ebbinghaus, the organism came to replace the psyche as the focus of their attention. Here, the skin forms a distinct boundary between the object of study, i.e. the individual, and the environment of that individual. The object of study is thus a bounded object, whether animal or human. The figure/ground relationship is a bold one when the figure is that of another human being. The distinction is much more clear cut than if mind is the object of study in psychology, as it had been for both Wundt and James. It is difficult to distinguish between the mind and its social and cultural context. Substituting the organism for the psyche was an important preliminary step along the path to psychology being considered wholly a branch of the natural sciences. It also marks a transition from philosophy to biology as the parent discipline for psychology.

In America this same progression took a slightly different turn. Watson proclaimed psychology to be wholly a branch of the natural sciences by declaring it to be the science of behaviour. Behaviour has the advantage over mind of being directly visible. This is a theme to which I shall return in subsequent chapters. The visibility of the individual and of the differences between individuals made it easier to study the latter. This is what J. McKeen Cattell did on his return to America from his studies in Germany and in England (see Sokal, 1981, esp. pp. 330–41). While Cattell had a Leipzig PhD and had been Wundt's research assistant, he was one of the young positivists (Danziger, 1979) who repudiated Wundt. Wundt in his experimental science was concerned with the mind in general, not with minds in particular. When Cattell, on his return to America, laid the basis of the mental test movement, he was more influenced by Galton, whom he had visited at Cambridge between September 1886 and December 1888 (see the letters from Cambridge edited by Sokal, 1981, pp. 218–313).

The distinction between the *Naturwissenschaften* and the *Geisteswissenschaften* also contributed to the subsequent neglect, in psychological circles, of Wundt's social psychology. In large measure this was because the history that mattered, in the eyes of subsequent generations, was the history of psychology as a branch of natural science. The objects of study in Wundt's *Völkerpsychologie* were language, religion, customs, myth, magic and cognate phenomena. These collective phenomena emerge from 'the reciprocal interaction of the many' (Wundt, 1916, p. 3) and, according to Wundt, they cannot be explained in terms of the consciousness of the individual which was the basis of his laboratory science. Wundt's social psychology was, thus, a form of *Geisteswissenschaft*. Psychology was still the science of mind but in the *Völkerpsychologie* Wundt analysed mind in its external manifestations, i.e. in terms of culture. It was still a science, but a different sort of science: a human and social science.

Science is one possible translation of the German word *wissenschaft*. The word 'science', unfortunately, is often used in a highly restrictive sense in England and Wales to refer to the natural sciences alone. This is very different from its usage on the continent of Europe where, typically, academies of science cover the whole spectrum of scholarship from the *Naturwissenschaften* to the *Geisteswissenschaften*. In this respect the Royal Society of Edinburgh (as distinct from the Royal Society of London) is more like a continental academy of science. In Britain, the Enlightenment was largely a Scottish affair and there were close cultural ties, at the time, between Scotland and France. Voltaire, for example, was proud of the fact that he was a Fellow of the Royal Society of Edinburgh. He would have been a highly improbable Fellow of the Royal Society of London.

The idea of studying mind in its external manifestations was a project that had first been mooted by Kant in his anthropology (Leary, 1982). It is difficult, at this remove in time, to appreciate the significance of Wundt's *Völkerpsychologie* without having a clear idea of what the human and social sciences comprised, i.e. the nature of the *Geisteswissenschaften*. Danziger (1983) has shown how history has not been kind to Wundt's vision of psychology. In part this is because, as noted above, experimental psychologists regard their discipline as being wholly a branch of the natural sciences; in part also because social psychologists, at least in the English-speaking world, lack a clear vision of psychology as a human and social science. Sociological social psychologists are more likely than their psychological cousins to entertain such a vision. This is because the latter, in the second half of the twentieth century, turned social psychology into a branch of the natural sciences (see chapters 1 and 10). First of all, psychology became a natural science, during the historical period covered in this book, and then, about half a century later (in what I here call the modern era) social psychology followed suit. What was *Geisteswissenschaft* for Wundt becomes *Naturwissenschaft* for Floyd Allport. When psychology was the science of mind it was easier to conceive of it as a human and social science than when it became the science of behaviour.

In Germany, Dilthey (1883) set out the foundational basis of the *Geisteswissenschaften*. The central discipline in this project was history, and the human mind was conceived of in historical terms. In Berlin there was clearly a clash between Dilthey's conception of psychology as *Geisteswissenschaft* and Ebbinghaus's conception of it as *Naturwissenschaft*. Dilthey was an influential figure in academic circles in Berlin and, although he was not a psychologist, he took an active interest in appointments to chairs in the subject. Stumpf was clearly more congenial to Dilthey's conception of psychology than Ebbinghaus had been. It was under Stumpf that Gestalt psychology flourished at the University of Berlin (Ash, 1982, see also chapter 6). Dilthey is also important in the context of the history of social psychology because he influenced G. H. Mead. Mead spent the years 1889–91 at the University of Berlin and Dilthey was his thesis supervisor. The thesis concerned the relationship between vision and touch in the perception of space. While Mead failed to complete his thesis before he had to leave Berlin to take up an appointment at the University of Michigan (see appendix 1), there is little doubt but that Dilthey influenced his thinking. When Mead was a student in Berlin he was influenced by both Ebbinghaus and Dilthey. He was thus acutely aware of the rivalry between the two forms of *wissenschaft*. This is discussed more fully in chapter 4.

The mandarin class

Ringer (1969) describes the high cultural standing achieved by the professoriate of the German universities in the course of the nineteenth century. He describes their standing within the wider German society as that of a mandarin class. He derives his model of a mandarin class from the work of the sociologist Max Weber. Professors acquired this status by becoming the indispensable advisers to an enlightened monarchy on matters of modern statecraft. They enjoyed the status of being civil servants of a sort. Ringer's book, more precisely, is a study of the decline in their influence between 1890 and 1933. This was occasioned by a crisis in culture as educational institutions in general adapted to the strains of a late industrialization. Ringer's book is a useful general guide to the historical background of the life and work of Wundt and of other pioneers, like Dilthey, in the emergence of psychology as both a natural and a social science.

The modern reader is fortunate to have available a contemporary account of what it was like to be a graduate student in the Psychologische Institut at Leipzig in the early 1880s. The account is contained in the pages of the private journals and family correspondence of J. McKeen Cattell, as edited and annotated by the historian Sokal (1981). Since Cattell's father was President of an American College, the letters reveal a great deal about the nature of university life both in Germany and in America at that time. The value in terms of an academic career in America of having a PhD from a German university, especially from Leipzig, is clearly evident in the pages of Sokal's book. So, too, is the power of the professoriate in Germany. Cattell, at his own expense, had a special piece of apparatus constructed (a modified gravity chronometer) for use in his experimental studies of reaction-time. He kept the apparatus in his lodging house where he carried out the studies for his thesis because he feared that if he brought the apparatus into the laboratory it would be impounded by the professor. Cattell, however, was more generous with regard to another piece of apparatus he had in his possession. When he left Leipzig he donated to Wundt the machine on which he had typed his thesis. Other professors in Germany felt that this American machine gave Wundt a distinct advantage in outpublishing them. Wundt was certainly a prolific publisher. Boring (1950), however, estimates that Wundt had a high published output even before receiving the gift of a typewriter.

Cattell appointed himself as Wundt's first assistant because he thought the laboratory at Leipzig needed to be organized. He was also the first of Wundt's doctoral students to choose the topic of his own research, as distinct from having it assigned to him by the professor. This was on individual differences in reaction-time, a problem that Wundt described as '*ganz amerikanisch*'. Wundt was probably too scholarly to be a great administrator and so the proffered help from Cattell was welcome. Wundt spent the mornings at home writing. In the afternoons he visited the laboratory, went for a short walk, and then gave his daily lecture at four o'clock in the afternoon. In the evenings he would occasionally relax and go to a concert or an opera. 'He avoided public ceremonies, never attended congresses, disliked travel, and hardly ever had a holiday' (Hearnshaw, 1979, p. 447).

Physiological Psychology/Social Psychology

Why separate the two?

Wundt did not consider it possible by means of introspection to study such higher mental processes as thinking. It was only possible in the laboratory to study basic sensory processes. This is because the mind cannot turn round upon itself and study that of which it is itself the product. To study the relation between language and thought, for example, was, for Wundt, part of his *Völkerpsychologie*. One can locate the antecedents of this approach to the study of language and thought in the social psychology of language as this had been developed by Humboldt, Herder and Hegel (Marková, 1983). It is also possible to see the further development of Wundt's ideas in the social psychology of G. H. Mead (1934) at Chicago (see chapter 4) and in the developmental psychology of Vygotsky in Russia. It is also faithfully preserved in the work on education of C. H. Judd at Chicago. Indeed, the thinking of the German expressivists (i.e. Humboldt, Herder and Hegel) concerning the social psychology of language, together with Wundt's treatment of language (Wundt, 1973), accounts for the remarkable similarity in the thinking of both Mead and Vygotsky. Although they were contemporaries, neither man, to my knowledge, was familiar with the work of the other.

The limitations of using introspection to study the mind were also evident to William James. Unlike Wundt, James was interested in studying the stream of consciousness. He likened the use of introspection for the study of consciousness to turning up the gaslight in order to see better the surrounding darkness. The brighter the light, the greater is the surrounding darkness. The task is almost futile, though not entirely so to such an astute observer of his own mind as James. Wundt's use of introspection, however, was quite precise. The introspective reports coming out of the Leipzig laboratory referred to events that were immediately present in consciousness. For Wundt, introspection was a form of inner perception (Danziger, 1980a). When the individual is approached from the outside, that is physiology; when the individual is approached from the inside, this is psychology. The two, together, comprise the field of physiological psychology. The generative processes involved in the production of collective mental phenomena, such as language, are interactional and, hence, social. This led Wundt to separate his social psychology from his physiological psychology. They were two independent, though related, projects. The one – social psychology – could not be reduced to the other – physiological psychology. The one concerned a community of individuals (a *volk*), while the other concerned the individual.

On the limitations of using introspection to explore collective mental phenomena, Wundt had this to say:

> It is true that the attempt has frequently been made to investigate the complex functions of thought on the basis of mere introspection. These attempts, however, have always been unsuccessful. Individual consciousness is wholly incapable of giving us a history of human thought, for it is conditioned by an earlier history concerning which it cannot of itself give us any knowledge. (Wundt, 1916, p. 3)

The mind, here, for Wundt is clearly a historical phenomenon. This is inherent in the notion of *Geisteswissenschaft*.

For Wundt, *Völkerpsychologie* 'relates to those mental products which are created by a community of human life and are, therefore, inexplicable in terms merely of individual consciousness since they presuppose the reciprocal action of many' (Wundt, 1916, p. 3). 'Language, for example, is not the accidental discovery of an individual; it is the product of peoples, and, generally speaking, there are as many different languages as there are originally distinct peoples. The same is true of the beginning of art, of mythology, and of custom' (Wundt, 1916, p. 2). Wundt's point is that language and religion were *in origin* the creation of a folk community even though by his day languages and religions had long since transcended the boundaries of a single people or *volk* and had become universal.

Differing conceptions of the origins of mind and of science

In the *Völkerpsychologie* (especially in the synchronic version *Elemente der Völkerpsychologie*, 1912), Wundt was searching for the origins of mind. This is integral to the conception of psychology as *Geisteswissenschaft*. The younger generation of positivists, however, who, in the words of Danziger (1979), repudiated Wundt, were seeking something rather different. They were attempting to identify when psychology ceased to be metaphysics and became science (i.e. wholly a part of the *Naturwissenschaften*). The contrast between the two forms of *wissenschaften* in regard to the issue of origins is neatly captured in the following extended quotation from Koch (1985, p. 7):

> It is rare that the pursuers of a broad field of inquiry hold an image of their field as having been 'founded' at some definite date. One does not encounter multimillennial celebrations of the founding of philosophy (or indeed, physics) by Thales or of history by Herodotus. Painting is not thought to have been initiated in some inaugural atelier, even one provided by a cave. If there be claimants to the invention of literature, they have not carried their case. Virtually all broad areas of inquiry or creative activity now 'institutionalized' are seen to meld into history and prehistory. It is ludicrous to think of them as having commenced on a determinably given date as it is to think of language as having been stipulated into existence by a persuasive primitive linguist. Any definition of what it is to be human must entail that psychological knowledge – both implicit and explicit – has been 'owned' and pursued by the race co-extensively with its emergence.

In the one case (the human and social sciences), history is co-extensive with the human race; in the other case (the natural sciences), it does not commence until the field of study ceases to be metaphysics and becomes science. When the latter occurs a clear break with the past is created. It might be more accurate, however, to claim that the break with the past is constructed by the historians of science, the writers of the next generation of textbooks (Kuhn, 1962) and the editors of *Handbooks* (see chapter 10). The historical changes themselves are likely to be much less distinct.

For Wundt, his *physiologische Psychologie* and his *Völkerpsychologie* were sufficiently different forms of psychology for him to distinguish between them and to treat them as separate projects. They were, however, not unrelated, though Wundt himself was unable to work out fully the details of those links. One link, of course, is provided by Darwin's theory of evolution. Mead saw this very clearly (see chapter 4). Evolution is a non-experimental form of natural science in which time (and, therefore, in terms of human affairs, history) is important. Darwin's theory is concerned with the prehistory of the human race. He worked with the varieties of species available in nature. In developing his theory he used the comparative method.

Wundt tried to emulate Darwin by tracing the evolution of the human mind. The material at his disposal had been collected by linguists and anthropologists. He had to work with the varieties of language spoken by man and with the varieties of human nature to be found around the world. The objects of study in his *Völkerpsychologie* were language and culture. This was a different project from his experimental science since collective mental phenomena, such as language and culture, were not amenable to being brought under experimental control. It was, however, still science, though not experimental science. As mentioned earlier, the modern research university was established by Humboldt, who also established the field of comparative linguistics. The comparative method was common to both the *Naturwissenschaften* and the *Geisteswissenschaften*.

Culture is not the only phenomenon that is outwith (as the Scots say) the consciousness of the individual. Wundt's strict conception of experimental psychology as being the study of consciousness forced Freud, for example, to describe his theory of the unconscious as meta-psychology. When Rosenzweig, an American clinical psychologist, offered Freud experimental evidence for repression, Freud rejected this evidence out of hand. Almost certainly this was because Freud equated experimental psychology with Wundt's version of it, i.e. concerned exclusively with what is present in consciousness. Külpe and his co-workers at Würzburg were not so restrictive in their conception of consciousness or in their use of introspection. They allowed introspective reports of events that were no longer present in consciousness. These formed part of their introspective studies of thinking. Wundt regarded this as just poor experimental technique. With Ebbinghaus in Berlin studying memory by means of his specially devised nonsense syllables, it seemed as though higher mental processes could, after all, be studied experimentally. This is the view that came to prevail in the official histories of psychology, at least in the English-speaking world.

The limitations of a laboratory science based on introspection

There was something deeply flawed about an experimental science that depended to a large extent on accepting introspective reports. The reports were of private events that were not accessible to anyone other than the person making them. No one else could gain independent access to the mind of the person making the report to check its veracity. Science, necessarily, is a public enterprise. Science cannot take as its primary data uncorroborated accounts of events. The problem with the use of introspection in the laboratory, as it had been with its use in the armchair, is that observer and observed are one and the same person. The only mind to which one has direct access is one's own. Such a science of mind cannot truly be a science because it is not social. Mead (see chapter 4) criticized Wundt because the latter's theory of mind, which underlay his experimental science, was Cartesian rather than Hegelian.

Danziger (1990), on the basis of his analysis of the journal *Philosophische Studien*, has given us a historical account of the social structure of experimentation in the Leipzig laboratory. The person providing the scientific data was clearly more important than the person presenting the stimuli. The distinctions with which we are more familiar today between experimenters and subjects did not then exist. Research was much more of a collaborative affair and persons often alternated between the roles of reporter and presenter. Wundt quite often acted as a subject but never as an experimenter. While introspection was quite widely used in the Leipzig laboratory, the research of the laboratory did not depend exclusively upon it. Behavioural techniques were quite often employed, especially in the reaction-time experiments. Great care was taken in the administration of stimuli and in the recording of responses. Figure 2.2 shows Wundt and some of his assistants at the Leipzig laboratory around 1910.

A problem with a laboratory science that depends to a significant extent on introspection is the absence of agreed-upon procedures for

Figure 2.2 Wilhelm Wundt and assistants at the Leipzig laboratory (c.1910) (*archives of the University of Leipzig, Wundt–Nachlass*)

resolving conflicting claims coming from rival laboratories. An example of such an unresolved conflict was whether or not thinking occurs in terms of images. Külpe, at Würzburg, maintained that thought was imageless. It proved impossible to resolve the issue by means of introspection. It was this feature of the mind's first science that prepared the ground, at least in the New World, for the emergence of behaviourism. Here observer and observed were two different persons or, in the case of animal studies, an observing human and an observed animal. Since the object of observation was behaviour, it was possible to obtain measures of inter-observer reliability. This was much more in keeping with the public nature of science. The transition from the armchair to the laboratory meant that psychology, in research practice if not in theory, was now a social science.

Distortions in the Perception of Wundt in the English-speaking World

Blumenthal (1975) claims that there is virtually no resemblance between the historical Wundt and the portrayal of him that emerges from the historical accounts available in English. How can this be so? I shall be brief in suggesting how these distortions may have arisen. The careful detective work that provides an answer to the question has already been done by Danziger (1979).

Experimental psychology as an Anglo-German achievement

Several writers believe that psychology first became a science when the experimental methods devised by physiologists in Germany were used to solve some of the problems psychology had inherited from philosophy. 'The Germans knew how the receptors worked; the British knew why they were important. Given the positivistic spirit of the times it was inevitable that the two lines of thought should converge. When this happened, psychology became an experimental science' (Miller and Buckhout, 1973, p. 25). O'Neil, an Australian historian of psychology, gives a similar account. 'Psychology as a methodical observational study began with the application of methods, mainly experimental, derived largely from physiology to problems derived largely from philosophy' (O'Neil, 1982, p. 2). It would seem that the convergence of German physiology and British philosophy resulted in the emergence of physiological psychology. Hearnshaw, a British historian of psychology, seems to endorse this general view. 'In Great Britain . . . Wundt never had much of a following, in spite of the fact that Wundt himself derived many of his ideas from British psychology; in particular, of course, the empirical, analytic, associational approach' (Hearnshaw, 1979, p. 449). In a way, all this is curious because the philosophical antecedents of Wundt are Leibniz and Kant and not Locke, Hume, James Mill, John Stuart Mill, Berkeley etc.

The chief source of distortion here is Titchener, an English gentleman from Cheltenham, who studied philosophy at Oxford before going on to Leipzig where he obtained his PhD from Wundt in 1892. Titchener assimilated Wundt to the tradition of philosophy he had been taught at Oxford, i.e. the empirical, associationist tradition of British philosophy. This led him to misperceive the key role of apprehension in Wundt's philosophy of the mind, together with his voluntaristic stance. This is all part of what Danziger (1979) calls the positivist repudiation of Wundt. It is Danziger's considered opinion that 'Titchener practically made a career out of interpreting Wundt in his own highly idiosyncratic fashion' (Danziger, 1979, p. 206). These gross distortions which Titchener introduced might be of no significance today had it not been for the fact that one of Titchener's prize doctoral students at Cornell was E. G. Boring. Boring was dependent upon Titchener for much of his information concerning the origins, in Germany, of psychology as an experimental science. Boring dutifully dedicated his *History of Experimental Psychology* (1929) to his former teacher and mentor who had died a couple of years before the publication of the first edition.

The influence of Wundt on the development of the social sciences

Boring published a list of those pioneers of experimental psychology in America who went to Leipzig and who were influenced by Wundt:

> America was close behind Germany in adopting the new psychology, and it also took its cue from Wundt. Stanley Hall visited Leipzig in the first years of Wundt's new laboratory and founded in America (six years after Wundt began the *Philosophische Studien*) the *American Journal of Psychology*, thus the second journal of experimental psychology in history. The proportion of Wundt's students from America was very large. Cattell was his first assistant. The following list, arranged chronologically is, I think, complete for Wundt's American students before 1900: G. S. Hall (Clark), J. McK. Cattell (Columbia), H. K. Wolfe (Nebraska), E. A. Pace

(Catholic University), E. W. Scripture (Yale), F. Angell (Stanford), E. B. Titchener (Cornell), L. Witmer (Pennsylvania), H. C. Warren (Princeton), H. Gale (Minnesota), G. T. N. Patrick (Iowa), G. M. Stratton (California), C. H. Judd (Chicago), G. A. Tawney (Beloit). (Boring, 1950, p. 347)

It is curious that Boring omits G. H. Mead and treats Titchener as an American

I have compiled a very short list of distinguished social scientists who were strongly influenced by Wundt. Most of the evidence is contained in the list of important dates set out in appendix 1. Some of these people were at Leipzig, for example, Malinowski who became the founder of British social anthropology. Others were enrolled as Wundt's students, as G. H. Mead, the Chicago pragmatist philosopher (see chapter 4), and W. I. Thomas, the distinguished Chicago sociologist who, in the 1920s, equated social psychology with the study of social attitudes. Others were people who visited Leipzig; for example, Durkheim visited a number of German universities in 1885–6 and was impressed by what he saw.

> It was, however, in the work of Wilhelm Wundt that he found the greatest evidence of advance in the sociological treatment of morality. He also greatly admired Wundt's experimental work in psychology, with its concentration on 'precise and restricted' problems and its avoidance of 'vague generalisations and metaphysical possibilities'. But it was Wundt's sociological work that excited, and influenced, him the most. (Lukes, 1973, pp. 90–1)

There were others who read and reacted to Wundt's *Völkerpsychologie*; for example, Boas, who created an important school of cultural anthropology in America. Freud wrote *Totem and Taboo* as a riposte to Wundt's account of the totemic age in the evolution of man. This short, and still incomplete, list is an impressive one. There is little or no trace of Wundt's influence on the *Geisteswissenschaften* to be found in official histories of psychology. It has taken me a long time to compile the list of dates and events contained in appendix 1. If Wundt's influence as a social psychologist is to be traced, it needs to be studied in other social and human sciences which are now independent of psychology; for example, in psychoanalysis, in linguistics, in American and French sociology, in British and American social and cultural anthropology and so on. There are a few autonomous traditions of social psychology which can be traced to the influence of Wundt but which, now, are independent of the dominant psychological tradition of social psychology discussed in chapter 1. These include the symbolic interactionist tradition of social psychology within

American sociology (see chapter 4); contemporary French research on 'social representations' which derives its inspiration from Durkheim; the now defunct tradition of comparative psychology reflected in the organization of Murchison's first *Handbook of Social Psychology* (1935) (see chapter 5). What all these forms of social psychology have in common is that they are 'sociological' rather than 'psychological' traditions of social psychology; that is, they derive from Wundt's *Völkerpsychologie* rather than from his laboratory science. They are thus genuinely *social* forms of social psychology.

Positivism in the historiography of psychology and of social psychology

Danziger (1979) has written incisively about the role of positivism in the history of psychology, especially in relation to the repudiation of Wundt by the younger generation of experimentalists. I am keen to trace its effects on histories of psychology, especially histories of social psychology; that is, I am concerned to identify the role of positivism in the historiography of psychology, especially in the historiography of social psychology. Here, in this chapter, I am dealing with the history of psychology, especially with the account written by Boring (1929, 1950). It was written during the period covered by the present book. In chapter 10 I shall return to this theme in much greater detail, specifically in relation to histories of social psychology, especially those written by G. W. Allport (1954) and by Jones (1985). Those histories were written during the modern era in social psychology. The one looks back at the roots of modern social psychology (Allport, 1954); the other chronicles its achievements (Jones, 1985). At the start of the modern era in social psychology, then, we have the relaunch of a positive history of psychology (the second edition of Boring, 1950), quickly followed by an account of the historical background to modern social psychology (Allport, 1954) in which Comte is identified as the founder of the discipline. Both of these histories were written in the Department of Psychology at Harvard University.

One way to counteract the distortions in the portrayal of Wundt to be found in histories of psychology in the English language is to consider his work in its contemporary setting. In 1862 Wundt set himself three tasks in life: the creation of (a) an experimental psychology; (b) a scientific metaphysics; and (c) a social psychology. He achieved the first of these tasks by writing a two-volume *Grundzüge der physiologische Psychologie* (1873–4); establishing, in Leipzig, the world's first Institut für Psychologie, in 1879; and founding a journal

Philosophische Studien in 1881 in which he could publish the results of his laboratory research (see appendix 1 for more detail). Historians of psychology often single out this particular decade in Wundt's highly productive life and declare it to have been the time when he accomplished his most significant work. Miller (1966, pp. 33, 34), for example, has this to say: 'With a handbook, a laboratory and a scholarly journal the new psychology was well under way.' To do this, however, is grossly to distort both the range and the significance of the tasks Wundt had set himself.

For the next two decades of his life Wundt was preoccupied with the second of his three tasks. Wundt here adopted an explicitly anti-positivist stance. Positivism was that movement of thought in philosophy which had originated in the middle of the nineteenth century in the writings of the French philosopher, Auguste Comte, and culminated in the middle of the twentieth century in the logical positivism of the Vienna Circle and in linguistic analysis. For a positivist, science replaces metaphysics. The idea of writing a scientific metaphysics is, therefore, for a positivist, a contradiction in terms. It is to put the clock back. It is to be concerned with metaphysics rather than with science. It is a retrograde step.

In the final two decades of his life Wundt turned his attention to the third of the three tasks he had set for himself back in 1862, creating a social psychology. He was 69 years of age when he published the first of the ten volumes of his *Völkerpsychologie* (1900–20). These volumes have remained largely inaccessible to historians of psychology and of social psychology who write in English. By the start of the modern era in social psychology the objects of study in Wundt's *Völkerpsychologie*, i.e. language, religion, customs, myth, magic and cognate phenomena, are widely believed to be the objects of study of other social sciences like linguistics, sociology and anthropology. How this came about is part of the story of the present book. It is primarily due to the working out of the forces of positivism in the period before the end of the Second World War. The effects of reductionism are dealt with in chapter 3 and the individualization and Americanization (Manicas, 1987) of social psychology is the topic of chapter 6.

Wundt kept meticulously to the plan of writing he had set himself back in 1862. He took one decade to accomplish the first task; two decades each to accomplish his second and third tasks. He finished the last volume of the *Völkerpsychologie* in 1920 and, for good measure, added a brief autobiography and then, two weeks later, he died. Boring estimated that he wrote some 54,000 pages in the course of his life.

The forces of positivism at work in the historiography of psychology, which I have identified under each of Wundt's three tasks above, cumulatively, can have a quite devastating effect on the way Wundt is portrayed in histories of psychology, especially those written in English. The following portrayal exemplifies those cumulative effects:

> Wundt's genius was the kind Thomas Edison described – one per cent inspiration and ninety-nine per cent perspiration. One cannot help marvelling at Wundt's energy and endurance over a period of 60 years. Yet it is his first achievement – the creation of a scientific, experimental psychology – that must command our greatest respect. His later work is now largely forgotten. His philosophy was undistinguished, and his social psychology came too late. (Miller, 1966, p. 39)

Nor is Miller alone in arriving at such a negative overall evaluation of Wundt. Hearnshaw, in an address celebrating the centenary of the Leipzig laboratory, could raise only two, not three, cheers for Wundt:

> Wundt was not a very original figure; his standpoint in psychology was questionable, and has been largely rejected; his writing was dull, and his views sometimes demonstrably wrong . . . So Wundt deserves at least one cheer for being lucky enough to be at the right place at the right time and for consciously seizing the opportunity which confronted him. He deserves a second cheer for being an exceptionally hard-working and competent organizer, and an honest investigator, in spite of his limitations of outlook. But we must withhold the third cheer, which we will keep for psychology's man of genius, its Newton, when he [sic] turns up. (Hearnshaw, 1979, pp. 450, 451)

The first two cheers sound rather faint to me. Hearnshaw's appraisal of Wundt is a highly patronizing account. Boring (1929) was also negative about Wundt's achievements: 'there have been no great psychologists. Psychology has never had a great man to itself. Wundt was not a great man of the order of Helmholtz or Darwin . . ..' Wundt was repudiated by the positivists because he claimed that the experimental science he had established was a limited project (Danziger, 1979). He was also repudiated, I would add, because he claimed that his social psychology was *Geisteswissenschaft* and not *Naturwissenshaft*.

Epilogue: The Wundtian Inheritance

Psychology emerged as a natural and social science in Germany at the end of the nineteenth century and the beginning of the twentieth century. Among the 10,000 Americans who flocked to Europe for their graduate studies in the half century between 1865 and 1914, Sokal (1981), Boring (1929, 1950) and Hilgard (1987) identify the pioneers of an experimental psychology in America. There were many more laboratories established in America than in Britain based on the Leipzig model (Hearnshaw, 1979).

In recognition of the origins of the discipline, German became a required language in most doctoral programmes in American universities and in some British universities. It is doubtful if even the pioneers who studied 'the new psychology' in Germany itself understood all they heard in lectures or read in books. I have identified, in this chapter, some of the sources of misunderstanding between teachers and students, e.g. Titchener's misunderstanding of Wundt. It is doubtful if the philosophical antecedents of 'the new psychology', as it came to be called, were understood by non-native speakers of German. The brass instruments of the new laboratory science, however, were much more portable. They were often items in the luggage of returning Americans who were quick to set up laboratories in the new graduate schools that began to mushroom at American universities. Hilgard (1987, pp. 32–4) lists some 41 laboratories that had been established in America by 1900. Very often, however, these were projects quite different from the Leipzig laboratory on which many of them had been modelled. The study of individual differences, for example, was very much a British, French and American innovation, rather than being German in its inspiration. It is also doubtful if the language requirements of American doctoral programmes – which continued well into the modern era – actually did bring about the international understanding they were designed to effect. The language requirements of American doctoral programmes were designed to preserve the links between the Old World and the New World. The emergence, in the modern era, of English as the language of international communication in science destroyed many of those links.

The misunderstanding of the social science component of psychology was much greater than the misunderstanding of the natural science component. This may be because it was much more culture specific. Certainly, the corpus of Wundt's work was not understood very well outside his native Germany; for example, the relationship between his experimental science and his social science. The inheritance from Wundt was an experimental psychology that was not social and a social psychology that was not experimental. If psychology first became an experimental science in Germany, then it was social psychology that became an experimental science in America.

3
The Psychology of the Masses and of Culture

At the turn of this century, it was quite usual for major figures in the human and social sciences to write both about the individual and about the collective. These, as we have seen already in the case of Wundt, were, quite often, separate projects. While the author could appreciate the significance of both projects, he could not work out how they were inter-related. He knew enough to separate the two objects of study, but not enough to demonstrate how they were inter-related. Occasionally, as in the case of Durkheim, the writer's motive in distinguishing between two objects of study was that he wished to study the one and not the other. By distinguishing between collective and individual representations, Durkheim (1898) was also distinguishing between sociology and psychology.

The drawing of distinctions is an important first step in the development of a field of study. It is akin to the scientist's desire to carve nature at its joints. Wundt's distinction between his physiological psychology and his social psychology is a case in point. The object of study in the one is a psychic or biological entity. The objects of study in the other are collective mental products that arise from 'the reciprocal action of the many' (Wundt, 1916, p. 3). The generative mechanisms underlying the phenomena that are the objects of study in the *Völkerpsychologie* are social and interactional. They are also historical. This is why the *Völkerpsychologie* is part of the *Geisteswissenschaften*.

The drawing of distinctions is important for another reason. It poses a problem to which others may respond. The social psychology of Mead (see chapter 4), for example, is a considered response to Wundt's distinction between his *Völkerpsychologie* and his physiological psychology. Mead shows how the individual, too, is a product of the reciprocal interaction of the many. He resolves the Wundtian antithesis by inserting self between mind and society (Mead, 1934). The mind, too, is a social entity. The antithesis is no longer, as it had been for Wundt, between biology, on the one hand, and either society or culture, on the other, because Mead sets all three terms within the context of Darwin's theory of evolution. In Mead's resolution of the problem posed by Wundt, a form of *Naturwissenschaft* (i.e. Darwin's theory of evolution) encompasses the *Geisteswissenschaften*. This is because man and his culture is but one among a number of other species. The posing of the problem by Wundt and its resolution by Mead occur within the same historical epoch (i.e. the epoch covered by the present book).

Sometimes the creation of an antithesis and its subsequent resolution occur in two different historical epochs. Durkheim, for example, proposed his over-sharp distinction between individual and collective representations at the end of the nineteenth century. A synthesis in terms of a theory of social representations had to await the publication by Moscovici (1961) of his study *La Psychanalyse: son image et son public* at the start of the modern era in social psychology. This timing takes it outside the time frame of the present study. Since Moscovici developed his theory within the context of sociology, as defined by Durkheim, it is, necessarily, a sociological form of social psychology. This makes it quite different from the psychological forms of social psychology which are dominant in America throughout the modern era. Differences between these two forms of social psychology are the subject of discussion in chapter 7. Since I am dealing with the roots of modern social psychology rather than with modern social psychology *per se*, I can here only deal with the prehistory of Moscovici's theory of social representations (Farr, 1994).

Occasionally, during the period here under review, a major theorist both poses a problem and proceeds to answer it himself. I think this is true of Freud. His early work, as befits a clinician, are case studies of individuals. His initial model of the mind distinguishes between different levels of consciousness, i.e. the conscious, the preconscious and the unconscious. The upheavals of the First World War and his assiduous reading of Le Bon (Moscovici, 1985) led Freud, in the 1920s, to revise his theory of mind to account for mass phenomena. His new model of the mind, in which he distinguishes between ego, id and superego (Freud, 1923), is much more explicitly social than his first model of the mind. The notion of self is central to his conception of mind, as indeed it was for Mead (see above). Freud's preoccupation in the 1920s with the analysis of collective phenomena is, in part, obscured in the English-speaking world by the rather quirky translation of the German word '*masse*' by the English word 'group' as, for example, in *Group Psychology and the Analysis of the Ego* (Freud, 1921). In the German it is *Massenpsychologie und Ich-Analyse*. To the modern reader, the word 'group' suggests a small group, as in Lewinian group dynamics. Freud's many contributions to our understanding of collective phenomena is in danger of being lost to the collective memory of scholars because the psychoanalytic inheritance is in the hands of clinicians rather than in the hands of social scientists. There are, of course, some notable exceptions, e.g. Badcock (1980, 1983, 1986).

Contrasts between the Individual and the Collective

Consciousness and culture: the Wundtian antithesis

One of the sharpest possible distinctions between the individual and the collective is that between consciousness and culture. This, essentially, is the distinction between Wundt's experimental science and his *Völkerpsychologie*. The juxtaposition of culture and consciousness is quite dramatic. It is not at all clear how one might get from the one to the other and back again. Consciousness isolates an individual from others; culture absorbs the individual and blurs the distinction between one individual and another. The reasons that led Wundt to separate his experimental science from his social science were fairly fully covered in chapter 2 and need not be repeated here.

The consequences, historically, of the juxtaposition, perhaps, are worth treating in a little more detail. We have seen already how the narrowness of Wundt's conception of consciousness forced Freud to describe his theory of the unconscious as meta-psychology. The dispute between the laboratories at Leipzig and at Würzburg over the use of introspection in the study of the mind can best be understood, perhaps, in terms of Freud's initial theory of mind. Wundt would admit only that which is immediately present in consciousness to be a legitimate object of scientific investigation. This is equivalent to Freud's conception of consciousness. Külpe, at Würzburg, however, was prepared to consider factors that once had been in consciousness but which, now, were so no longer. In other words, Külpe permitted memory to play a role in the production of introspective reports, whereas Wundt confined the data of his new experimental science to the facts of inner perception alone. The practice of the Würzburg laboratory, but not that of the Leipzig laboratory, included a role for the operation of what Freud called preconscious thought. Freud's first theory of mind, in which he distinguished only between the conscious, the preconscious and the unconscious, thus enables us to appreciate what Wundt saw only too clearly – namely, that his experimental science was a strictly limited project. Freud showed, in relation to mental phenomena, that consciousness is only the tip of the iceberg. Most of what is significant in human life is not present in consciousness and this relates to culture as well as to Freud's notion of the unconscious.

Jahoda (1992) has demonstrated that the issue of the relationship between culture and mind is part of a much longer debate in the history of ideas concerning the nature of human nature. Jahoda traces this debate to its roots in eighteenth-century thought. His book is also valuable because he is able to compare and to contrast French and German thought on the same issues. In part III of his book, Jahoda (1992) provides the reader with a far better account of the historical background needed for appreciating the significance of Wundt's *Völkerpsychologie* than does Danziger (1983). Jahoda's book is highly germane to the theme of this chapter. The time frame of his study, however, is much deeper than the strictly limited, and somewhat arbitrary, one I have adopted for the purposes of writing this book.

For Wundt, as well as for both Durkheim and Freud (see below), culture is something that is beyond the awareness of the individuals who both embody and transmit it. It is something which is outwith (as the Scots say) the consciousness of individuals. It comprises what Durkheim (see below) called collective representations. These collective representations are now objects of study in such human and social sciences as psychology, sociology, anthropology and linguistics. The idea, proposed by Jung, that individuals may be linked to one another through some form of collective unconscious is a faintly preposterous one, from a strictly scientific point of view. The consideration of it need detain us no longer. It does illustrate, however, the difficulties involved in moving from the study of culture (i.e. myths and other archetypes in this particular case) to an understanding of the minds (and especially of the dreams) of individuals. Equally preposterous hypotheses have been proposed in the modern era by people taking a similar route, e.g. moving from the study of language to a consideration of the linguistic competence of the individual. The inferential leap is the assumption that a generic linguistic competence must also be genetic. The confusion here is acoustic as well as real.

For Wundt, but not for either Durkheim or Freud, language was an important object of study in his *Völkerpsychologie*. Indeed, the first two volumes in the series were devoted to *Die Sprache*. Mead (1904), who was then in Chicago, reviewed these first two volumes in *Psychological Bulletin* (see appendix 1 for more details). Part of this work was translated into English for the first time comparatively recently (Wundt, 1973). In his valuable introduction to this translation, Blumenthal (1973) has this to say about Wundt's influence, at the turn of the century, in the field of linguistics:

> to understand the history of psycholinguistics no less than that of psychology in general, one must attempt seriously to comprehend Wundt and his times . . . He was the one living psychologist who had the most influence on the thought of linguists at that time. His lectures on the psychology of language were the most heavily attended in the world and those who heard him included de Saussure, Paul, Delbrück and Bloomfield. Most who undertook the study of the psychology of language in the decades around the turn of the century were either guided by him or had to deal with him at their great effort. (Blumenthal, 1973, pp. 12, 13)

Blumenthal has done a useful job in rehabilitating the image of Wundt in histories of psychology more generally (Blumenthal, 1975) and not just in relation to the history of psycholinguistics. His motivation, in part, is to show the continuing relevance of some of Wundt's ideas in the context of modern cognitive science; for example, Wundt's treatment of attention and also his work on the psychology of the sentence. I am not so sure that this is a worthy motive since the two situations – the one in which Wundt developed his ideas and the other to which Blumenthal applies them – are so dramatically different from each other. I am sure it is wrong to think of Wundt in terms of cognition; but not so wrong to think of him in terms of mind. In this respect Miller (1966) and Gardner (1985) have a better sense of history than Blumenthal. Blumenthal (1973) thinks the time is now ripe for psycholinguists to appreciate the historic significance of Wundt's work for their own discipline and in this I am sure he is correct. Blumenthal, himself, has done much to bring about this highly desirable state of affairs.

Individual and collective representations: the Durkheimian antithesis

In choosing representations as his key theoretical term, Durkheim privileged a private/public dimension to the contrast between the individual and the collective. The contrast enabled him to focus on the public and to ignore the private. He claimed the study of collective representations to be the peculiar province of the sociologist. He was content to leave the study of individual representations to the psychologist. What he produced was a sociology of knowledge rather than, say, a psychology of widespread beliefs. This is because knowledge is public, whereas beliefs are personal, psychological and private. This is why Moscovici's book *La Psychanalyse: son image et son public* (1961) is within the Durkheimian tradition. It is a contribution to the sociology of knowledge as well as being a major study in modern social psychology. The French word '*savoir*' is only imperfectly translated into English by the word 'knowledge'. The latter is closer in semantic space in English to 'belief' than *savoir* would be if there were an exact English equivalent.

Durkheim, therefore, is an important figure when it comes to the drawing of disciplinary boundaries within the human and social sciences. He is often portrayed as the most anti-psychological of all the major sociologists. The psychology to which he was so strongly opposed was the psychology of the individual. His choice of suicide as the topic of one of his major studies was of strategic significance. Suicide would appear to be wholly the act of an individual, yet Durkheim succeeded in demonstrating variations in rates of suicide across both societies and social categories and, over time, within those societies and categories; for example, Protestants were more likely to commit suicide than Catholics; single people were more liable than people who were married, etc. Social facts need to be explained in terms of other social facts. They cannot be explained at the level of the individual. This is a strongly anti-reductionist stance. Durkheim maintained this stance in relation both to theory and to methods of research.

In his article of 1898, in which he argues for the independence of sociology from psychology, Durkheim reviews some of the arguments advanced by James (1890) for asserting the independence of psychology from physiology. Wundt later used somewhat similar arguments to justify the separation of his *Völkerpsychologie* from his experimental psychology (see chapter 2). Both men adduced the same anti-reductionist arguments. The objects of study in Wundt's *Völkerpsychologie* – language, religion, customs, myth, magic and cognate phenomena – were very similar to the collective representations that, according to Durkheim, were the objects of study in sociology. Wundt thought language was very important; Durkheim thought religion was very important. It seemed to be the same project, but with a difference in emphasis.

At an early stage in his career Durkheim had been influenced by Wundt (see appendix 1). In 1885–6 Durkheim visited various German universities, including Leipzig, and was impressed by what he saw (Lukes, 1973). He was particularly impressed by Wundt: by the exactness and precision of Wundt's laboratory science; by his organizational skills in creating the new subject of psychology; by his establishment of an Institute and founding of a journal in which to publish the research of his laboratory. Back at his base in Bordeaux, Durkheim adopted some of the same tactics in establishing sociology as a distinct discipline. The similarities between Wundt and Durkheim were probably greater than the differences. Durkheim was not averse, for example, to calling sociology 'collective psychology', providing that one recognized that the laws of 'collective psychology' were very different from the laws of psychology. In this opinion he was clearly influenced by Wundt.

A major difference, however, between Wundt and Durkheim, was that the former regarded his *Völkerpsychologie* as part of the *Geisteswissenschaften*. This was clearly a fundamental difference, though the debate about the different forms of *wissenschaft* was a German rather than a French debate. Durkheim was certainly a positivist; and Wundt, as we have seen, was an anti-positivist. The debate in France was in terms of positivism rather than in terms of *wissenschaft*. This reflects the difference between the two cultures but, essentially, it is the same debate. There is, however, a subtle difference. The debate in Germany concerned two different forms of *wissenschaft*. In France, positivism was a movement to model the human and social sciences on the natural sciences. It was not concerned with distinguishing between two different forms of *savoir*. The debate in France was not as neutral as that in Germany. This is also the sense in which G. W. Allport (1954) nominates Comte as the founder of social psychology. This choice of ancestor (see chapter 8) is part of the process, in the modern era, of social psychology becoming a branch of the natural sciences, following the successful example of the parent discipline, psychology. In France, the counterpoint to considering the social sciences to be natural sciences is to consider history as a social science.

Durkheim is important, in the context of the present volume, because of his over-sharp distinction, at an early stage, between psychology and sociology. This made possible the development of social psychology as a subdiscipline of either psychology or sociology. This, in

replaced his brother, F. H., as editor of the social psychology half of the journal, a position he held for a period of some 12 years (appendix 1). The emergence of a cognitive social psychology in America during the modern era is, at least in part, a reaction to this historic link between the social and abnormal. This is clear, for example, from the general tenor of Asch's classic text on *Social Psychology* (1952).

While Wundt dealt with culture and Durkheim with society, Le Bon dealt with society in transition. Nye (1975), as we have already noted, observed that the psychology of crowds was a product of the crisis in democracy in the Third Republic. Crowds had played a revolutionary role in French politics ever since the Revolution. Formulating the issue, as Le Bon did, it terms of the relation between the individual and the crowd, privileged an interpretation of social phenomena in terms of individuals. This is because crowds and masses are aggregates of individuals. This is a process that we shall call the individualization of the social (Graumann, 1986). Le Bon and, to a lesser extent, Durkheim were concerned with individualization as a societal process. My concern in this volume is with the individualization of the social in the context of the history of academic disciplines. The two processes are related, though in complex ways.

Case studies and the psychoanalytic critique of culture

All of the major theorists I have considered to date in this chapter draw a sharp contrast between the study of the individual and the study of the collective. They were better able to state antitheses than they were to propose syntheses. Freud is an exception. As a clinician, most of his early writings were reports of clinical cases. Part of his therapeutic technique involved the interpretation of dreams. He regarded the dream and its analysis as the royal road to the study of the unconscious. His first model of mind was a theory of the unconscious. The unconscious, here, is a personal unconscious and the dreams to which it gives rise are the dreams of an individual. In the 1920s Freud moved on from the interpretation of dreams to the interpretation of culture. This is now the basis of a whole hermeneutic enterprise. This, truly, is part of the human and social sciences, i.e. the *Geisteswissenschaften*.

In a whole series of volumes he wrote in the 1920s, Freud developed a psychoanalytic critique of culture. He was influenced by a number of factors, apart from his own abiding interest in cultural issues. Like Morton Prince, he was influenced by the mass phenomena of a world at war. His writings after the war were much more explicitly social than they had been before the war. Moscovici (1981, 1985) has shown how Freud was Le Bon's most assiduous disciple. The masses for Le Bon were masses of individuals. Freud believed that the masses were not as unstructured as Le Bon seemed to claim. What united the members of a crowd with each other was their common identification with a leader. The leader emerges as a type of superego. It was during this period that Freud revised his theory of mind in a more explicitly social direction by distinguishing between ego, id and superego where, previously, he had only distinguished between the conscious, the preconscious and the unconscious. So Freud provided his own synthesis between an analysis of the psyches of individuals and his critique of culture.

The psychoanalytic contribution to the social sciences is in danger of being overlooked, especially in histories of social psychology. It did feature in the 1954 *Handbook of Social Psychology* edited by Lindzey and again in the 1968–9 edition edited by Lindzey and Aronson, but not in the subsequent edition. The psychoanalytic inheritance in psychology, more generally, is mainly in the hands of clinicians rather than in the hands of social psychologists. It is biased, therefore, more in favour of the individual than in favour of culture as the focus of its interest.

The single most important study in the history of social psychology to be inspired by psychoanalysis was *The Authoritarian Personality* by Adorno et al. (1950). The inspiration and thinking behind the project were the product of the Frankfurt School of sociology whose Institute had been shut down on the orders of Hitler himself. Many, nowadays, see this as sociology rather than as psychology. The book itself, which was close on a thousand pages, was a brilliant study of the nature of anti-Semitism in a modern context. It was an attempt to understand, on the part of a group of German and Austrian emigrés, the nature of fascism in their native countries. All of the empirical data in the study, however, were American. The best-known output from the study was 'The Californian F Scale', where F stood for fascism. It was a measure of anti-Semitism.

The Authoritarian Personality was a landmark publication in social psychology and recognized to be so as soon as it appeared. It was, literally, a monumental achievement. It was cited in 1965 by the editors of the new *Journal of Personality and Social Psychology* as a prototypic study in the field of the new journal. This was when the dominant psychological tradition of social psychology in America severed its links with the abnormal and espoused the normal (see above). While the study flowered at the beginning of the modern era in social psychology (it was published in 1950), its roots are clearly in the period here under review. It is also a particularly fine example of the claim advanced by Cartwright (1979) that Adolf Hitler was the single most influential figure in the history of social psychology (see chapter 1).

It is difficult for the modern reader trained in the dominant psychological tradition of social psychology in America to appreciate that the inspiration for *The Authoritarian Personality* was as much sociological as psychological. The synthesis worked out at the Institut für Sozialforschung in Frankfurt was between psychoanalysis and Marxism. The ideological element was at least as important as the psychoanalytic element. The modern reader referred to above is probably totally oblivious to the towering reputation within sociology of the Frankfurt School or its importance in fields like media studies and theories of modern culture. This is almost certainly due to the individualization and the Americanization (Manicas, 1987) of social psychology in the modern era. This is a product of the expansion of the *Naturwissenschaften* into the realm of the *Geisteswissenschaften*. Cultural studies and media studies are not natural sciences. Hermeneutics is a form of literary criticism and not a recognized technique of scientific research.

Yet the roots of this tradition are to be found in Freud's critique of culture during the period following the end of the First World War. This raises the issue of the status of psychoanalysis in terms of the rivalry between the two different forms of *wissenschaft* within the German academic tradition. Members of the Vienna Circle were certainly clear it was not a branch of the *Naturwissenschaften*. Perhaps the whole corpus of Freud's work is best conceived of as *Geisteswissenschaft*. Since he worked out his own synthesis between the individual and the cultural, his work should be judged as a whole. He was as strong an anti-reductionist as either Wundt or Durkheim. In this, however, he was in the Jamesian mould, stressing the independence of psychology from physiology. This is at the level of theory. Durkheim had taken James as a model in developing his own arguments for the independence of sociology from psychology (see above). It isn't that Freud didn't try to make the reduction – his training, after all, was as a research physiologist. It was for purely domestic reasons that, reluctantly, he became a clinician. He did have 'a project for a scientific psychology' which would have made it a branch of the natural sciences because the aim of the project was to reduce the language of psychology to the language of physiology. His decision not to publish the project was a consciously taken one that we must respect. He was not satisfied that it could be done. Wundt produced a physiological psychology that was only in part a branch of natural science. Freud produced psychoanalysis which was wholly a human and social science.

It is because psychologists aspire to be treated as natural scientists that they are ambivalent about Freud. This is beautifully captured by Marie Jahoda in her book *Freud and the Dilemmas of Psychology* (1977; but see also Jahoda, 1972, 1983; Farr, 1975, 1981). She notes that Freud does not enjoy an assured status in histories of psychology. This, Jahoda suspects, is because the logical positivists in Freud's native Vienna judged that psychoanalysis was not a science. Perhaps the arguments they marshalled in coming to this conclusion could equally be applied to psychology, she mischievously surmises. In the interests of scientific and academic respectability, it might be better to distance oneself from psychoanalysis and its claims to be a science. This, by and large, is what academic psychologists (including social psychologists) have done in the United Kingdom and in the United States of America. A notable exception to this, of course, is Marie Jahoda. There is also in Britain a great suspicion of theory. The ashes of Freud are in Hampstead and the bones of Karl Marx are in Highgate but any meeting between their two minds is more likely to occur in Frankfurt, Paris, New York, Budapest, Rio de Janeiro or Buenos Aires than in London.

Mind, self and society: the Meadian synthesis

Wundt pitted the consciousness of the individual against culture because, unlike Freud, he could not see how they were inter-related. The American pragmatist philosopher, G. H. Mead, produced a synthesis in response to Wundt's antithesis. He resolved the antithesis, as Freud had done, by producing a social theory of mind. For Mead, even more than for Wundt, language was of central importance. He worked backwards from Wundt's concept of the human gesture in the opening volumes of the *Völkerpsychologie* to a critique of Wundt's essentially Cartesian theory of mind underlying his experimental psychology. He interpolated the notion of self between those of mind and of society. Mead's work is so important in this respect, not least because he was a professional philosopher, that I have devoted a separate chapter to its exposition (see chapter 4).

Minor Variations

Masse und publikum: *the role of the journalist in modern society*

Masse und publikum was the title of Park's thesis that he submitted at the University of Heidelberg in 1904 (see appendix 1). It was not translated into English until quite some time later. As a journalist, Park resented the association between the masses and irrationality as presented in the social psychology of Le Bon. He was more influenced by the inter-mental social psychology of Tarde and by the latter's notion of public opinion. Most of Le Bon's psychology of the crowd related to consociate crowds who were together in one place and influenced by the oratory of their leaders. While this was the prototypic crowd in Le Bon's writings, he did also envisage the masses as being dispersed but responding to the same social events at the same time. This latter model is more appropriate to the modern mass media of communication, especially newspapers, radio and television.

As a journalist, Park was concerned with the rationality of public opinion as this emerges from the opinion pages of national newspapers. Hence his preference for the social psychology of Tarde over the social psychology of Le Bon. The emphasis is on rationality rather than on irrationality. The emphasis is on reading the printed word rather than on being swayed by oratory. Park on his return to America from Heidelberg worked with his colleague Burgess at Chicago and together they co-authored a textbook of *Sociology* which became the standard text in the subject at most American universities. Park was an important figure in the development of sociology at Chicago.

Table 3.1 Levels of theorizing

| Theorist | Level of phenomenon | | |
	Individual	Intermediate	Collective
Wundt	Physiological psychology		Völkerpsychologie
Durkheim	Individual representations		Collective representations
Le Bon	The individual		The crowd
Freud	Clinical studies	Ego, id and superego	Psychoanalytic critique of culture and society
de Saussure		*Parole*	*Langue*
Mead	Mind	Self	Society
McDougall	Instincts		Group mind
F. H. Allport	Behaviour of individuals		Institutional behaviour; public opinion

Parole et langue: the social and the collective in language

De Saussure is widely regarded as the founder of modern linguistics. He distinguished between '*langue*' at a collective level and '*parole*' at an interpersonal level. The latter, but not the former, was a form of social psychology. Indeed, de Saussure regarded semiotics as a form of social psychology. This illustrates a point that I hope is becoming clear to the reader as this chapter progresses. Social psychology as a discipline (if it is a single discipline) exists precariously at an intermediate level between the individual and the collective. This is illustrated in table 3.1. What is interesting about de Saussure is that language does not exist at the level of the individual. This was true also for Wundt and for Mead. Wittgenstein also asserted that there was no such thing as a private language. Language is social *tout court*. This is the tradition in Europe. Psycholinguistics is a Cartesian fallacy that emerged in American cognitive science during the modern era (Marková, 1982).

A British contribution to the debate

'A sketch of the principles of collective psychology with some attempt to apply them to the interpretation of national life and character': this is the subtitle of McDougall's book on *The Group Mind* which he published in 1920 as he left the post of the Wilde Readership in Mental Philosophy at Oxford to take up an appointment at Harvard. This was his version of collective psychology which was meant to complete his much earlier *Introduction to Social Psychology* of 1908. The two together comprised his social psychology. McDougall was clearly dealing with national life and character and so was operating at the same level as Wundt in his *Völkerpsychologie* and of Durkheim in his studies of collective representations. His approach is more explicitly biological than that of either Wundt or Durkheim. In this respect he is much closer to Mead and to Freud in seeing impulsivity as the basis of life in society. When McDougall arrived in America he sailed into a storm of criticism. In the previous decade, especially under the influence of behaviourism, Americans had come seriously to question the utility of instinct as a concept for understanding specifically human behaviour. This had been the basis of his 1908 text. Shortly after he arrived in the States he was attacked by F. H. Allport (see below) for appearing, in his notion of group mind, to assign agency to entities other than individuals (Farr, 1986).

Reductionism in the Social Sciences

The Americanization of social psychology: the role of F. H. Allport

All of the major theorists whose work appears in table 3.1, with the singular exception of F. H. Allport, were anti-reductionists. They all believed it was impossible to explain the collective in terms of the individual. F. H. Allport (1924), in his seminal textbook *Social Psychology*, turned social psychology into a behavioural and experimental science. One consequence of this, as Graumann (1986) has shown, was the individualization of the social. This is such an important theme in the context of the present book that chapter 6 is devoted solely to it. F. H. Allport (1933) went on to write a book about institutional behaviour, that is, a form of collective behaviour. In this respect he is similar to all of the other theorists listed in table 3.1 (with the exception, this time, of de Saussure). Where he differs from the others, however, is in his belief that as one moves from the level of the individual to the level of the collective it is not necessary to change one's model: the collective can be explained in terms of the individual. F. H. Allport in the 1930s was also a strong supporter of public opinion polling. The technology of opinion polling was completely consistent with his own form of methodological individualism. Manicas (1987) talks about the Americanization of the social sciences. I would want to argue that, in the work of F. H. Allport, we have a particularly fine example of the Americanization of one of the social sciences – social psychology.

4

George Herbert Mead: Philosopher and Social Psychologist

Philosophically, Mead was a pragmatist; scientifically, he was a social psychologist. He belonged to an old tradition – the tradition of Aristotle, Descartes, Leibnitz; of Russell, Whitehead, Dewey – which fails to see any sharp separation or any antagonism between the activities of science and philosophy, and whose members are themselves both scientists and philosophers.

C. W. Morris, in G. H. Mead, *Mind, Self and Society: from the standpoint of a social behaviorist*, 1934, p. ix

In my earliest days of contact with him as he returned from his studies in Berlin forty years ago, his mind was full of the problem which had always occupied him, the problem of individual mind and consciousness in relation to the world and society.

J. Dewey, at the memorial service for Mead in 1931

The Significance of Mead in Relation to the History of Social Psychology

Mead is important in the context of the present volume for a number of different reasons. He was one of those 10,000 Americans (Sokal, 1981) who flocked to German universities to pursue a graduate education in psychology and philosophy (see chapter 2). Unlike many, he remained in Germany for three years before returning to his native

America. Even after his return he kept himself informed about new
developments in Europe. He reviewed, for example, the first four
volumes of Wundt's *Völkerpsychologie* as they came off the presses in
Leipzig (Mead, 1904, 1906). As Dewey observed at the memorial
service for Mead in 1931, Mead spent a lifetime trying to resolve the
antithesis proposed by Wundt – 'the problem of individual mind and
consciousness in relation to the world and society' (Dewey, 1931). The
Meadian synthesis (as we noted in chapter 3) was to interpolate self
between mind and society. Mead was also (see below) a completely
consistent Darwinian. He thus had a sophisticated understanding of
comparative psychology. He derived this not only from Darwin but
also from Wundt's *Völkerpsychologie* (1900–20). This was the intellectual framework of the first *Handbook of Social Psychology* to be
published in America, edited by Murchison (1935) (see chapter 5).

The relevance of Mead to the themes treated in this volume does not
end here. He demonstrated the dialectical nature of the relationship
between the individual and society. Individualization is the outcome of
socialization and not its antithesis. The self in humans needs to be
understood both phylogenetically, in terms of the evolution of the
species, and ontogenetically, in terms of the development of each
individual member of the species. The self in humans is an emergent
property in the full Darwinian sense of the term. Mead was critical of
what he quaintly called Watsonism. Watson was one of his junior
colleagues at Chicago (see appendix 1). Mead was thus opposed to the
reductionist tendencies at work in the historical development of social
psychology in America (see chapter 6). This was mainly associated
with behaviourism, especially the behaviourism of F. H. Allport
(1924). Allport cites many of the published papers of Mead. He did not
have available, in 1924, any of the posthumously published books of
Mead. He cites Mead in the main (e.g. chapter 15), though not exclusively, as reducing the social to the individual. In this respect he treats
Mead as a fellow behaviourist and fails to appreciate that Mead is an
anti-reductionist.

The social behaviourism of Mead differs, quite radically, from the
behaviourisms of Watson, F. H. Allport and Skinner, principally because he treated language as an inherently social phenomenon. In this
respect his starting point for the development of his social psychology
was Wundt's *Völkerpsychologie*. He provided an account, in terms of
natural history, of mind and of self-reflexive intelligence in the human
species. This was at a time when behaviourists in psychology and
social psychology (namely Watson and F. H. Allport) were treating
mind, the self and consciousness as metaphysical concepts. The behav-

iourists in psychology (Watson) and social psychology (F. H. Allport), but not the social behaviourist in philosophy (Mead), were over-valuing what they could see and under-valuing what they could hear. Language is central to the social psychology of Mead.

When Mead died in 1931 his annual course of lectures in social psychology at Chicago was taken over by Blumer. Mead's course had become central to the development of sociology at that university. Blumer was a sociologist and not a philosopher. He named this tradi-tion of social psychology 'symbolic interactionism'. The name is Blumer's and not Mead's. This is how it became a sociological, rather than a psychological, form of social psychology (see chapter 7) during the modern era. Sociologists regard Mead as the originator of symbolic interactionism which is still an active tradition of research in modern American sociology. It is, of course, a serious misinterpretation of Mead (McPhail and Rexroat, 1979; Blumer, 1980; McPhail and Rex-roat, 1980). The effect on the historical development of sociology in America of Blumer's misinterpretation of Mead was to free sociology of its dependence on Darwin's theory of evolution. Yet Mead was a fully committed and completely consistent Darwinian (much more so than either Watson or Skinner in psychology, for example).

Mead was rejected by the psychologists because he was not a behav-iourist, as they understood the term, and accepted by the sociologists because he appeared to set the social sciences free of their dependence on the life sciences (which was not, in fact, Mead's own position). Watson and Blumer have little in common apart from the fact that they were both taught social psychology by Mead at Chicago. Neither could really have understood what they were listening to. Watson, at least, is honest about this. 'I took courses and seminars with Mead. I didn't understand him in the classroom, but for years Mead took a great interest in my animal experimentation, and many a Sunday he and I spent in the laboratory watching my rats and monkeys. On these comradely exhibitions and at his home I understood him. A kinder, finer man I never met' (Watson, 1936, p. 274). Blumer (1980) is less honest.

I hope it will soon be apparent that Mead was exceptionally well qualified to talk to psychologists but they were not particularly in-clined to listen to him. Like Wundt and William James, Mead was, and chose to remain, a professor of philosophy. This, at least in the minds of psychologists, associated him with the metaphysical past of their discipline rather than with its scientific present and even more scien-tific future. When the University of Chicago was established in 1894, Dewey was appointed to the Foundation Chair of Philosophy. This appointment included psychology and education as well as philosophy, and Dewey brought Mead with him to Chicago from Ann Arbor (see appendix 1). When Dewey left Chicago for Columbia in 1904, the psychologists at Chicago under Angell formed a separate department. Mead remained with the philosophers while Watson transferred with the psychologists. One consequence of this quite early separation between the two disciplines was that the psychologists at Chicago were unlikely to look back to the philosophers for their inspiration. It was the sociologists at Chicago and not the psychologists who attended Mead's course of lectures in social psychology. The fact that the social psychology of Mead has been preserved within American sociology (albeit in a distorted form) has led to its neglect by modern social psychologists trained in the dominant psychological forms of social psychology (see chapter 1).

As we have already seen (chapter 1), G. W. Allport (1954), at the start of the modern era in social psychology, distinguished between the roots of modern social psychology and its flowering, which he considered to be a characteristically American phenomenon. The social psychology of Mead is firmly rooted in the distinctive soil of the whole Western tradition of thought in philosophy and it is also a characteristically American phenomenon. It flourished, however, before the modern era in social psychology. G. W. Allport (1954), in his historical background to modern social psychology, singularly failed to appreciate the significance of Mead's social psychology. He referred to Mead briefly and, then, only with regard to the inadequacy of imitation as a single explanatory principle in accounting for social phenomena. Interestingly, he thought that Mead was less damaged by this criticism than the other theorists who used imitation as an explanatory principle. Mead devised his social psychology at a time when psychology had become an experimental science (in Germany in the last quarter of the nineteenth century) and before social psychology became an experimental science (Jones, 1985), in America in the later half of the twentieth century. This is why it is easy to overlook the significance of what he achieved.

Mead provides an interesting link between positivism in Europe and in America in that he was a student of Ebbinghaus (see below and appendix 1) and a teacher of Watson (see above). Ebbinghaus and Watson were the spearheads, in Europe and America respectively, of the move to make psychology wholly a branch of the *Naturwissenshaften*. They were both opposed to Wundt's own view that psychology was only, in part, a branch of the natural sciences. Ebbinghaus, in his studies of memory, challenged Wundt's view that higher mental processes could not be studied experimentally in the laboratory. Watson challenged the dependence of experimental psychology on introspection. He did so by challenging the one person in America who was widely regarded as Wundt's representative there – Titchener. The functionalist school of thought in psychology which originated in Chicago under Dewey's leadership was set against the structuralism of Titchener and it was the functionalists who emerged victorious. Functionalism, as Mead himself argued, was only a transitional phase in the move to behaviourism. Watson claimed the whole of psychology to be a branch of the natural sciences by advocating the extension to the study of humans of the objective methods of research that had proved successful in the study of animals and human infants. These could in no way depend upon introspection since neither animals nor infants talk in a manner that is intelligible to the adult experimenter. For Mead, of course, language was central to psychology as a social science, as it had been for Wundt also.

The prototypical natural science for Watson was physics; for Mead it was evolution. This, at first, may seem surprising since Watson was an acknowledged expert in the study of animal behaviour (this apparent paradox is discussed more fully below and, again, in chapter 5). Mead provided a basis in natural science for Wundt's *Völkerpsychologie*, i.e. he grounded it in Darwin's theory of evolution. Wundt, himself, had consciously used the comparative method in his exploration of language, religion, customs, myth, magic and cognate phenomena. Mead naturalized mind, while Watson dispensed with it. Watson was a philosophically naïve positivist; Mead was a philosophically sophisticated pragmatist. They were two quite distinctly different types of scientist. Mead made psychology a branch of the *Geisteswissenschaft*; Watson made it a branch of the *Naturwissenschaften*.

Mead, like Wundt before him, was repudiated by the positivists in psychology. He does not appear as a major (or even a minor) figure in histories of social psychology (Allport, 1954; Jones, 1985) or in handbooks of social psychology (Lindzey, 1954; Lindzey and Aronson, 1968–9, 1985). The extent to which those histories were informed by a positivist philosophy of science was a theme that I treated in chapter 1. The extent to which the modern series of *Handbooks of Social Psychology*, edited by Lindzey and by Lindzey and Aronson, is informed by the same philosophy of science is the topic of chapter 10.

Figure 4.1 George Herbert Mead at the time of his 1927 course of lectures in social psychology

G. H. Mead: the Man and his Work

His education

Mead (see figure 4.1) was born at South Hadley, Massachusetts, in 1863 and died in Chicago in 1931. He obtained a general arts degree in 1883 from Oberlin College, where his father had been a professor of homiletics. He was expected to follow his father into the ministry of the Church but began to develop serious doubts about the truth of Christianity. He shared these doubts with a fellow student, Henry Castle, who was the son of wealthy American missionaries in Hawaii.

By the time they graduated from Oberlin College in 1883 the two friends were agnostics. Mead's father had died a year or so before George Herbert enrolled as a student at Oberlin. Mead shielded his mother, who was a pious woman, from knowing about his increasing doubts concerning Christianity. The source of his agnosticism was his conviction that Kant was right about the limits of human knowledge.

After graduating from Oberlin, Mead tried his hand, briefly, at teaching in a primary school but this proved disastrous for all concerned. He then worked for three years as a member of a survey crew involved in the construction of the Wisconsin Central Rail Road, and was impressed by the accuracy and precision of such work. On Castle's advice, he enrolled at Harvard for a master's degree in philosophy and psychology. Castle was reading law at Harvard. The two friends jointly took Royce's course on Kant and this proved a revelation to both of them. Royce was a Hegelian and his interpretation of Kant was very different from what they had been taught at Oberlin. At Harvard, Mead was more influenced by Royce than he was by James. James, however, recruited Mead to tutor one of his children and so, for a period of months, he became a member of the James household. James had been impressed by an essay Mead had written for him. Mead needed the money and James needed someone in the household with whom he could talk metaphysics. It proved to be a symbiotic relationship over the summer months of 1888.

Mead's friend, Henry Castle, returned to Europe to study philosophy at various German universities where he had studied before his decision to study law. Mead joined Castle in Europe where he studied first in Leipzig and then in Berlin. In the winter semester of 1888–9, he enrolled in Wundt's classes in Leipzig. This was the phase in Wundt's highly planned career (see chapter 2) when he was developing his scientific metaphysics. Mead, on the advice of G. Stanley Hall, then left Leipzig in 1889 for Berlin, where he specialized, over a period of two years, in the study of physiological psychology and experimental psychology, both of which he learned from Ebbinghaus. He also studied psychology, anthropology, philosophy and education under Paulson and philosophy under Dilthey.* He was supervised, in his doctoral studies, by Dilthey (Joas, 1985). His thesis, which he failed to complete before returning to the United States, was on the perception of space and concerned the relationship between vision and touch.

* I am grateful to my former colleague, Dr David Frisby, of the Department of Sociology at the University of Glasgow, for some of the information in this paragraph which he obtained from the archives of the Humboldt University in Berlin. Joas (1985) also contains some of the same information.

While vision provides the individual with information about objects at a distance, this needs to be supplemented by the actual experience of contact with the object concerned. Mead is very much a haptic philosopher, concerned with the relationship between the hand and the development of the central nervous system. This, together with language, makes the human species different from all other species.

Mead and Castle corresponded when they were not actually lodging or studying together at Harvard, Leipzig or Berlin. Some of this correspondence has been analysed by Coughlan (1975) for the light it sheds on the young John Dewey (see esp. ch. 7, pp. 113–33). It is interesting to set this correspondence alongside that of J. McKeen Cattell (see chapter 2). Since Mead and Castle were peers, the correspondence is much more informal than the letters Cattell sent to his parents describing his student days in Leipzig and Cambridge. Castle was restive and frequently changed his career plans. He often returned home to Hawaii and vacillated between the study of philosophy and qualifying to practice law. One option open to him was to work with his brother in the family law firm in Hawaii. Castle's friends had originally gone to Hawaii before the Civil War to manage the finances of the Calvinist Mission there. They became wealthy landowners in their own right and Castle's father, among other things, managed a sugar plantation there.

In 1889 Castle married the beautiful 19-year-old daughter of their German landlady in Berlin. Later that year he returned to Hawaii via Harvard and Columbia where he had vaguely (and it turned out vainly) hoped to finish his law degree. Mead continued in Berlin with his studies and became engaged to an American girl. In Hawaii, Castle's wife was killed by a fall from a horse, and, in November 1890, Castle returned to Germany and rejoined his friend. Castle's sister Helen had been in Europe when her brother's wife was killed; she joined Mead and Castle in Berlin. Mead's engagement had been broken off earlier that summer. Mead then unexpectedly received an offer from the University of Michigan of a post as instructor in philosophy and psychology. He married Helen Castle; tried, unsuccessfully, to complete his doctorate; and then returned to America with his bride to take up his new post. In 1895 Henry Castle was drowned in a shipwreck on the River Elbe. His parents published a memorial edition of their son's letters and Mead contributed a preface for the volume. This is the correspondence analysed by Coughlan (1975), to whom I am indebted for much of the information presented in the previous paragraphs.

Mead's career

Mead left Berlin in 1891 to take up the instructorship in philosophy and psychology at the University of Michigan. It was at Michigan that Dewey and Mead met and became firm, lifelong friends. It was also at Michigan that Mead met C. H. Cooley who, at the time, was writing his doctoral thesis in economics. It was Cooley who introduced Mead to the writings of Adam Smith which is the source of Mead's idea about assuming the role of the other. In everyday market transactions, buyers and sellers assume each other's roles and their ability to do so significantly enhances the efficiency of markets. It is possible to interact commercially with a wide range of others with whom one does not share a common language or a common culture. Mead believed that trade had done more to unite the world than any of the world's major religions. It is not too difficult to see in the social psychology that Mead was to develop at Chicago a similarity to Adam Smith's *The Theory of Moral Sentiments* (Smith, 1759).

When Dewey was appointed in 1894 head of the Department of Philosophy at the newly established University of Chicago, he brought Mead with him from Michigan, as an assistant professor, and Mead remained in Chicago until his death there in 1931 (see appendix 1 for further information on this and other events in the life and work of Mead). Dewey, however, left Chicago for Columbia in 1904. Watson went up to Chicago in 1900 to study for his doctorate under Dewey. Watson claimed, in a brief autobiography which he wrote in 1936, that he had never really understood Dewey. Instead, he completed his doctorate under Angell on the topic of educating rats to negotiate mazes.

Mead first began to give his annual course of lectures in social psychology in 1900. It is highly likely that Watson took this particular course, probably in its first year on offer. In 1908 Watson, at the age of 30, left Chicago and went to Johns Hopkins as a full professor. It was in the period between 1912 and 1915, when he became President of the American Psychological Association, that Watson formulated, and then put into effect, his behaviourist manifesto (Watson, 1913, 1916). This was a movement that was dedicated to ridding psychology of the notions of consciousness, of self and of mind. These were the very notions that were central to the form of social psychology that Mead was working out at Chicago. It is a measure of the success of Watson's crusade that James's definition of psychology, as the science of mental life, rapidly became obsolete. Psychologists followed Watson much as the inhabitants of Hamlyn followed the pied piper.

Albion Small, the Foundation Professor of Sociology at Chicago, was quick to appreciate the importance of Mead's course of lectures in social psychology for the development of sociology. This became a strongly recommended course for graduate students in sociology at Chicago. Lewis and Smith (1980) show that Mead's influence among sociologists at Chicago was greater after 1920 than it was before that date. The key figure here was Faris who replaced Thomas in 1920 and who strongly recommended Mead's course in social psychology to graduate students in sociology. This involved them in attending an ancillary course in another department (the Department of Philosophy). When the sociologists heard Mead attack Watson I believe they assumed that he, like them, was an anti-positivist. In fact, what Mead was saying was that Watson had not gone far enough: he had not come up with a natural history account of the origins of mind and of self-awareness in the human species. Watson had ignored mind rather than attempting to explain it.

One of the problems that Mead poses for the historian of social psychology concerns the development of his own thinking, especially in the field of social psychology. Mead lectured without the aid of notes. That we have even the knowledge we do of his course of lectures in social psychology is a tribute to the notes his students made in the classroom. It was also due to their initiative (and the financial generosity of an ex-student) that a stenographer was smuggled into the class to record his 1927 course of lectures in social psychology. This formed the basis of the posthumously published volume *Mind, Self and Society: from the standpoint of a social behaviorist*, edited by Morris (Mead, 1934). All of the books bearing Mead's name were published posthumously and comprised edited versions of student's notes and draft manuscripts. There is even another version of Mead's 1927 course of lectures in social psychology (Mead, 1982, edited by D. L. Miller) that is quite different from the version edited and published by Morris in 1934. Miller can only suppose that Mead must have taught the course twice in that year.

I agree with the view expressed by Joas (1980) that Miller's (1973) biography of Mead is of little use in helping us to trace the development of Mead's thinking. This is largely because it is arranged in terms of topics rather than in terms of progression in his thinking. Some idea of the development in Mead's thinking can be obtained from the selection of his writings edited by Reck (1964). These are a selection of the papers by Mead that were published during his lifetime and they are arranged in chronological order of publication. The best, and easily the most detailed, study of the development of Mead's thinking is to be found in Joas (1980, English edition 1985). This is because it is based on extensive archival research and on a detailed linguistic analysis of his various texts. More significantly, it is an interpretation of the development in his thinking and not just a list of important facts. Being a European rather than an American exegesis of the life and work of Mead, it does full justice to the role of German idealism in the development of Mead's thinking, especially in the early years. It also contains an unrivalled exposition of the development of Mead's political thinking (see esp. ch. 2, 'The development of a radically democratic intellectual: George Herbert Mead, 1863–1931', pp. 15–32 in Joas, 1985).

I have been able to identify only five Americans who understood the significance of Wundt's *Völkerpsychologie* (1900–20). These were Mead, Judd, Baldwin, Thomas and Murchison. It is no accident, I believe, that three of the five were at the University of Chicago: Mead in philosophy, Judd in education and Thomas is sociology. Even the philosophers who understood Mead didn't necessarily understand Mead's relation to Wundt. Morris, for example, states (Mead, 1934, p. xiii) that Mead studied at Berlin, but fails to mention that he also studied at Leipzig. Miller (1973), in his biography, thinks that Mead was influenced by Wundt's physiological psychology. He was, but Mead was highly critical of it because the conception of mind underpinning Wundt's experimental science was essentially Cartesian. He was, however, strongly influenced by Wundt's *Völkerpsychologie*, reviewing the first four volumes of it in *Psychological Review* in 1904 and 1906 (see appendix 1). Clearly, the American philosophers to whom I refer had only a tenuous knowledge of the Germanic origins of much of Mead's early thought. This is why Joas's interpretation of Mead is an antidote to the views of those American philosophers who edited and interpreted the work of Mead as it appears in the books that were published posthumously.

At the end of his life Mead, as Chairman of the Department of Philosophy at Chicago, was involved in an increasingly acrimonious dispute with Hutchins, the President of the University. Miller (1973) is suitably circumspect in reporting the details of this dispute. A rupture occurred in the spring of 1931, the year in which Mead died. Miller states that an outline of the events surrounding this dispute are in his own personal file (Miller, 1973, p. xxxviii, n. 28). Joas, who has read the file, is able to be more precise (Joas, 1985, p. 221, n. 51). This dispute came to a head with the appointment of a neo-Thomist, Mortimer Adler, to a professorship at Chicago, against the express wishes of the department and of its chairman. Joas (1985, p. 221,

n. 51) explains the consequences of the appointment: 'Hutchins and Adler became important figures for the conservative emigrants from the Third Reich, for whom the University of Chicago became a gathering place – very much in contrast to the traditions of that university's first decades.' These disturbing events interfered with Mead's preparation of the courses of lectures which he gave at the University of Berkeley in December 1930. These lectures were later published as *The Philosophy of the Present* (Mead, 1932). Murphy, who edited the texts of these lectures, explains:

> Unfortunately, Mr Mead, in his capacity as chairman of the department of philosophy at the University of Chicago, was forced to surrender the time he had set aside for the completion of the lectures to administrative concerns of an unexpected and disturbing character. As a consequence the lectures were written hurriedly, in large part on the journey from Chicago to Berkeley; and he had not opportunity in the weeks immediately following their delivery to begin the revisions he already had in mind. By the end of January he was seriously ill and he died within a few weeks. (Murphy, in Mead, 1932, p. vii)

According to Miller (1973, p. xxxvii), Dewey visited Mead during this last illness and Mead agreed to leave Chicago and go to Columbia University in the autumn of 1931. He died before he was able to take up this appointment.

Mead as a Philosopher

Mead tackled most of the major problems addressed by philosophers. He worked out his own system in philosophy through the medium of his annual course of lectures in social psychology which he started in 1900–1 and continued until his death in 1931. He knew, when he was a student in Germany, that he needed to work out his own system in philosophy if he was to obtain an academic post in America. He needed, however, to conceal his own agnosticism since most academic positions were still in denominational colleges. The solution he hit upon was to work out his system at the level of physiological psychology. He discussed this with his friend Castle. Castle, in a letter home to his parents dated 3 February 1889 (see Coughlan, 1975, p. 124), explained his friend George's strategy: 'it would be hard for him to get a chance to utter any ultimate philosophical opinions savouring of independence. In Physiological Psychology on the other hand he has a harmless territory in which he can work quietly without drawing down upon himself the anathema and excommunication of all-potent Evangelicism.'

His early preoccupation with the problems of physiological psychology were just as important in the development of his thinking as his later concern with the principle of sociality. This is most clearly evident in his conversations with Dewey which resulted in the latter's publication of his classic paper 'The reflex arc concept in psychology' (Dewey, 1896). This was published while Dewey and Mead were together at the University of Chicago, but it had been a lively topic of conversation between the two men when they had been colleagues at the University of Michigan. The close links between Dewey and Mead at that time justified, in the eyes of Coughlan (1975), devoting a complete chapter in a book on *Young John Dewey: an essay in American intellectual history* to an analysis of the correspondence between G. H. Mead and his friend Henry Castle (see above). Mead, by all accounts (Miller, 1973, pp. xxxiv–xxxviii) was a great conversationalist. Dewey's daughter, Jane, also attests to this: 'Since Mead published so little during his lifetime, his influence on Dewey was the product of conversation carried on over a period of years and its extent has been underestimated . . . from the nineties on, the influence of Mead ranked with that of James' (Dewey, 1951, pp. 25–6).

The best interpretation of the development of Mead's thought in the late 1890s and the opening decade of the twentieth century is Joas (1980). Joas devotes an entire chapter to an analysis and discussion of Mead's article on 'The definition of the psychical' (Mead, 1903). The starting point of this analysis is Dewey's critique of the reflex arc concept in psychology. Joas thinks that Mead's mature work begins with the publication of this paper on defining the nature of the psychical (Joas, 1985, p. 63). He regards it as 'certainly his most significant work prior to the development of his fundamental premises for a theory of interaction and a social psychology' (1985, p. 64). These latter Joas considers to have been in place from about 1912 onwards. 'From my study I have concluded that the development of Mead's thought after about 1912 is to be understood more as the unfolding of his conception of symbolic interaction' (Joas, 1985, p. 10). Joas is not, here, referring to Blumer's notions of symbolic interaction. He, like myself, regards that as a serious misinterpretation of Mead (see below). He describes Blumer's social psychology as being 'achieved by means of an extremely fragmentary appropriation of Mead's work' (Joas, 1985, p. 7). The English translation (1985) of the original German text (Joas, 1980) uses Blumer's phrase 'symbolic interaction'. In the German original, Joas used the phrase coined by Habermas '*symbolvormittelte Interaktion*', which Joas himself translates as 'symbolically mediated interaction' (Joas, 1985, p. 228, n. 1). Joas's claim that the fundamentals of Mead's social psychology were already in place by 1912 is confirmed by the publication by Miller of a transcript of Mead's 1914 class lectures in social psychology (Mead, 1982, pp. 27–105).

Cartesian dualisms

As a major pragmatist philosopher, Mead was committed to overcoming the various dualisms that Descartes introduced into philosophy when he inaugurated the modern era in that discipline. The best-known dualism was that of mind and body. This is but a special case of the more fundamental dichotomy between mind and matter. The more fundamental dualism is also the source of the much later distinction between the *Geisteswissenschaften* (the sciences concerned with mind) and the *Naturwissenschaften* (the sciences concerned with matter) (see chapter 2). Matter is extended in space, while mind is not. The problem that this posed for Descartes, in the special case referred to above, was: how can mind, which is immaterial, be causally efficacious in the physical world? How can thoughts give rise to actions? The interaction between mind and body, Descartes concluded, is a divine miracle that occurs in the pineal gland. This is scarcely an acceptable answer in a scientific age. Mead saw Darwin's theory of evolution as offering philosophy the prospect of a new beginning in its search for an answer to such a question. 'For Mead . . . the key figure for a new beginning in philosophy was Darwin . . . Darwin's theory about the origin of species offered an escape from the dilemma of the alternative mechanistic and teleological explanations of evolution' (Joas, 1985, p. 53).

There were other dualisms in Cartesian philosophy besides the mind/body dualism. The dichotomy between knower and known was important in relation to epistemology and to the philosophy of knowledge. In the form in which Descartes posed the question, the knower is an isolated individual. The pragmatisms of Dewey and of James set out to resolve this particular dichotomy. The answers, like the question they address, are individualistic. I agree broadly with the view of Lewis in Lewis and Smith (1980) that, among the four major pragmatist philosophers, Dewey and James can be best considered nominalists, while Peirce and Mead are realists. The latter two are much more explicitly social than the former two in relation to their theory of truth. It is no accident, I would argue, that Mead worked out his system in philosophy through the medium of his course of lectures in social psychology.

The form of dualism that is of greatest significance to both Peirce and Mead is the dualism between self and other. In his attack on the Cartesian theory of knowledge, Peirce argued that the knowledge which each of us has of himself or herself as a unique 'thinking subject' is not as obviously 'intuitive' as Descartes had suggested. Gallie notes 'A plausible conclusion . . . is that our self-knowledge is always in fact inferential, although the inferences on which it is based have become for the most part so habitual to us, and as a result of this habitualism so "telescoped", that we very easily come to regard our self-knowledge as immediate or intuitive' (Gallie, 1952, p. 66). Peirce, therefore, questioned the very form of knowledge that Descartes thought was most secure in relation to his method of radical doubt, i.e. the '*cogito, ergo sum*'.

Mead showed how self emerges from social interaction. By assuming the role of the other with regard to ourselves, we become an object to ourselves. Our awareness of others is a necessary prerequisite to our awareness of self (Marková, 1987). The nature of consciousness in humans is an awareness of self in relation to others. Consciousness is thus an inherently social process. Between 1912 and 1920 Mead offered, on six separate occasions, a seminar on 'social consciousness'. This was in addition to, though usually in a separate semester from, his course of lectures in social psychology (see Lewis and Smith, 1980, p. 267). To my knowledge, we do not have any record of the programme of this series of seminars. Lewis and Smith present a much firmer data base for Mead after 1920 than they do before 1920. The timing of this supplementary seminar on social consciousness is, I believe, highly significant. It precisely coincides with Watson's development and elaboration of behaviourism (see appendix 1 for various relevant dates and events). This is discussed more fully in the section below on social behaviourism. Clearly, the nature of the self in humans preoccupied Mead throughout this period and his concern was not confined to his course of lectures in social psychology.

Here I am trying to place Mead (and, to a lesser extent, Peirce) in the much wider context of the history of Western philosophy. More specifically, however, I am concerned with how separately, and yet together, they set out to refute Cartesian dualism. Peirce does it by stressing the derived and inferential nature of the self in humans; Mead by stressing the inherently social nature of the self in humans. In both cases the self is an emergent rather than a given in terms of human experience. They are, in this sense, both process philosophers. I must be careful not to overstate the links between Peirce and Mead since, at best, they are indirect (Joas, 1985). The lines of influence, according to Joas, probably run from Peirce to Mead through Royce. I wish to suggest two further possibilities that might account for some of the similarities between the pragmatisms of Peirce and Mead. If, as I believe, they are both realists, then their philosophies will be informed by the findings of science. As philosophers, this sets Peirce and Mead apart from James and Dewey. There are still clear differences between Peirce and Mead since Peirce is concerned mainly with the natural sciences, while Mead is concerned with the biological and social sciences. The social psychology of Mead is closer to the 'pragmaticism' of Peirce (see below) than it is to either the pragmatism of James or the instrumentalism of Dewey. Language is also important to both Mead and Peirce (see below). The work of both Mead and Peirce is taken up and developed by semioticians.

The other possibility concerns the personalities of the four pragmatists and the dynamics of their friendships. James and Dewey were much more charismatic figures then either Peirce or Mead. Peirce and Mead, I would want to argue, were more profound thinkers than either James or Dewey. They published comparatively little during their lifetimes and we are indebted to their former students, colleagues and others, who collected and edited their papers after their deaths, for our understanding of the scope and significance of their work. Part of the charisma of James and Dewey is that they were able to popularize science. Peirce and Mead differed most radically from James and Dewey in their conceptions of the social nature of science. It was James's failure to appreciate the inherently social nature of truth that lay at the root of his failure to understand Peirce's pragmatism. That is what led Perry (1935), the biographer of James, to claim that 'the philosophical movement known as Pragmatism is largely the result of James's misunderstanding of Peirce' (quoted in Gallie, 1952, p. 30). Since, at the time, Peirce was dependent on the personal charity of James, he did not like to publicise his friend's misunderstanding of his own philosophy. He rather gallantly offered to re-name his own philosophy 'pragmaticism' since this was such a barbaric word that no one (not even a friend) would want to borrow it and popularize it. The close friendships within the quartet of pragmatist philosophers were between Dewey and Mead and between James and Peirce. I think that it is no exaggeration to claim that, while James individualized Peirce's theory of truth, Mead socialized Dewey's philosophy of the act. This may account, in part, for the similarity between James and Dewey and the more indirect and distant similarity in the thought of both Peirce and Mead.

The issue of Cartesian dualism – especially the dualism between self and other – has been inimical, historically, to the development of the social sciences. Mead clearly saw this and set out to solve the problem. Others, who did not see it as a problem, failed to appreciate the significance of what Mead had achieved. I should like to elaborate this point since it is an important theme elsewhere in this volume. It may also help to explain why Mead has not had the influence, historically, on the development of psychology and of psychological forms of social psychology that the quality of his ideas deserves. I hope I have established that Mead was exceptionally well qualified to talk to psychologists but they, in the main, were not inclined to listen to him. In part, I have suggested, this may have been due to the fact that the psychologists at Chicago associated him with the metaphysical past of their discipline, as a branch of philosophy, rather than with its future as a branch of the natural sciences. I think the matter goes even more deeply than that. It concerns what Kuhn (1962) refers to as an incommensurability between paradigms.

In her book *Paradigms, Thought and Language*, Marková (1982) notes that histories of Western philosophy are often accounts of the conflict between rationalism and empiricism. Such histories obscure the fact that these rival philosophies are both Cartesian in their inspiration. The real incommensurability between paradigms is between Descartes and Hegel. Here Marková uses the word paradigm to refer to a system of thought in philosophy rather than to one in science. I think this is a legitimate use of the word paradigm. It helps to explain why certain forms of thought run very deep and shape enquiry in both philosophy and natural science for centuries without their influence being detected. This is especially the case when a certain field of enquiry, like psychology, which used to be a branch of philosophy, suddenly declares its independence from the parent discipline by claiming to be a branch of the natural sciences. This is what happened in what Mead, rather quaintly, called Watsonism. The Cartesian paradigm can continue to exist undetected. The alternative, Hegelian, paradigm which is incommensurable with the Cartesian paradigm (Marková, 1982) is much more explicitly social than the latter. Instead of the self/other dualism, self is considered in relation to other. Instead of an either/or dichotomy we have a both/and contingency. Mead developed his own system of philosophy in the context of German idealism and it is, thus, no accident that it was a form of social psychology. 'Mead's approach to a theory of intersubjectivity is incomprehensible without an understanding of his relationship to German idealism' (Joas, 1985, p. 11). Joas develops the thesis 'that Mead went through a Hegelian phase before he founded his inter-subjectivist pragmatism' (1985, p. 54). Marková's notion of a paradigm helps to explain why, to date, Mead has had little or no detectable influence on the historical development of psychology. That development had been wholly within a Cartesian paradigm. Mead solved a problem that psychologists did not even recognize to exist.

Descartes' method of radical doubt led him to doubt the evidence of his own senses. If, as in a visual illusion, our eyes sometimes deceive us, let us assume, he argued, that they might always deceive us. In extrapolating his method from a consideration of the physical world to a consideration of the social world, he was led to doubt that other people had minds. What he could not doubt, however, was his own doubting; that is, that he, himself, had a mind. Hence the importance of his famous '*cogito, ergo sum*'. Descartes is the *fons et origo* of the individualization of the social and not F. H. Allport as Graumann (1986) claims. The latter, however, is important specifically in relation to the history of social psychology and is dealt with at some length in chapter 6. Descartes' *Discourse on the Method of Rightly Conducting the Reason and Seeking Truth in the Sciences* (1637) is the principal reason why psychology, in the modern era, has not developed as a social science. Society becomes the problem of whether or not minds other than one's own exist.

Histories of modern psychology are written as if behaviourism had laid to rest the ghost of Descartes. During the period between 1912 and 1920, when Mead was offering his seminar at Chicago on the social nature of consciousness in humans, psychology ceased to be the science of mind and became, instead, the science of behaviour. Watsonism was a systematic crusade to rid psychology of all reference to consciousness, mind or self. Those who followed Watson could plausibly claim to have laid to rest the ghost of Descartes. The argument of Marková (1982), in *Paradigms, Thought and Language*, is that the ghost of Descartes continues to haunt the modern study of language and thought. We have already noted, in chapter 1, how the conflict between Chomsky and Skinner in 1957 is best interpreted as a conflict within what Marková calls the Cartesian paradigm between rationalism and empiricism in relation to the study of language.

Psychological, as distinct from sociological, forms of social psychology are also haunted by the ghost of Descartes. These two forms of social psychology, which are discussed more fully in chapter 7, differ precisely because they belong to different paradigms (Farr, 1990). They are also located in different academic disciplines, a topic that is dealt with more fully in chapter 6. Here I am concerned with an exposition of the philosophy of G. H. Mead and, more narrowly still, with trying to understand why he failed to influence the way in which psychology developed. The conclusion I have come to, after much thought, is that psychologists failed to realize that behaviourism, far from laying to rest the ghost of Descartes, is merely the other side of Cartesian dualism. The Cartesian inheritance in psychology is a mental philosophy of the self (accessible by means of introspection) and a behavioural science of the other. This is the nature of the self/other dualism in Cartesian philosophy. When psychology became the science of behaviour, it did not progress beyond Cartesian dualism. Mead saw this very clearly in the 1920s and solved the problem. Psychologists falsely thought that they had exorcized the ghost of Descartes by accepting behaviourism. They failed to see that the behaviourism they espoused and the mentalism they rejected belonged to one and the same paradigm.

Let me illustrate this 'failure of self-insight', as Ichheiser (1949) would describe it. Behaviourists generally, with the notable exceptions of Mead (1934) and of Bem (1967, 1972), don't believe that there is a self to be insightful about. One of the early textbooks of behaviourism, written by Max Meyer (1921) at the University of Missouri, was intriguingly entitled *The Psychology of the Other One*. After centuries of philosophers meditating in their armchairs concerning the nature of mind it was time, Meyer thought, to develop a science of the other one. This was a clarion call to abandon metaphysics and to establish a science. It is a particularly fine example of the clean break with the past that a positivist philosophy of science inspires. The other one, who would be the object of study in this new science, could be a plant, an animal, a mechanical device, a human infant or, even, another human being. Meyer intended his book as a practical guide for Robinson Crusoe on his desert island. Crusoe would be able to apply the various tests outlined in the book to ascertain what sort of a creature Man Friday was.

Language

Mead, Wundt and Vygotsky, in their respective social psychologies, were part of a tradition in Western thought that goes back to the writings of Herder, Humboldt and Hegel (Marková, 1983). Language, here, is a form of dialogue and, hence, is intrinsically, and irreducibly, social. This is much more explicit in Mead than it is in Wundt. For Wundt, language was the product of mind; for Mead, mind was the product of language. There are several light years between these two positions. Mead showed that by searching for the origins of language in behaviour (or gesture), Wundt was on the right track to solving the problem of mind but because his theory of language presupposed the existence of mind, the latter was left as something mysterious and unexplained. Mead was much bolder. He showed how mind emerges naturally from the conversation of gestures that occurs at a lower level in the evolutionary scale from the sorts of conversation that characterize human intercourse. 'Mind arises through communication by a conversation of gestures in a social process or context of experience – not communication through mind' (Mead, 1934, p. 50). Mead thus used Darwin to exorcize the ghost of Descartes from Wundt's theory of language.

The uttering and understanding of sentences is a tradition of research in the modern era that is more Cartesian than Hegelian in its inspiration. Speaker and listener are, here, two quite distinct persons who do not necessarily engage each other in conversation. They can only really converse if, in Mead's terms, each assumes the role of the other. It is important that speech is listener-orientated and listening is speaker-orientated (Rommetveit, 1974). It is also an integral part of Mead's theory of language that speaker and listener are also one and the same person. When a person speaks, she speaks to herself as well as to others. Language is very much a species-specific form of behaviour and it accounts for the self-reflexive nature of human intelligence. This is why, for Mead, thinking is a social activity. It involves carrying on a conversation with oneself that is comparable to the sorts of conversation one has with others. This is why, for Mead as well as for his fellow pragmatist Peirce, thinking is dialogical in form. For Peirce 'words, or signs of whatever description, are things whose function is not confined to expressing our own private thoughts, i.e. that "sign reading" is essentially of the same kind, whether the signs we read are made by ourselves or made by other people' (Gallie, 1952, p. 82).

This explicitly social treatment of language and thought which is to be found in the work of both Peirce and Mead is lost within the Cartesian paradigm. Watson did treat thinking as sub-vocal speech. The speech, however, is a monologue and not a dialogue. It is potentially detectable as minute innervations in the larynx. The divine miracle whereby mind interacts with body is to be found now in the larynx rather than in the pineal gland – except that Watson wasn't as pious as Descartes and so didn't believe in divine miracles. The larynx is also much closer to the surface of the human body and so is potentially detectable from the perspective of an outside observer. With a suitably sensitive instrument to record minute innervations, it should be possible to observe people thinking. Descartes chose the pineal gland as the locus of his miracle because nobody in his day knew what its function was and because it was difficult to gain access to it. The social nature of language is equally destroyed whether one accepts the rationalism of Chomsky's *Syntactic Structures* (1957) or the empiricism of Skinner's *Verbal Behavior* (1957), though the latter is more explicitly social than the former. Chomsky is, quite explicitly, a Cartesian. Cartesian assumptions were smuggled into cognitive science (see chapter 1) when Miller helped to establish psycholinguistics in the mid-1950s. The phantom of Descartes is scarcely invisible in this particular project: it lurks in the word 'psycho' as a qualifier for linguistics.

Joas (1985) tells us how he came to make his critical and detailed reappraisal of the work of George Herbert Mead:

> Mead's work seemed to me . . . to hold the key to the desired convergence of two very different philosophical and scientific traditions: the dialogical approaches of linguistic theory in the German tradition of the hermeneutic humanities, and the approaches to a 'generative' theory of grammar that followed upon the great strides made by Noam Chomsky toward an investigation of human language which is both universal in orientation and empirically fruitful. (Joas, 1985, p. 1)

My own view of Joas's dilemma would be that, following Marková (1982), these two conceptions of language belong to two different and incommensurable paradigms: the Hegelian and the Cartesian. One needs to choose one's paradigm rather than work out a compromise.

The philosophy of the act

The basic unit of analysis for Mead is the communicative or social act (Farr and Rommetveit, 1995). The former is best understood in the context of language, which is a uniquely human mode of communication. The latter is best understood in a broader, more evolutionary, context that need not be specifically human. It is a part action that others complete. For Mead, the meaning of an act is the nature of the response it elicits from others. Others react to the beginning of an act in terms of its end and self then reacts to their reactions. This applies at any level in the evolutionary scale. Language, for Mead, is a peculiar complication in the gesturing mechanism that occurred in the evolution of the human species and makes that species different from all others. The meaning of an act, then, is not to be equated with the intention of the actor. The actor, however, on the basis of her experience, can anticipate the reactions of others – especially of familiar, particular others – and adjust her actions accordingly. This is the social matrix out of which mind and awareness of self as an object in the social world of others emerges both phylogenetically in the evolution of the species and ontogenetically in the development of each member of the species. Mind is thus for Mead, but not for Watson, a purely natural phenomenon. For Watson, it is a supernatural phenomenon; Watson continues to be haunted by the ghost of Descartes because that is his own conception of mind. This is why, as a philosopher, Mead is a pragmatist but, as a scientist, he is a social psychologist (see the quotation from Morris at the beginning of this chapter). It also explains why he is a process philosopher.

Mead's philosophy of the act has its origin in Dewey's article on the reflex arc concept in psychology (Dewey, 1896). In the article Dewey warned of the dangers of taking the reflex arc as the basic unit of behaviour. This warning did not prevent Watson from doing just that some 20 years later. An act is a meaningful unit in its own right. Why focus on that segment of the act that happens to be visible from the perspective of an outside observer? The beginning of an act is not visible from the outside. It originates in the central nervous system of the actor. Nor is the consequence of an act always predictable from the perspective of the actor. The perspective of the observer and the perspective of the actor are both limited perspectives. Psychologists, in the course of the short history of their discipline, have adopted either one or other of these two perspectives but without being able to demonstrate how they are inter-related. For Mead, a perspective is an objective point in space/time from which events are viewed (Mead, 1927). Mead derived this notion of perspective from his reading of Einstein. 'Adopting the perspective of the other' came to replace his earlier notion of 'assuming the role of the other'. Behaviourism in psychology, therefore, is something very different from Mead's philosophy of the act. In his social psychology Mead is able to demonstrate how these two limited, partial and incompatible perspectives can be combined (Farr and Anderson, 1983). Speech, for Mead, is social rather than laryngeal. It is something to be understood rather than observed.

Mead as a Social Psychologist

The originality of Mead as a thinker, of which Dewey claimed Mead himself was totally unaware, comprised the fact that the key to understanding his philosophy is to be found in his social psychology and the key to understanding his social psychology is to be found in his philosophy. Since Mead worked out his own system of philosophy through the medium of his annual course of lectures in social psychology, the latter necessarily contains the key to the former. The problem is that philosophers, psychologists and sociologists usually only ever read the one literature but not the other and so fail to see how they are inter-related. The separation between academic disciplines, which was virtually complete by the time of Mead's death (see chapter 6), has exacerbated a problem that was already present during his lifetime. Miller (1973), a philosopher, noted that most psychologists unfamiliar with Mead's thinking start with *Mind, Self and Society: from the standpoint of a social behaviorist* (Mead, 1934). He has no quibble with this as a starting point. Miller's advice is that if you then become familiar with the whole of the rest of Mead's philosophy and then return to *Mind, Self and Society* you will discover that it is a totally different book. This is certainly my own experience. I have tried to convey something of this to the reader of this volume by discussing Mead's philosophy before coming to a consideration of his social psychology.

Mind, self and society: the course and its interpretation

This is the course that Mead first offered in 1900–1 and which he continued to offer most years until his death in 1931. We now have transcripts of two different versions of the course both of which were offered in 1927 (Mead, 1934, 1982). Miller, the editor of Mead (1982), also includes a transcript of Mead's 1914 class lectures in social psychology. In all three transcripts of this course of lectures in social psychology, Mead starts with mind (or its origin in perception and action) and goes on to deal with the self. Finally, he deals with society. His coverage of this latter topic depended, presumably, on the time available for completing the course, given his treatment of the first two topics. It is more extensive, for example, in *Mind, Self and Society* (Mead, 1934) than it is in *The Individual and the Social Self* (Mead, 1982), yet these two courses were both offered in the same year. In the transcript of his 1914 course (see Mead, 1982) society, as a topic, is treated at greater length than in Miller's version of the 1927 course. The progression of topics is the same in all three texts: from mind to society through self. For a course of lectures in philosophy, this is a natural order of progression. For a course of lectures in sociology, which is what it became when Blumer took over the course from Mead on the latter's death in 1931, it might not be the most suitable order of progression. There is some indication of this in the review of *Mind, Self and Society* by Faris who suggested that the order of topics should be reversed. 'Not mind and then society; but society first and then minds arising within that society – such would probably have been the preference of him who spoke these words' (Faris, 1936, p. 910). Faris certainly echoed Mead's belief that society is prior to the individual. All of the historical evidence, however, points to mind, self and society as Mead's actual order of progression in his lectures on social psychology.

Mead was critical of Watsonism. We have noted this already in the context of the rival paradigm of Descartes and of Hegel (see above). Mead compared Watson to the Queen in *Alice in Wonderland* – 'off with her head' – nothing above the spinal cord. I think the sociologists who heard Mead criticize Watson thought that, like them, he was an anti-positivist. In fact, what he was saying was that Watson had not gone far enough. He had not come up with an account of the natural history of mind and of the peculiarly self-reflexive nature of human intelligence. There is both continuity and discontinuity between humans and other species. Two very different models of man emerge depending upon whether one stresses the continuity or the discontinuity between man and other species. Watson stressed the continuity, while Mead stressed the discontinuity. There are characteristics, according to Mead, which set the human species apart from all other species: a close relationship between the hand and the development of the central nervous system and language as a form of species-specific behaviour. Language, which is inherently social, has been dealt with fairly extensively in the section on Mead as a philosopher. For Mead, as it had been for Wundt, the study of human intelligence is a form of social psychology. Watson reduced human rationality to the rationality of rats. We now know a lot about the laws of learning that are common to mice and men.

The hand is important in the evolution of the human species as it is, too, in the evolution of the higher primates. Especially important, here, is the opposable thumb that enables apes and humans, alike, to create and to use tools. This gives rise to the notion of the physical object. The value of an object relates to its role in the completion of human tasks. This is the pragmatist viewpoint. The hand is important in the manipulative phase of an act. Our experience of contact with physical objects leads to a three-dimensional perception of the world. Mead's most distinctive notion is that of sociality, i.e. our relation to other people. That is why the key to understanding his philosophy is to be found in his social psychology. He used the words 'social psychology' well before others did. This was the title of his course of lectures in 1900–1, some eight years before the words appeared in the titles of books by McDougall (1908) and Ross (1908). The physical object arises in human experience within the context of this sociality. It is a necessary prerequisite to the later experience of self as an object in the social world of others. These others, following Meyer (1921), could be objects, animals or people. Mead discusses all three, though without any specific reference to Meyer with whose work he was probably unfamiliar. Mead's point is that our relationship to each of these categories of other is quite different. We relate differently to objects than we do to people. Indeed, the categories themselves emerge from our own experience of the world. In each case the relationship is between self and others. Hence the fundamental importance of sociality since self is social. Heider (1958) also distinguished between our relationship to objects and our relationship to others. He did so from a phenomenological, rather than from a pragmatic, perspective.

Joas (1985), in his careful linguistic analysis of the work which Mead published during his lifetime, stresses the important role of the physical object in the evolution (i.e. the phylogenesis) and development (i.e. the ontogenesis) of human intelligence. The physical object arises in the coordination of hand and eye in relation to the experience of contact with the world of physical objects. Something further is added with the acquisition of language. In her autobiography, Helen Keller (1902), who became blind and deaf after an illness when she was only 19 months old, describes how her life was transformed when she came to realize that each object has a name. Language enables the mind to grasp and to handle objects without overworking the hands. Joas (1985) shows how, in the development of Mead's thinking, assuming the role of the other, when the other is a physical object rather than a person, is critical to the emergence of the physical object in the experience of the person. 'The breakthrough for Mead's theory of the constitution of the object came, then, when he recognised that the co-operation of the hand and the eye creates "things", permanent objects, only when the capacity for role-taking, which has been developed in social intercourse, is also utilised in the individual's dealings with non-social objects' (Joas, 1985, p. 153).

The difference between Mead's philosophy of the act and what he quaintly called Watsonism can be found in the difference between Dewey's analysis of the infant reaching to grasp the bright flame of a candle (1896) and, more than 20 years later, Watson's conditioning of little Albert (Watson and Rayner, 1920). Dewey showed how any analysis of the infant's action in terms of stimulus and response destroyed the unity and coherence of the act and undermined the agency of the actor. This was the article (see above) in which Dewey warned psychologists of the dangers of taking the reflex arc as the basic unit of behaviour. Watson not only ignored the warning – he openly defied it. Dewey's article in *Psychological Review* was entitled 'The reflex arc concept in psychology'. Watson's article in the same journal (it was his Presidential address to the American Psychological Association) was entitled 'The place of the conditioned reflex in psychology' (Watson, 1916). Watson, the reader may recall, went up to Chicago in 1900 with the express purpose of completing a PhD under the supervision of Dewey (see appendix 1). Watson induced in little Albert a conditioned fear of white rats. The philosophy of the act to which Dewey and Mead subscribed was much closer to the work of Thorndike than it was to the work of Watson. Watson, in his conditioning of little Albert, borrowed his technique from Pavlov. This latter form of learning became known as classical conditioning in contrast to the operant conditioning model of learning developed by Skinner who took Thorndike rather than Watson as his prototype.

While Wundt separated his physiological psychology from his social psychology (see chapter 2), Mead inter-related the two. Experience is stored in the central nervous system, especially in the association tracts of the brain. 'The act . . . and not the tract is the fundamental datum in both social and individual psychology when behaviouristically conceived, and it has both an inner and an outer phase, an internal and an external aspect' (Mead, 1934, p. 8).

If the tract, rather than the act, were the fundamental datum, then physiological psychology would, indeed, be quite separate from social psychology. The skin would then be a very important boundary between these two quite distinct and separate branches of psychology. This is how it appears from a phenomenological perspective. Strange as this may seem, this is the perspective of the behaviourist (Mackenzie, 1977). The behaviourist is an observer of others. In the full Meadian (and Einsteinian) sense of the term, perspective is here an objective point in space/time from which events are viewed. Events occurring in the cortex of the brain are not directly visible from this perspective. In this respect Skinner is more radical than Watson. He criticized Pavlov for speculating about the patterns of excitation and inhibition in the cortex of the brain when these could not be observed directly. Watson had taken Pavlov as a model of how psychology could become an objective discipline and a branch of natural science.

The act, especially the communicative act, involves the physiology of the individual as well as the social context in which the act takes place. It is artificial, therefore, to separate the physiological from the social and Mead was too good a Darwinian to do so:

> comparative psychology – and behaviorism as its outgrowth – has extended the field of general psychology beyond the central nervous system of the individual organism alone, and has caused psychologists to consider the individual act as a part of the larger social whole to which it in fact belongs, and from which, in a definite sense, it gets its meaning; though they do not, of course, lose interest thereby in the central nervous system and the physiological processes going on in it. (Mead, 1934, p. 8, n. 8)

Mead's comparative perspective provides a link between Wundt (chapter 2) and Murchison (chapter 5). His perception that behaviourism is the outgrowth of comparative psychology, at least in America, also helps to account for the individualization of social psychology (chapter 6).

Mead acknowledges that an act has both an inner and an outer phase. The question arises as to how the two phases are related. Mead is critical of Wundt for presupposing mind in his physiological psychology and of Watson for dismissing it in his behaviourism. The one corresponds to the inner phase of the act (i.e. mind) and the other to its outer phase (i.e. behaviour). Both perspectives, however, are partial and, being the perspectives of two quite different individuals, they are incompatible with each other. Consciousness, the basis of Wundt's experimental science, can only be the consciousness of an individual. There is nothing inherently social about either conception. What Mead did was to suggest how they might be related. He showed how an actress, in the course of interacting, might incorporate the perspective of the other in her own perspective and thus become an object to herself, i.e. become self-conscious rather than being merely conscious.

In his critique of the psychophysical parallelism underlying Wundt's physiological psychology, Mead points out that the parallelism is, in fact, incomplete on the psychic side: 'the required parallelism is not in fact complete on the psychical side, since only the sensory and not the motor phase of the physiological process of experience has a psychic correlate' (Mead, 1934, p. 42, n. 1). The blind spot, from the perspective of psyche as the actress, relates to the motor phase of the act. The outer phase of the act, however, is present in the consciousness of the observer even if it is not present in the consciousness of psyche herself.

The parallelism is between the physiology of the organism and 'what goes on in the experiences that the individual recognizes as his [her] own' (Mead, 1934, p. 42).

From the perspective of the observer (i.e. the standpoint of the behaviourist), the blind spot is the significance for the actor of the situation (i.e. the inner phase of the act). This divergence in perspective between actor and observer is in the visual modality (Farr and Anderson, 1983). The skin, here, is an important boundary when it comes to visual perception. It is an impenetrable barrier to seeing what it is that other people have in mind. Due to the location of our eyes at the front of our heads, we are only rarely an object in our own visual field. This is why the motor phase of an act is not present in the consciousness of the actor. This is also why, humans, in the natural state (i.e. without the assistance of mirrors, cameras and CCTV), are no different from any other species. In the visual modality humans, generally, are not self-reflexive. They are, however, in the auditory modality (Farr and Anderson, 1983; Farr, 1991a). Language is a form of expressive behaviour that is unique to humans and, here, as Skinner (1964) himself observed, the skin is not a particularly important boundary. When we speak, provided we are of normal hearing, we hear ourselves speak more or less as others hear us. When we talk, we talk to ourselves as well as to others. This is why the self-reflexive nature of human intelligence is more closely related to speech than it is to vision. This is the essence of the social psychology of George Herbert Mead. It is also a particularly fine example of Wundt's claim that the study of higher mental processes is a form of social psychology.

I have stressed the extent to which Mead depended on science in the development of his philosophy, e.g. on Darwin, Einstein and others. It is also clear from his writings that he had read Freud. Mead took science seriously – and what he produced when he did so was social psychology. Many who were influenced by Mead may have failed to appreciate the extent to which his theorizing was constrained by the available scientific evidence. Since Mead did not conduct his own scientific research, it is easy to make such a mistake. In the section on society in the 1927 course of lectures in social psychology (Mead, 1934) it is quite clear that Mead had read the literature available to him on insect societies, etc. On the basis of this evidence, for example, he agrees that it is possible to have society without mind but not mind or self without society. In trying to figure out how societies of insects differed from societies of humans, Mead speculated that the principle of organization in the former was probably of a chemical nature, while in the latter it was of a linguistic nature. This was in 1927, some two decades before pheromones were identified, isolated and their relationship established in the organization of such societies as those of ants, bees and other insects.

Social behaviourism/symbolic interactionism

Mead's course of lectures is listed in the university calendar simply as social psychology. His own approach to social psychology is quite distinct. After his death the problem arose of devising a name for this distinctive approach. Morris, a philosopher who edited a transcript of the 1927 course of lectures in social psychology, called it 'social behaviourism'; Blumer, a sociologist who took over the teaching of the course from Mead, called it 'symbolic interactionism'.

I hope I have said enough to convince the reader that the behaviourism of Mead is very different from that of either Watson or Skinner and that Mead was a much more consistent Darwinian than either of them. This is relevant to the theme of the next chapter because behaviourism, more than anything else, led to the demise, at least in America, of comparative psychology. Social psychology for Wundt (chapter 2), for Mead and for Murchison (chapter 5) was part of a truly comparative psychology. On six occasions before 1912, but never thereafter, Mead offered a course at Chicago on comparative psychology (see Lewis and Smith, 1980, app. I). This was in addition to his course of lectures on social psychology. This, like the seminars he offered between 1912 and 1920 on social awareness (see above), was probably incorporated into his later courses of lectures in social psychology in the 1920s. It certainly informed his whole approach to social psychology.

It is possible that Morris's description of Mead as a social behaviourist is unhelpful or even positively misleading in the literal sense. Mead was a pragmatist rather than a positivist. Morris was one of the New Encyclopaedists who were concerned to stress the unity of science. It was his personal ambition to inter-relate pragmatism and positivism. He went on in his book *Foundations of the Theory of Signs* (Morris, 1938) to provide a behavioural basis for semiotics. Mead did not use the term 'social behaviourism' to describe his own position. Morris, as the editor of the volume, acknowledges this: 'Though not used by Mead, the term "social behaviourism" may seem to characterize the relation of Mead's position to that of John B. Watson' (Morris, Introduction to Mead, 1934, p. xvi). Morris was aware that Mead was highly critical of Watsonism. Morris expresses the hope that 'The judgment of time will perhaps regard Watsonism as behaviorism methodologically simplified for [the] purposes of initial laboratory investigation' (1934, p. xvii).

Perhaps Morris was too sympathetic to positivism to appreciate adequately the significance of Mead's criticism of Watson. In terms of the history of psychology positivism was Watsonian behaviourism. The natural science that Watson had in mind was physics rather than evolution. The starting point for Mead's social psychology was Wundt's *Völkerpsychologie*, i.e. a branch of the *Geisteswissenschaften*. It could be argued that Mead extended the *Geisteswissenschaften* to incorporate the *Naturwissenschaften*. To classify Mead as a social behaviourist is to focus rather narrowly on his relation to Watson and seriously to underestimate the significance of his relations to Wundt and, more generally, to German idealism. Fortunately, Joas (1985), in his careful study of the development of Mead's thinking, helps to counteract this latter deficiency. Morris inaccurately states that Mead was not at Leipzig: 'Although he was at Berlin, and not at Leipzig with Wundt, there can be ...' (Morris, in Mead, 1934, p. xiii). I have personally established that Mead was at Leipzig with Wundt before going to Berlin (see above).

The sociologists at Chicago were none too pleased with Morris's editing of Mead's course of lectures in social psychology. Ellsworth Faris (1936), a former student and colleague of Mead, in his review of *Mind, Self and Society* had this to say:

> But Mead never wrote his book on social psychology. The present volume was assembled from the notebooks of students who heard him in the latter part of his career. The editor has, unfortunately, seen fit to give it another title and has taken the liberty to re-arrange the material in a fashion that will be deprecated by many who knew Mead and thought they understood him. The task of the editor under such circumstances is one of unusual difficulty; and disappointment over the imperfections of the result yields to the feeling of gratitude to those men who did the best they could, according to their lights, and all who are interested in social psychology should be thankful for even this much. (Faris, 1936, p. 809)

Whether the sociologists at Chicago (especially Blumer who called Mead's social psychology 'symbolic interactionism') better understood Mead than the philosophers is an issue I shall pick up and develop more fully in chapter 7 where I deal with sociological forms of social psychology. There I shall argue that 'symbolic interactionism' is a sociological form of social psychology in its own right which is only loosely related to what Morris calls the 'social behaviourism' of G. H. Mead.

5
The Murchison *Handbook* of 1935: a Truly Comparative Psychology

A distinction was drawn in Europe before the First World War between physiological psychology, on the one hand, and *Völkerpsychologie* on the other (see chapter 2). Wundt, who was the source of this distinction, contributed significantly to both fields. The two fields were united by a common conception of psychology as the science of mental life. In the one field, mind was studied in its inner aspects; in the other, it was studied in its outer manifestations. The two fields were divided by a difference in their respective methodologies. One was experimental; the other was comparative. Essentially, the contrast was between the laboratory and the field; between what could, and what could not, be brought under experimental control; between what was artificial and contrived, on the one hand; and what was natural, social or cultural on the other. The inheritance from Wundt was a physiological psychology that was not comparative and a comparative psychology that was not physiological. This left open the possibility, at some future date, of developing a truly comparative and physiological psychology. Such a unitary discipline would only have been possible in the context of Darwin's theory of evolution. This was the synthesis that Mead produced from Wundt's antitheses (chapter 4). It was not appreciated at the time he worked it out. This is also the unstated rationale of the first *Handbook of Social Psychology* edited by Murchison and published in 1935. Murchison, however, was much closer to Wundt than he was to Mead: he was better at posing the question than he was at supplying an answer. This, perhaps, is the difference between being an editor and being a scientist.

Courses, Journals, Textbooks and Handbooks

Textbooks v. handbooks

Some historians (e.g. Sahakian, 1974, esp. ch. 8; Jones, 1985; Hilgard, 1987, esp. ch. 6; Collier et al., 1991) believe that they can identify the origins of social psychology with the publication, in 1908, of the first two textbooks in the English language with social psychology in their titles (McDougall, 1908; Ross, 1908). Since the author of one of these textbooks was a biologically orientated psychologist (namely, McDougall) and the author of the other was a sociologist, these same historians often claim, with apparent reason, that psychological and sociological forms of social psychology (the topic of chapter 7) were twin-born in 1908. The strongest such claim is that made be Collier et al. (1991, p. 6): 'since its inception, American social psychology has existed not as one but as two separate disciplines, each with its own literature and interests.'

The danger, here, is that historians of social psychology read back into their reconstruction of the past distinctions between academic disciplines that characterize their own age. All four of the histories referred to above were published in the last quarter of the twentieth century (± one year), when the separation between psychological and sociological forms of social psychology was almost total. It is tempting to imagine that the difference, which is so evident now, was there from the very start. My own position is that the inter-war years were important in terms of the emergence of the main academic disciplines in the biological, social and human sciences, but that distinct traditions of social psychology did not develop within those disciplines (i.e. psychology and sociology) until the modern era (i.e. after the Second World War). I also think that handbooks are more important than textbooks in establishing the identity of disciplines.

Of the two textbooks published in 1908, the one written by McDougall was the more important in terms of its subsequent impact. It was influential because it was controversial. His advocacy of instinct as an appropriate explanatory device at the level of human behaviour was controversial among psychologists and sociologists alike, especially in America. As a textbook it was incomplete. It was intended as an *Introduction to Social Psychology* (McDougall, 1908). It was the first volume of a two-volume work, the second volume of which (McDougall, 1920) did not appear for another 12 years (see chapter 3). It, too, was controversial but for a different reason (Farr, 1986). The issues raised by McDougall do feature in the Murchison *Handbook of Social Psychology* (1935) but neither McDougall nor Ross was a contributor to that first handbook. The work of McDougall is referred to more often in the *Handbook* than the work of Ross. Biology and sociology appear as academic disciplines in their own right in the Murchison *Handbook* rather than as rival forms of social psychology. This accurately reflects the nature of the academic disciplines at the time.

Handbooks are important in the historical development of a discipline. This is especially the case when there are established doctoral programmes in the subject. In the case of social psychology this did not occur until after the end of the Second World War. Before that we can reasonably talk only of the roots of modern social psychology, and the Murchison *Handbook* of 1935 is one of those roots. It is not a particularly coherent handbook in terms of cross-references between the various contributors. Indeed, virtually the only thing that the various contributors have in common is that their work appears between the same set of covers. The integration is more in the mind of the editor than in the minds of the contributors. It is a strong statement, on the part of Murchison, of the comparative nature of psychology.

If I were asked to identify a textbook from the period here under review that had a formative influence on the development of social psychology as a discipline it would have to be the text *Social Psychology* (Allport, 1924). This helped to establish social psychology in America as an experimental and behavioural science. It is so important in this respect that it features prominently in the next chapter on the individualization of social psychology in North America. Its twin emphases on behaviourism and experimentation undermined the whole conceptual framework of the Murchison *Handbook*. It was not just social psychology that became individualized under the twin influences of these two forces; so, too, did comparative psychology. The laboratory replaced the field as the preferred location for observing the behaviour of animals, and the number of different species being studied was dramatically reduced (Beach, 1950, 1960). This did not happen to anything like the same extent in Europe as it did in North America. The ethological studies of Tinbergen, Lorenz and others continued to be part of a truly comparative approach in the life sciences. Lorenz (1950) once remarked, with reference to the American *Journal of Comparative and Physiological Psychology*, that, to the best of his knowledge, 'no really comparative paper has ever been published in it.'

Courses of lectures and journals

There were few, if any, established traditions of social psychology at the time the Murchison *Handbook* was published. Two inter-related traditions of social psychology, however, are worth mentioning. They both began in 1900, some eight years before the appearance of the textbooks of McDougall and of Ross. I refer to Mead's course of lectures on social psychology at the University of Chicago and to the first two volumes of Wundt's *Völkerpsychologie* which were devoted to the study of language. The latter was published at the rate of about two volumes a year between 1900 and 1920. In many ways it was like a research journal except that it only ever contained the work of its editor. Wundt had borrowed his title from the recently defunct journal *Zeitschrift für Völkerpsychologie und Sprachwissenschaft* which had been edited by Lazarus and Steinthal between 1860 and 1890 (see Jahoda, 1992, for a further account of Wundt's *Völkerpsychologie*). Some 20 years earlier (see appendix 1) he had established the journal *Philosophische Studien* as the house organ for the work of Leipzig laboratory. Now, through the pages of *Völkerpsychologie* he set out, single-handedly in his old age, to accomplish the third of the three tasks he had set himself some 40 years earlier: the creation of a social psychology.

The social psychology of Mead remained largely an oral tradition until Morris, in 1934, published an edited version of Mead's 1927 course of lectures at Chicago under the title *Mind, Self and Society* (see chapter 4). This would have appeared in print just as the Murchison *Handbook* was going to press. Murchison's preface to the work is dated 17 January 1935. It is scarcely surprising, then, that there is no reference to *Mind, Self and Society* in the course of the *Handbook*. Only one of the contributors to the *Handbook* cited any of Mead's published work. G. W. Allport (1935), in his classic chapter on attitudes, refers to Mead's motoric theory of attitudes. Above all else, Mead is a comparative psychologist in his whole approach to social psychology. This reflects the extent to which Darwin influenced his whole philosophy. Comparative psychology is the organizing principle behind Murchison's *Handbook of Social Psychology*. In the course of his lectures Mead deals with the behaviour of various species including snakes, insects, birds, cats, dogs, horses, cows and the higher primates.

The framework of the *Handbook* is very comparable to Wundt's ten-volume project on *Völkerpsychologie* (Wundt, 1900–20). The objects of study in the latter project were language, religion, customs (including ritual), myth, magic and cognate phenomena. Here Wundt was dealing with the varieties of language and of human nature to be found around the world. He drew freely on the work of linguists and of anthropologists. This is why his critics (who included no less a person than William James) accused him of being an encyclopaedist. The phenomena he was studying changed over time and across space. They were extensive in both the temporal and spatial senses of the term. Jahoda (1992) comments on the number of pages in the *Völkerpsychologie* devoted to a mere listing of ethnographic details. Science is a collaborative enterprise which depends heavily on the work of others past, present and future. There is no reason why an individual should personally collect all of the data used in the development of a theory. Scholarship is at least as important as research in the development of good theory. One can assemble the work of others for the purposes either of research, as in the case of Wundt, or of teaching, as in the case of Murchison. The Murchison *Handbook* is probably the highwater mark in America of Wundt's influence on the development of social psychology.

Murchison: the *Handbook* and its Editor

That comparative psychology is the organizing principle behind the first *Handbook of Social Psychology* will become readily apparent to the reader from even a cursory glance at its table of contents (see figure 5.1). Murchison is an editor rather than a researcher. While the scope of his *Handbook* may be as ambitious as that of the three tasks Wundt set himself (see chapter 2), Murchison, unlike both Wundt and Mead, is not, himself, concerned with tracing the evolution of mind in the human species. Instead he commissions, edits and arranges material that is relevant to such a concern. His preface is brief (less than a page) and to the point. He expresses a concern to identify the mechanisms involved in the generation and transmission of social phenomena. His concern is a moral, as well as a scientific, one:

> The social sciences at the present moment stand naked and feeble in the midst of the political uncertainty of the world. The physical sciences seem so brilliant, so clothed with power by contrast. Either something has gone all wrong in the evolution of the social sciences, or their great day in court

TABLE OF CONTENTS

[XI]

[XI]

Figure 5.1 Table of contents of the Murchison (1935) *Handbook of Social
Psychology*

has not yet arrived. It is with something akin to despair that one contemplates the piffling, trivial, superficial, damnably unimportant topics that some social scientists investigate with agony and sweat. And at the end of all these centuries, no one knows what is wrong with the world or what is likely to happen to the world. (Murchison, 1935, p. ix)

The division of the work into sections, the titles of these sections and of the chapters within each section are clearly the work of the editor or, at least, the outcome of negotiations between the editor and the various contributors to the volume. The overall conception is of social psychology as part of a truly comparative psychology. The work makes no sense outside of an evolutionary perspective. Why else would there be chapters on bacteria, plants, insects, birds, mammalian herds and packs, and infrahuman primates in a handbook of social psychology? Wundt had separated his *Völkerpsychologie* from his experimental science because he believed that the generative mechanisms underlying the objects of study in the *Völkerpsychologie* were different in kind from those that could be isolated and studied by means of introspection in the artificial context of a laboratory. Collective representations such as language, religion, customs, myth, magic and cognate phenomena were the outcome of 'the reciprocal action of the many' (Wundt, 1916, p. 3). Murchison, in assembling the highly heterogeneous material he did for his *Handbook*, hoped that he, or at least some of his readers, might be able to identify the nature of those mechanisms of social interaction. This is what he refers to in the preface as 'social mechanics'. We have seen already (chapter 4) how Mead picked up Wundt's notion of 'the human gesture' from the early volumes of the *Völkerpsychologie* and related it to language as a specifically human mode of communication.

Only a minority of the contributors to the *Handbook* actually cite the work of Wundt. When they do it is usually the *Völkerpsychologie*. The majority of the contributors (there were only two Europeans among them) may not have been sufficiently fluent in German to read the *Völkerpsychologie*. The most extensive references to Wundt are in the chapter by Esper on language. Others refer to his work, *en passant*, but without citing a specific reference; for example, G. W. Allport refers to Wundt's treatment of attitude in terms of feeling. Dashiell, in distancing himself from the whirlpool of debate concerning whether or not groups, as distinct from individuals, have minds cites Wundt as siding with Allport (presumably F. H.) in this debate, which is rather curious. Another contributor, Thorleif Schjelderup-Ebbe, in his chapter on the social behaviour of birds, cites Wundt in his references but not in the body of his text. I suspect that this chapter was substituted for another at the last minute, which would account for the mismatch between text and references (this mismatch is by no means confined to the work of Wundt). The editor, in his brief preface, expresses regret 'that the interesting work in the Clark laboratories on the experimental measurement of social hierarchies in animals is not developed far enough for inclusion in this book' (Murchison, 1935, p. ix). Clark University is the editor's own institution. The chapter by Schjelderup-Ebbe is concerned with studies of the pecking-order among birds (which he rather quaintly refers to as despotism). Some of the observations he reports concerning social hierarchies in societies of birds were made in the Zoological Gardens at Leipzig though whether these observations were made by the author himself or by Wundt is unclear from the context. Schjelderup-Ebbe's chapter appears in the section of the *Handbook* devoted to 'Experimental Constructions of Social Phenomena'. This may have been the slot originally intended for the work of the Clark laboratories on the experimental measurement of social hierarchies in animals.

Social phenomena in selected populations

Part I of the *Handbook* comprises a trilogy of chapters on populations as disparate as those of bacteria, plants and humans. This directly raises the issue, at three very different levels of evolution, of the relationship between the individual cell, plant or human and the populations of which it is but a part. All three authors are concerned with the individual, with relations between individuals (families, colonies, communities etc.) and with the link between such groupings and wider populations both of conspecifics and of other species with whom they share a habitat or an ecosystem. The social phenomena are located at the intermediate level of these groupings. There can be colonies of cells as well as of plants; communities of plants as well as of humans etc. The chapters by Buchanan on bacteria and by Thompson on demography seek to identify the environmental conditions under which these respective populations either increase or decrease.

The habitat is treated as both cause and effect in relation to plants, animals and humans. Animals are treated only in their relationship to and dependence upon plants. Clements, in his chapter on plants, stresses the greater importance of studying processes than of devising taxonomies. He is also opposed to the notion of instinct as an explanatory device. In discussing the dynamics of populations of plants, Clements distinguishes between the action of the habitat, the reaction of the group to the habitat, and co-action between members of the group. Although he is dealing with plants, his conceptualization of the processes involved is more explicitly social than those of the other two contributors to part I. There are no cross-references between the three chapters.

Social phenomena in infrahuman societies

Part II of the *Handbook* comprises three chapters on insects, birds and mammals. Each is, respectively, about 20 pages shorter than its predecessor, less lavishly illustrated in terms of photographs and less fully referenced. The bibliographies of all three contributors are multilingual with 119 items on insects, 69 on birds and 19 on mammals. Society is a theme common to all three chapters.

Plath (p. 83) notes that 'Nowhere in the animal world has social organization reached such a high degree of perfection as in the social insects.' He discusses the social behaviour of wasps, bees, ants and termites (with, respectively, 7, 14, 13 and 8 pages devoted to each) before going on to discuss processes such as social parasitism, 'the temporary or permanent enslavement of the members of one colony by those of another' (pp. 133, 134). The most striking feature of such societies, from a human perspective, is the division of labour. Some of these societies 'are very ancient in comparison with human social organization, having been fully perfected at least 65,000,000 years ago, since which time they have undergone little or no change' (p. 83). Friedmann (p. 142), in his treatment of bird societies, notes the contrast with insects: 'birds show but little social evolution.' He distinguishes gregariousness from society, with the latter being most clearly evident in the breeding colony. He discusses other forms of aggregation such as roosts and flocks. Flocking for the purposes of migration is different from winter feeding flocks of birds that, during summer, are solitary. Alverdes, before discussing families, packs and herds of mammals as forms of infrahuman society, notes that in most mammalian species 'every male, as a rule, exhibits a temporary or lasting relationship to one or several females' (p. 185). He identifies various patterns of mating (promiscuity, monogamy and polygamy), each of which may be either seasonal or permanent.

Historical sequences of human social phenomena

Part III comprises a remarkable quartet of chapters on the social histories of the negro (Herskovits), the red man (Wissler), the white man (Wallis) and the yellow man (Harvey). Each is 50 ± 10 pages long. The authors, who come, respectively, from Northwestern, Yale, Minnesota and Dartmouth, write as social, rather than as biological, scientists. They discuss the three main races of *homo sapiens*: Negroes, Caucasians and Mongols. Harvey, though not Wissler (the author of the chapter on the red man), treats aboriginal Americans as being of mongoloid origin. Wallis (p. 312) is careful to point out that 'race is a concept rather than an objective fact.' It is something, literally, only skin deep. In all four chapters the focus is on culture. 'Whilst culture is conservative it is never static' (Herskovits, 1935, p. 251). Wissler is also the author of the chapter, in part IV, on material culture. Degler (1991), in his discussion of human nature (see below), stresses the salience of culture over biology in the 1920s and 1930s in America. This quartet of chapters would support his point of view.

Herskovits covers the civilizations of Africa, the history of the slave trade and he presents an ethnographic account of the negro cultures of the New World. He shows how Africanisms are most clearly evident in songs (e.g. negro spirituals), folklore (e.g. stories about animals, the widespread use of proverbs and riddles), religious beliefs (e.g. magic and the use of charms) and religious ceremonies (e.g. the importance of priests and links between river cults in the Old World and baptism in the New). He links the popularity, in America, of the Charleston to the cult of royal ancestors amongst the Ashanti of West Africa. He suggests that the slave trade can be viewed, in retrospect, as an experiment in acculturation set up for the social scientist by history. The children of slaves absorbed and perpetuated the behaviour patterns of their parents and associates rather than those of their masters.

Wissler's primary concern is with the aboriginal inhabitants of the Americas before the arrival of Christopher Columbus in 1492. He distinguishes between city states, agricultural tribes and hunting tribes. He describes at some length the great empires of the Aztecs and Incas, stressing the importance of ceremonialism and social discipline: 'the wheel as a driving principle was wholly absent, and the same may be said of the plow and the broadcast sowing of grain. The ox and the horse were conspicuously wanting. Iron was unknown' (p. 298). The domestication of plants was a significant achievement. The use of tobacco was unique to aboriginal America. It was a religious ceremony, as well as being a symbol of good will. Among the cultural artifacts of aboriginal Americans, Wissler notes the hammock, the cigar, the pipe, birch canoes, lacrosse, the toboggan and the rubber ball.

Wallis claims that Caucasians had closer links, throughout the historical period, with Mongols than they had with Negroes, from whom they were cut off by the deserts of North Africa. He traces the expansion of the white man around the world after 1600, with discovery being followed by exploration and exploitation through settlement. He traces early and late Mediterranean civilizations and pagan Europe beyond the Mediterranean. He notes cultural differences and stresses contact between cultures: 'the white man has been in recent centuries the greatest creator of civilization and also the greatest destroyer of both human and natural resources' (Wallis, 1935, p. 358). Whites have little in common apart from the colour of their skin and Indo-European languages. Wallis notes that 'the linguistic unity is apparent only to the grammarian, not to the users of the respective languages' (p. 358). He discusses at some length the evolution of various customs associated with the celebration of Christmas. He notes that 'In most lands which have been claimed by whites few natives survive to curse their destroyers' (p. 359).

Harvey notes that the mongoloid peoples are the most numerous of the three human races. He refers to the military expansion of the Mongols westwards into Central Europe under Genghis Khan. He also notes the Asiatic origin and kinship of the Amerindians with the yellow races of Asia. He covers the cultural histories of China (25 pages), Korea (6 pages), the Mongols (2 pages) and Japan (18 pages). Before discussing the great dynasties of China, Harvey discusses the importance of fire as a divine element in the taming of nature and the domestication of man. 'The possession and control of fire freed the yellow race from fear of wild animals, from fear of the demons of the earth and air and sky' (Harvey, 1935, p. 363). It cooked their food and the hearth became the rallying point of the family. He then discusses civil government and the flourishing of the arts and of education in the great dynasties of China. He discusses Japan in recent years as an unrivalled and uniformly successful military power. He was writing some six years before the Japanese invaded Pearl Harbor in 1941.

Analyses of recurring patterns in social phenomena

Part IV comprises three chapters in which the contributors analyse recurrent patterns of social life such as language, magic and material culture. The patterns are recurrent in that they (a) are transmitted from one generation to the next and (b) appear in one form or another in most societies. Esper, in his chapter on language, for example, deals with the child's acquisition of language. The treatment of each topic is

general rather than specific and the treatment across topics is diachronic rather than synchronic. In this latter respect the trilogy of
chapters is reminiscent of Wundt's *Völkerpsychologie*. So, too, are the
titles of the various chapters; for example, language, magic (including
religion) and such cognate phenomena as customs and ritual, and
material culture.

Esper is critical of Wundt's treatment of language. He rejects the
dualistic assumptions concerning mind on which it is based. In this
respect his critique of Wundt is comparable to that of G. H. Mead to
whom he makes no reference. Bloomfield, too, had been critical of
Wundt, and Esper was a pupil of Weiss who was a pupil of Bloomfield.
In support of some of his arguments, Esper quotes such behavioural
sources as Watson, F. H. Allport, Max Meyer and also Hull. Willoughby, in his treatment of magic and cognate phenomena, presents an
hypothesis inspired by Freud rather than by Wundt (whom he does not
mention). He deals at some length with the nature of anxiety and spells
out the social significance at both a collective and an individual level
of being able to control anxiety. He links the psychopathology of the
individual to recurrent social practices in the fields of magic and
religion. The rituals are those of priests and of obsessive-compulsives.
Recurrent, here, carries the connotation of repetition. Wissler, in his
contribution, deals with the material possessions of man, both savage
and civilized. 'The most despised savage carries about with him a
material equipment that puts all other creatures to shame' (1935a, p.
520). He treats the material cultures of all ages and regions as continu-
ous trains of events. In all ages material culture (i.e. possessions) sets a
standard of well-being.

Analyses of some correlates of social phenomena

Part V comprises five chapters on such varied topics as the physical
environment, age, sex, attitudes and adjustments. These are correlates
of social phenomena since they cannot be brought under experimental
control. Part VI, by way of contrast, is concerned with experimental
constructions of social phenomena.

Shelford notes that the ecology of plants and of animals is a more
advanced form of science than the ecology of man. He attempts to
make good the deficiency, especially with regard to the white man. He
shows how humans, progressively, gain control over their physical
environment. In this respect they are much less at the mercy of the
elements than other species. Walter R. Miles, from the Institute of
Human Relations at Yale, in a very long chapter (86 pages), deals with

changes in human capacity over the life-cycle. He also deals, in an imaginative manner, with the societal implications of generational differences. 'Men are not all equal partly for the reason that they cannot all be born at the same time' (Miles, 1935, p. 596). He cites the ages at which people from different academic disciplines write their *magna opera*. He notes that Pavlov retained his skill as a surgeon into his eighties. He also observes that J. McKeen Cattell continued to achieve a high level of publishing into his old age. Perhaps he was trying to outpublish Wundt! This is the same J. McKeen Cattell whose letters home to his parents, while he was a student in Leipzig, we found useful in chapter 2. Catharine C. Miles, also from the Institute of Human Relations at Yale, deals, at even greater length (114 pages), with what, today, we would call gender differences. Most of the differences relate to test scores, mainly on measures of intelligence. Earlier in her career the author had worked collaboratively with Terman.

The best known chapter in part V is the one by G. W. Allport on attitudes. He describes attitude as 'probably the most distinctive and indispensable concept in contemporary American social psychology' (1935, p. 798). He identifies attitude as a form of readiness for action and then differentiates it from other types of readiness. After considering numerous definitions (by sociologists as well as by psychologists), he provides his own definition of attitude as 'a mental and neural state of readiness to respond, organized through experience, exerting a directive and/or dynamic influence upon the individual's response to all objects and situations with which it is related' (p. 810). Part V concludes with a rather obscure chapter by Wells from the Harvard Medical School on adaptive and maladaptive forms of regression. Regression, here, could be from adult to childish forms of behaviour. The theoretical inspiration is, in the main, psychoanalytic (though with more references to Jung than to Freud).

Experimental constructions of social phenomena

Part VI, the final section of the Murchison *Handbook*, comprises five chapters reporting experimental studies of (a) relatively simple animal aggregations; the social behaviour of (b) birds, (c) infrahuman primates, (d) children, and (e) adults. The principal difference between the trilogies of chapters devoted to the study of animals in parts II and VI of the *Handbook* is that in the former trilogy the experimenter is nature, while in the latter it is man. Part VI closes with two chapters devoted to the study of humans, the first of which deals with the child and the second with the adult. Common to all five chapters in part VI is the experimental study of behaviour. The focus on behaviour and the preference for experimenting led, ultimately (see below), to the demise of the comparative perspective in psychology, at least in America. Without this perspective, the Murchison *Handbook* would lose its coherence.

The simple animals whose aggregations are the focus of interest to Allee include, among others, fruit flies, grasshoppers, beetles, cockroaches, goldfish, fish and domestic fowls. Experimental treatments include placing mirrors in fish tanks; blinding fish to ascertain the role of vision in the forming of schools; training cockroaches and also fish to negotiate mazes; and varying the density of domestic fowls in cages to study the effect on the size and number of eggs laid etc. Schjelderup-Ebbe argues that 'every bird is a personality' (1935, p. 947), but that it takes the human observer some time to recognize the individuality of each. After a separation of two to three weeks, birds fail to recognize each other. The memory of parent birds for their own fully grown offspring is quite limited. Schjelderup-Ebbe, as we had occasion to note earlier in the chapter, goes on to study the establishment of pecking orders in birds, or what he quaintly calls 'despotism'.

In a richly illustrated chapter, containing some 22 photographs of infrahuman primates, Yerkes and Yerkes review their own experimental studies of primates as well as discussing Köhler's work on *The Mentality of Apes* and Zuckerman's observations in London Zoo of the social life of monkeys and apes. The progression from monkey, through ape, to man is characterized by a longer period of gestation; increased helplessness at birth; a longer period of infancy and, hence, the increased importance of parental tuition; a longer time to reach sexual maturity etc. The authors stress the importance of social order among infrahuman primates. 'The trend toward an increase of altruistic interest and activity would appear to be one of the most significant aspects of primate evolution' (Yerkes and Yerkes, 1935, p. 1029).

Lois and Gardner Murphy, who, four years earlier, had published their text on *Experimental Social Psychology* (Murphy and Murphy, 1931), review research by themselves and others on the influence of social situations on the behaviour of preschool children. They are at pains to stress the importance of both the situation and the child. While they subscribe to the notion of traits, they do not conceptualize the traits as inherent in the child. The final chapter in the *Handbook* is by Dashiell. It concerns experimental, mainly laboratory-based, studies of the influence of social situations on the behaviour of individual human adults. Today this field of research would be called social facilitation effects. The editors of the modern series of *The Handbook of Social Psychology* (see chapter 10) single out this chapter as a harbinger of the future of social psychology as an experimental science. It is, therefore, one of the roots of modern social psychology. In its contemporary setting, with its twin emphases upon the behaviour of individuals and experimental methods of research, Dashiell's chapter was a significant contribution to the individualization of social psychology in America (chapter 6). The experimental studies of F. H. Allport on co-action feature prominently in Dashiell's review of the literature.

The Multi-disciplinary Nature of the Murchison *Handbook*

It is tempting to identify the origins of a discipline with the appearance of the first textbooks or handbooks in the subject. We have already seen how deceptive this can be in the case of the textbooks. The textbook by Ross (1908), for example, reflected the past rather than established the future of social psychology. McDougall (1908) anticipated a future for the discipline (with instinct as his main explanatory) that did not materialize in the form in which he envisaged it. It is not until Allport (1924) that we come across a textbook that is foundational at least in relation to psychological forms of social psychology (see chapter 6).

The Murchison (1935) *Handbook of Social Psychology* is quite unlike its successors, the modern series of *Handbooks* edited by Lindzey (1954) and by Lindzey and Aronson (1968–9, 1985). The latter series of *Handbooks* reflects the establishment of a discipline or, perhaps more accurately, of a subdiscipline. The Murchison *Handbook* enshrines a conception of the discipline that is no longer current. Its coherence and unity was in the mind of its editor rather than in the collaborative efforts of the contributors. Murchison was a professional editor who owned and edited journals and handbooks in other areas of psychology besides social psychology. The different disciplines on which Murchison drew in editing the first *Handbook of Social Psychology* became, and remained, quite distinct disciplines. According to Manicas (1987), the separation between academic disciplines in the human and social sciences was more or less complete at American universities by about 1925 (see chapter 7 of this book).

The Decline of Darwinism

There is a further reason, beyond the separation between academic disciplines, why Murchison's conception of social psychology is no longer current. The coherence of his 1935 *Handbook* depended upon an acceptance of Darwin's theory of evolution, together with an appreciation of its relevance to the human and social sciences (i.e. to the *Geisteswissenschaften* of chapter 2). In America there had been an early appreciation of the potential relevance of Darwinism in the area of the newly emergent human and social sciences. This was in the form of Social Darwinism, rather than of Darwinism *per se*. Spencer was much more influential in America than he was in his native Britain. The Darwinism was social because it was applied to human society rather than to the varieties of species to be found on the planet earth. It was not social in the sense of the social sciences since the basic unit of analysis was the individual rather than society. It was the survival of the individual and of the family in a period of rapid industrialization and urbanization that was the focus of concern and interest to the social scientist. Since Darwin's theory was all about the survival of the fittest it seemed appropriate to an understanding of social transformations.

While industrialists may have thought Darwin's theory was appropriate also at the level of the firm (in terms of its survival in a fiercely competitive market), social scientists were more concerned with the effects of industrialization and urbanization on individuals and their families. This was especially the case at the University of Chicago where the metropolis itself served as one huge laboratory of the social sciences. As research in the social sciences gathered momentum, it moved further and further away from purely biological explanations of social phenomena. The social scientists at Chicago were very much concerned with studying the metropolis in which they lived and worked. They produced, collectively, an impressive ecology of urban life in terms of crime, juvenile delinquency, mental illness, suicide etc. This was the study of anomie and egoism in the strictly Durkheimian sense of those terms.

At a broader, more cultural, level the Social Darwinism of Spencer was compatible with the individualism of American culture. Degler (1991), an American historian, is concerned to trace the decline and revival of Darwinism in American social thought. It is a wide-ranging and interesting study. The revival of Darwinism, to which his title refers, is a comparatively recent phenomenon; that is, it occurs during what, here, I call the modern era in social psychology. He is careful to point out that the revival does not include Social Darwinism. It is reflected, for example, in the emergence of such novel fields as behaviour genetics and sociobiology. Here the unit of analysis is no longer the individual but the gene pool and it becomes possible to deal with altruism as well as egoism. This, however, is not the focus of concern in the present book.

The section of Degler's book that is highly relevant in the present context is his treatment of the decline of Darwinism. Anthropologists, such as Boas, and sociologists, especially those at Chicago, played an important role in this process. Their attack on the utility of instinct as an explanatory concept in the human and social sciences is one important theme. They were in the vanguard of what Degler calls the decline of Darwinism. This made the approach to social psychology of McDougall (1908) controversial, especially in an American context (Farr, 1986). The attack by Dunlap (1919) on instincts, entitled 'Are there any instincts?', was important here. This came essentially from the behaviourist camp. Degler (1991) sees the separation between behaviour and nature as part of the decline of Darwinism. The differences between Mead and Watson (discussed in chapter 4) derive mainly from the fact that Mead was a more consistent Darwinian than Watson. Degler shows how culture came to prevail over biology, especially in the work of Boas and his students. I think the move away from Darwinism led the social scientists at Chicago increasingly to misunderstand Mead. It is possible to consider the symbolic interactionist tradition of social psychology within American sociology as being Mead without Darwin (chapter 7). I would exempt Baldwin (1986) from this criticism.

The Demise of Comparative Psychology in America

In part, this is the working out in psychology of what Degler called the decline of Darwinism. The device by which this came about during the period under study was behaviourism of the Watsonian variety. This theme is neatly delineated in the beautifully illustrated history written by Boakes (1984) which he entitles *From Darwin to Behaviourism: psychology and the minds of animals*. Once behaviour becomes the focus of study in psychology, the latter soon ceases to be a truly comparative discipline. This is especially the case if the stated objectives of the new science are the prediction and control of behaviour. The range of species is restricted to one or two (e.g. white rats, fan-tailed pigeons etc.) and the behaviour studied is that of the isolated animal in response to an artificial and standardized laboratory environment. This is a pity since Watson (1909) set out as an excellent comparative psychologist; for example, in his studies, with Lashley, of the behaviour of noddy and sooty terns on the Tortuga islands off the coast of Florida.

With the acceptance of behaviourism not only does mind drop out of the frame, so, too, does culture, since infrahuman species (to borrow a phrase from Murchison), in general, lack culture. The study of customs and ritual becomes, instead, the study of habit and the habits studied are those of isolated individuals (whether animal or human). The force of behaviourism in psychology in general is to individualize the discipline. I refer, here, to psychology. In the next chapter I shall work out the same theme specifically in relation to the history of social psychology. Behaviourism in the American context destroyed the comparative perspective adopted by the editor of the first *Handbook of Social Psychology.*

Degler (1991), in discussing the uncoupling of behaviour from nature, argues that Watson, in favouring nurture over nature, was in the same tradition of social thought in America as Boas and Kroeber who favoured culture over biology. I would also want to add that behaviourism in America also uncoupled behaviour from history. Darwin, with his theory of evolution, introduced the dimension of time into what, now, are referred to as the life sciences. He made it respectable to search for the origins of species. The genetic perspective (in the broad sense of the word genesis) appears in phylogeny and ontogeny. This is reflected in comparative and developmental psychology. It is no accident, I would argue, that Murchison, the editor of the *Handbook*, was also the owner and editor of *The Journal of Genetic Psychology.* The temporal dimension appears in his *Handbook* not only in terms of phylogeny and ontogeny but also in terms of social history.

All three elements are present also in Russian psychology, especially in the sociohistorical school of Vygotsky and his followers. Vygotsky and Luria (1930) produced three essays on the behaviour of apes, primitive man and the child. The common theme was the history of behaviour in terms of phylogeny, social history and ontogeny. Their conception is thus similar to that of the Murchison *Handbook* of 1935. The point at issue, here, is that the phenomena which are the objects of study in both psychology and social psychology are historical phenomena. It is the historical dimension in terms of phylogenesis and social history that is lost, in America, with the acceptance of behaviourism. Ontogenesis becomes the past history of reinforcement of the individual organism in relation to its various environments. The temporal dimension is restricted to the life-span of the individual organism.

The comparative perspective in psychology has always been stronger in Europe than in America. In large measure this is due to the work of distinguished ethologists like Tinbergen, Lorenz and Hinde. The perspective is better preserved in Europe because behaviourism has not had the pervasive effect there that it has had in America. Traditionally, comparative psychology stood in opposition to experimental psychology since it was primarily concerned with studying the variations that exist in nature. It was not confined to the study of animals in their natural habitats. It frequently included social and developmental psychology. This was the context in which I first taught social psychology at University College London in the late 1960s. The reader can glean some idea of the syllabus relating to comparative psychology by reading the rubric covering the University of London Honours Degree in Psychology which is reproduced in appendix 2.

6

The Individualization of Social Psychology in North America

At least since the time of the Renaissance individualism has been a key component in the Western intellectual tradition (Burckhardt, 1860). It is the tap root of modern social psychology, at least in its psychological forms. It is a more central value in some Western cultures than it is in others; for example, in America (Riesman, 1950) in comparison, say, to Russia. In this broad cultural sense (what Allport, 1954, calls the whole Western intellectual tradition) it is, more or less, synonymous with humanism. In more recent times it is part of the *Geisteswissenschaften* (see chapter 2).

Within the Western branch of Christendom the Reformation quickened the cause of individualism. The invention of the printing press and the spread of literacy further promoted it by producing active minorities who could read holy writ for themselves rather than accept the word of others, who protested at the propaganda, who dissented from the former consensus, and who failed, generally, to conform. The spokesmen (for they were men) for the pious majority represented these deviants as Protestants, Dissenters and Nonconformists. Once the representation had been formed, individuals could be identified and then persecuted. Persecution in the Old World led to selective migration to the New. This, in turn, led to individualism being a more central value in North America than, say, in Central Europe.

Social scientists such as Weber (1922), the sociologist, and Tawney (1926), the economic historian, identified links, of a historic nature, between the spirit (i.e. the *geist*) of Protestantism and the rise of capitalism in various Western cultures. This created its own dynamic in terms of the industrialization and, then, the urbanization of those societies. This was the context in which the social sciences themselves were born (Dahrendorf, 1995). Before the Industrial Revolution had come the Enlightenment. This was part of the whole Western intellectual tradition. Individualism here became secularized. The scepticism engendered by the Enlightenment was often used against the truths of revealed religion as, for example, in the writings of Hume and of Voltaire. The values of the Enlightenment were also used to justify the French and the American Revolutions.

When individualism becomes a dominant ideology within a culture, it is no longer visible to those whose ideology it is. Indeed, they often write books celebrating the end of ideology (Bell, 1960). They equate ideology with collective beliefs (see chapter 3). When the object of these collective beliefs is the individual, this is not thought to be an ideology – rather, it is thought to be the antithesis of ideology. This is curious since Ichheiser (1949) showed how a collective representation of the individual as an autonomous moral agent lay at the heart of the ideology of success and failure as this developed in various Western cultures, most notably in the Austro-Hungarian Empire. His compatriot, Heider (1958), showed how it is on the basis of this collective representation of the individual that we praise people when they succeed and blame them when they fail. These are the cultural assumptions underlying many of the attributions we make in everyday life.

When, at the beginning of the modern era, Moscovici (1961) initiated a sociological form of social psychology, he nominated Durkheim as its ancestor (see chapter 7). He rejected Durkheim's notion of a collection representation (chapter 3) in favour of his own notion of a social representation. He did so on the grounds that there were few, if any, collective representations in modern societies. I would argue that in many modern societies individualism is a collective representation in the full Durkheimian sense of the term. This is a collective representation that is enshrined in the legal codes of many of these countries.

The roots of individualism lie buried in the soil of the whole Western intellectual tradition but its flowering is a characteristically American phenomenon. Its roots are to be found in Cartesian dualism, right at the start of modern philosophy. If individualism is a core value within a particular culture then it should be possible to detect its effect in the history of the social sciences. I believe this to be true in the case of the history of social psychology in America. The effects of individualism might not be so evident in the history of psychology since the latter is, plausibly, the study of individuals.

Individualism, as I use the term here, is a core value and, as such, would appear in the right-hand column of table 3.1 (see p. 50). I said, there, that individualism as a collective representation is to be distinguished from individual representations that are collectively distributed. The myriad manifestations of individualism as a core cultural value are to be found in the entire left-hand column of table 3.1. The historical consequences of individualism as a collective representation are to be found in what Graumann (1986) calls 'the individualization of social psychology' and in what Manicas (1987) calls 'the Americanization of the social sciences'.

Of the two processes, the one described by Graumann is the more limited. It relates to a single social science, namely social psychology. It is of limited duration because the behaviourism of F. H. Allport, which is the object of Graumann's study, had its maximal influence on the historical development of social psychology in America during the period between the wars. The two processes, however, are linked because individualism is common to both. In the period following the Second World War the social sciences in America became individualized when, collectively, they became known as the behavioural sciences. This enlarges the scope and prolongs the duration of Graumann's thesis by applying it to social sciences other than social psychology and by extending it into the modern era of social psychology. The emergence of the behavioural sciences during the period of the Cold War (see also chapter 9) fits in with Manicas's thesis concerning the Americanization of the social sciences since behaviourism is a characteristically American phenomenon. Changing the name was a successful ploy in terms of attracting funding for the behavioural sciences that would not have been available for the social sciences (since the politicians who vote the funding fail to distinguish between the social sciences and socialism). The price of success, however, was the individualization of the social sciences in America.

The wider influence of behaviourism beyond psychology produced, in the late 1960s, a number of interdisciplinary fields of study in which psychology played a central role. This is scarcely surprising since these erstwhile social sciences were now thought of, collectively, as the behavioural sciences. The birth of such interdisciplinary fields as cross-cultural psychology, environmental psychology and the history of the behavioural sciences were the outcome of these postwar developments. They are an extension into the modern era of the individualization of the social sciences. To trace these developments in any detail would take us well beyond the time frame set for the present work.

Defining the Discipline: the Two Allport Brothers

There is little doubt that F. H. Allport's 1924 textbook *Social Psychology*, which is the focus of Graumann's study, played an influential role in shaping the discipline of social psychology. In his preface to the book, F. H. Allport notes that, to date, it is sociologists rather than psychologists who have written most of the textbooks in the discipline. He sets out in his own textbook to establish social psychology as a behavioural and experimental science. The links between his behaviourism and his individualism are quite explicit in the way in which he delimits the field of social psychology.

> There is no psychology of groups which is not essentially and entirely a psychology of individuals. Social psychology must not be placed in contradistinction to the psychology of the individual; *it is a part of the psychology of the individual*, whose behavior it studies in relation to that sector of his environment comprised by his fellows . . . There is likewise no consciousness except that belonging to individuals. Psychology in all its branches is a science of the individual. (F. H. Allport, 1924, p. 4)

This way of delimiting the field clearly does lead inevitably to the individualization of the social and provides the basis for Allport's reductionism which was commented on in chapter 3. His methodological commitments also lead in the same direction; for example, his advocacy of experimentation. His own experimental studies of co-action effects were included in Dashiell's review of the field in the final chapter of the 1935 Murchison *Handbook of Social Psychology* (see chapter 5). Dashiell and F. H. Allport were academic colleagues at the University of North Carolina in the 1920s.

F. H. Allport was a stern critic of anyone who appeared to assign agency to any entity other than individuals. I commented, in chapter 3, on his attack on McDougall in relation to the latter's notion of group mind. F. H. Allport was an enthusiastic supporter of public opinion polling when this was introduced in the 1930s since it was completely consistent with his own methodological individualism. This will become evident if we consider Allport's own definition of public opinion.

The term public opinion is given its meaning with reference to a multi-individual situation in which individuals are expressing themselves, or can be called upon to express themselves, as favoring or supporting (or else disfavoring or opposing) some definite condition, person or proposal of widespread importance, in such a proportion of number, intensity, or constancy, as to give rise to the probability of affecting action, directly or indirectly, toward the object concerned. (F. H. Allport, 1937, p. 23)

While the two Allport brothers differ from one another in their theoretical orientations – with G. W. being cognitive while F. H. is behavioural – they share a common representation of the individual. G. W. Allport defines the field of social psychology in similarly individualistic terms to his brother: 'With few exceptions, social psychologists regard their discipline as an attempt to understand and explain how the thought, feeling, and behavior of individuals are influenced by the actual, imagined, or implied presence of others' (G. W. Allport, 1954, p. 5). The others, of course, are other individuals. G. W. Allport is the only author to have contributed both to the Murchison *Handbook* of 1935 and to the modern series of *Handbooks of Social Psychology* edited by Lindzey (1954) and by Lindzey and Aronson (1968–9, 1985). He has thus contributed chapters to handbooks for over half a century. In his contribution to the Murchison *Handbook* he individualized the notion of attitude by effectively editing out the social and collective components in other people's definitions (Jaspars and Fraser, 1984) before offering one of his own (see chapter 5).

Attitude is not the only theoretical concept in social psychology that G. W. Allport has individualized. According to Craik (1993), he also individualized the notion of personality. He did this in his book *Personality: a psychological interpretation* (G. W. Allport, 1937). Craik compares and contrasts Allport's approach to personality with that of Stagner (1937) who published a book on personality in the same year. Craik (1993) describes Allport's approach to the study of personality as 'the individual *per se*' in contract to Stagner's more explicitly social approach which Craik characterizes as 'the individual in society'. While Graumann (1986) was writing about F. H. Allport and the individualization of social psychology, it would be quite possible also to write about G. W. Allport and the individualization of social psychology. Despite the quite sharp differences between them in terms of their theoretical perspectives, they share the same collective representation of the individual. The individualism which is common to both brothers is a characteristically American phenomenon, though it is also part of the whole Western intellectual tradition.

The Individualization of Social Psychology in America: Phase One

Graumann (1986) proposed that the attempt by F. H. Allport (1924) to establish social psychology as a behavioural and an experimental science resulted in its becoming individualized. This happened before the start of the modern era in social psychology. The arguments which Graumann adduces for his thesis are logical rather than historical, though he does set Allport's own research in the context of earlier, experimental, research in Germany. He rests his case on an analysis of *Social Psychology* (Allport, 1924), especially chapter 12 on the crowd.

Behaviourism was the principal, though not the sole, cause of the individualization of social psychology in America during the inter-war years. Graumann's thesis is a sound one in this respect. During the same period, behaviourism also resulted in the demise of a truly comparative psychology (see chapter 5) – again, through the individualization of the social. For F. H. Allport the ultimate reality is behaviour. Only individuals behave. It is a misuse of words, in Allport's opinion, to attribute actions to entities other than individuals. We have seen already (chapter 3) how this was the basis of Allport's critique of McDougall's notion of the group mind. Despite his behaviourism, Allport is not averse to talking in terms of consciousness or mind. The consciousness, however, is the consciousness of individuals. It is loose to talk of crowd consciousness, for example, since, as Allport (1924) observed, the crowd lacks a central nervous system.

F. H. Allport, in his book *Institutional Behavior* (1933), analyses the main institutions of society – the family, the Church, the nation, the school, politics, economic life etc. – in terms of the actions of individuals. In each of these domains he demonstrates how our use of language and our tendency to think in terms of institutions as though they are independent of the people who comprise them lead to the loss of moral autonomy on the part of the individual: 'Living as we do in this complex institutional era, the lack of awareness which many of us display concerning the nature of institutions and our own participation in them is little short of astonishing' (F. H. Allport, 1933, p. 29).

F. H. Allport describes in some detail (in a chapter entitled 'Justice takes its course') the role many different individuals played in the execution in Massachusetts of Sacco and Vanzetti on 23 August 1927.

His account foreshadows, by more than a couple of decades, the experimental studies of Milgram, in the modern era, on obedience to authority. The gist of both accounts is identical: when individuals become the agents of institutions they cease to be autonomous moral agents. In the conclusion to his book, Allport expresses the hope that a new form of individualism will emerge that dispenses with the need for institutions. 'Our most vexing dilemmas arise not from the fact that we lack the *right* institutions but from the fact that we have institutions at all' (F. H. Allport, 1933, p. 411). Individualism, for him, is the core value. 'A better world can only be a world of better and of freer individuals' (p. 520).

In developing his thesis, Graumann (1986) made no reference to *Institutional Behavior* (Allport, 1933). Allport's strong advocacy in that volume of the individualization of institutions merely adds strength to Graumann's thesis. Graumann argues that the individualization of the social goes hand-in-hand with the desocialization of the individual. I do not think that this follows logically. I also believe that it is wrong. Individualism is itself the product of a particular type of society. Individualism and socialization go hand-in-hand in the social psychologies of both G. H. Mead and F. H. Allport.

The Americanization of the Social Sciences

Manicas (1987) is concerned with the development of the social sciences in America. His interests, therefore, are much more wide-ranging than my own. He is concerned with many disciplines; I am concerned with but one discipline (though one which can be considered to be a subdiscipline of two other disciplines). He tends to skip over the historical development of the social sciences in America during the inter-war years, whereas, for me, these are crucial years. His realist philosophy of science is rooted in Marx; mine is rooted in the pragmatism of C. S. Peirce and of G. H. Mead.

The account by Manicas of the Americanization of the social sciences is compatible with the account being presented here. Indeed, he takes psychology to be paradigmatic for his own purposes; for example, Watsonian behaviourism is clearly an American and not a German form of science. He also notes that the individualism of the Anglo-Saxon tradition is much stronger in America than in Europe. Graumann's thesis concerning the individualization of social psychology in America fits neatly within Manicas's much broader treatment of the Americanization of the social sciences.

The Individualization of Social Psychology in America: Phase Two

There is a further phase in the individualization of social psychology in America beyond the one described by Graumann (see above). This is associated with the migration of the Gestalt psychologists from Austria and Germany to America. Koffka is the key figure in this migration. He emigrated to America in 1927 when he was appointed to a chair at Smith College. He was also the most fluent in English of the group and he helped to arrange jobs for the others when, at different stages and for various reasons, they were forced to emigrate. The letters which he wrote to one of his doctoral students, Molly Harrower, constitute, in the words of the latter, 'an unwitting self portrait' (Harrower, 1983).

Heider joined Koffka at Smith College in 1930 (appendix 1 contains the dates of many events relevant to these various migrations). Heider originally intended to stay only for a short while since Stern at Hamburg was keeping his post open for his return. Shortly after arriving in America, Heider married Grace Moore, an American citizen, and decided to settle in America. In 1947, at the age of 51, he left Smith College and went to the University of Kansas where he remained until his death in 1988. He published his autobiography some five years before he died (Heider, 1983).

When Hitler rose to power in 1933 Germany became impossible for academics who were Jewish. Among the first to leave were Wertheimer and Lewin (figure 6.1) Koffka (Harrower, 1983) wrote references for them in connection with possible appointments at the London School of Economics and Political Science. Harrower approached Ginsburg, 'the leading British sociologist and social psychologist', at the LSE in an effort to secure posts for Lewin and Wertheimer. In a letter dated 19 May 1933, Harrower wrote to Koffka: 'At Ginsburg's request I sent you a cable the meaning of which I hope will be clear, since he cannot get a direct statement from either Lewin or Wertheimer he wants your statement concerning their dismissal and will then use this as a basis for his appeal either to Jewish Relief Societies, or The London School of Economics.' In a letter dated 27 May 1933, Koffka replied: 'The Ginsburg news is splendid, I do not think that you will find the same spirit of personal sacrifice in any country except England. I hope the statements I sent about Wertheimer and Lewin are all right. Although I probably went too far in their qualifications . . . [later] Yesterday in the *New York Times* it stated that the London School of Economics has already invited four German professors. It is absolutely marvellous. Is Wertheimer or Lewin among them?' (Harrower, 1983). The School decided against offering them appointments.

Wertheimer accepted a post at the New School for Social Research in New York which became a veritable European University in exile with many distinguished French and German academics, including, among others, Levi-Strauss and Adorno, as faculty members. Lewin went first to Cornell, to the Faculty of Home Economics there, between 1933 and 1935 when he moved to the Child Welfare Center at the University of Iowa. During the Iowa years (1935–45), he gathered around him, just as he had at the Psychological Institute in Berlin in the 1920s, a group of talented graduate students, some of whom transferred with him to the Research Center for Group Dynamics when it was established at MIT in 1945 (see appendix 1 for more details). The group of doctoral students who assembled at MIT for those two years (see chapter 1) were to become the pioneers of social psychology in America during the modern era (Patnoe, 1988). On Lewin's death in 1947 the Research Center for Group Dynamics moved from MIT to the University of Michigan where, under the direction of Cartwright, it became part of the Institute for Social Research. Given his close links with Lewin, it is scarcely surprising that Cartwright (1979) should have such a vivid appreciation of the extent to which the history of social psychology in America was shaped by events in Germany (see chapters 1 and 9). The biography of Lewin by Marrow (1969), though a little sycophantic, is a mine of information concerning Lewin's years in America and of his considerable influence there, especially in the field of social psychology.

Another key figure in the Gestalt group was Köhler, though, from the rather narrow perspective of a history of social psychology, he was a less important figure than either Lewin or Heider. He remained in Berlin as Director of the Psychological Institute, showing courageous opposition to the Nazi regime until his position became untenable (Henle, 1986b). He accepted an invitation to deliver the William James lectures at Harvard in 1934 and then returned to America as a professor at Swarthmore College (1935–58). At Swarthmore, he influenced his colleague there, Asch, who played an important role in the development of a cognitive social psychology in the modern era. Köhler's book on *Gestalt Psychology* (Köhler, 1947) is important, from my perspective, because in it he worked out his own opposition to behaviourism which was the dominant form of psychology in America. It was not until they were immigrants in America that the Gestalt psychologists encountered behaviourism. When they did, they

Figure 6.1   Kurt Lewin, founder of social psychology as an experimental and
applied science

were opposed to it. It was a radically different perspective from their own. I believe it was in the context of behaviourism in America that a number of them (most notably Lewin and Heider) became social psychologists. They had not been social psychologists back home in their native Austria or Germany.

I think I can best make this point by means of an extensive quotation from Koffka's *Principles of Gestalt Psychology* (1936). The book is written with the explicit purpose of introducing the American reader to this German tradition of research, mainly in the field of visual perception. Koffka is acutely aware that the dominant perspective in America is very different from that of the Gestalt psychologists. In this passage Koffka is at pains to distinguish between the geographical and behavioural environments. He does so by citing a German legend:

> On a winter evening amidst a driving snowstorm a man on horseback arrived at an inn, happy to have reached a shelter after hours of riding over the wind-swept plain on which the blanket of snow had covered all paths and landmarks. The landlord who came to the door viewed the stranger with surprise and asked him whence he came. The man pointed in the direction straight away from the inn, whereupon the landlord, in a tone of awe and wonder, said, 'Do you know that you have ridden across the Lake of Constance?' At which the rider dropped stone dead at his feet. (Koffka, 1936, pp. 27–8)

Koffka goes on to ask in which environment does this behaviour take place? This is where the distinction between the natural and the behavioural environments becomes important.

> The Lake of Constance. Certainly, because it is a true proposition that he rode across it. And yet, this is not the whole truth, for the fact that there was a frozen lake and not ordinary solid ground did not affect his behaviour in the slightest. It is interesting for the geographer that this behaviour took place in this particular locality, but not for the psychologist as the student of behaviour; because the behaviour would have been just the same had the man ridden across a barren plain. But the psychologist knows something more: Since the man died from sheer fright after having learned what he had 'really' done, the psychologist must conclude that had the stranger known before, his riding behaviour would have been very different from what it actually was. Therefore the psychologist will have to say: There is a second sense to the word environment according to which our horseman did not ride across the lake at all, but across an ordinary snow-swept plain. His behaviour was a riding-over-a-plain, but not a riding-over-a-lake. (Koffka, 1936, p. 28)

The perspective of the geographer or natural scientist is like that of the innkeeper in the present context – an observer who knows the nature of the natural environment. This is the perspective of the behaviourist in psychology. Koffka goes on to cite an example that will be more familiar to his American readers 'Does the rat run in the maze the experimenter has set up?' There is clearly a divergence in perspective between actors and observers in all of these examples. The Gestalt perspective is that of an actor in the social scene, i.e. that of the rider on horseback or the rat in the maze. In order to understand the behaviour of the rider, one needs to understand the environment as he believes it to be. In contrast to the perspective of the detached observer of others, this will appear to be a highly 'subjective perspective'. Interestingly, it is an equivalent perspective to Thomas's theorem in sociological forms of social psychology, i.e. 'if men define a situation as real, then it is real in its consequences.' The Gestalt perspective is the distinctive input that makes cognitive social psychology, in the modern era, a characteristically American phenomenon.

What Koffka describes as the behavioural environment is equivalent to Lewin's notion of the psychological life-space of the individual. The point I wish to make here is that the Gestalt perspective also resulted in the individualization of the social, this time in terms of perception rather than in terms of behaviour. Coming as it did after the first phase of the individualization of the social, it had a dramatic effect. The coexistence in the modern era of social psychology of two incompatible, individualistic perspectives – those of the observer and of the actor – does not make for a social science. These are the 'consistency of response' and 'view of the world' approaches to the study of attitudes to which Campbell (1963) drew attention in the context of modern social psychology.

The Gestalt perspective tends to be individualizing. This is very true of Lewin's notion of the psychological life-space of the individual. It is much less true of Heider's psychology of interpersonal relations (1958). This falls just outside the historical period here under review. It is interesting, though, that Heider was unable to use his friend Lewin's notion of psychological life-space because it was too individualistic to form the basis of a psychology of interpersonal relations. Heider claimed that it was difficult to represent the life-space of one individual within the life-space of another individual when dealing with social relations. While Lewin generated a great deal of research on the dynamics of small groups, his model of the individual (e.g. his work on personality) was a curiously non-social model. It is almost as though he empathically put himself in the place of the person whose behaviour he was trying to understand rather than, as Heider does, retaining his own perspective on the other. Heider's P-O-X (Person, Other, Object) model is more behavioural and more explicitly social than Lewin's model of the psychological life-space of the individual.

This difference in the theoretical formulations of Lewin and of Heider is important in relation to the theme of this chapter. Lewin's formulations of the psychological life-space of the individual is much more individualizing than Heider's conception of a psychology of interpersonal relations. It was Lewin rather than Heider who decisively influenced the development of experimental social psychology in America at the start of the modern era. He established social psychology as a cognitive and experimental science in much the same way as F. H. Allport, some two decades earlier, had established it as a behavioural and experimental science. They both individualized social psychology in terms of both their theory, i.e. behaviourism and Gestalt psychology, and in terms of their methodology, i.e. experimentation.

The difference, within the Gestalt tradition, between Lewin and Heider is brought out in this quotation from Heider:

> When Lewin developed topological psychology, I had at first great hopes that it would furnish the tools for the representation and analysis of interpersonal phenomena. However, though the concepts of topology were of great help in disentangling the underlying means-end structures in the actions of a person, they were rather cumbersome and in many cases inadequate in dealing with two-person situations. It is difficult or impossible to describe in topological terms how one person's life space is represented in another person's life space – how, for instance, the sentiment of A can be a goal for B, or how A reacts to what B does to him. (Heider, 1958, p. 14)

Wertheimer at the New School for Social Research in New York strongly influenced Asch (figure 6.2), whose textbook *Social Psychology* (1952) became extremely influential throughout the modern era in social psychology. It played a prototypical role in regard to that era that was comparable to Allport's 1924 text of the same title for the

Figure 6.2   Solomon Asch, an important figure in the emergence of a
cognitive social psychology in the modern era

inter-war years. It was a clear articulation of the Gestalt perspective and it contributed substantially to the emergence of a cognitive social psychology in America during the modern era.

Individualism in the Period of the Cold War

While there is a strong theoretical contrast between Asch (1952) and Allport (1924), which corresponds to the difference in perspective between Gestalt psychology and behaviourism, respectively, they share a common representation of the individual. This common element of individualism is part of American culture. We have seen earlier in this chapter that the same was true of the two Allport brothers, despite their quite different theoretical perspectives – cognitive in the case of G. W. and behavioural in the case of F. H.

Individualism as a core cultural value is also evident in relation to the history of psychology and not just the history of social psychology. An important series of books available to the historian of modern psychology is the series on *A History of Psychology through Autobiography*. More than seven volumes have appeared to date. The editors of these volumes will be familiar to the readers of the present volume. They are Murchison, Boring and Lindzey. The idea that one can write history through the medium of autobiography is attractive and also absorbingly interesting but it betrays the importance of individualism as a cultural value. When Luria, the distinguished Russian neuropsychologist, contributed to the series he wrote about the history of his laboratory rather than providing an autobiography.

If social psychology is a distinct discipline – and I believe it is – then it concerns the relationship between the individual and the community (or society). During the period of the Cold War individualism became the ideology of the West and communism the ideology of the East. This, I believe, led to gross distortions in the development of the social sciences on both sides of the former Iron Curtain. When either the individual or the community becomes the privileged term, it becomes impossible to formulate the relationship between the individual and the community. Now that the Cold War is over there is as much conceptual re-thinking called for in the former West as in the former East. This, however, falls outside the historical period covered by this book. At the beginning of the modern era of social psychology in America, which does just come within our ambit, the activities of Senator McCarthy did have a detectable effect on the development of the social sciences. I think the history of this period still needs to be written. This was the context (see above) in which the social sciences found it beneficial to be referred to as the behavioural sciences. It is part of the history of the individualization of social psychology in America during the modern era.

7

Sociological and Psychological Forms of Social Psychology

In the opening chapter I observed that there are few, if any, links in the modern era between sociological and psychological forms of social psychology. This is especially true in America. When G. W. Allport first spoke, in 1954, of the flowering of social psychology as a characteristically American phenomenon he clearly intended to include sociological as well as psychological forms of the discipline. When Jones (1985) published his short account of modern American social psychology it was the achievements of what he saw as the dominant psychological form of the discipline that he was celebrating. So what happened, during the modern era, between these two dates? The simple answer is that social psychology flourished in the context of two quite separate disciplines (namely, sociology and psychology), assuming a different form in the two contexts.

Sociology and Psychology

Sociology and psychology are, today, distinct disciplines. It has not always been like that. The majority of the theorists whose work is considered in chapter 3, for example, wrote both about the individual and about either society or culture. This includes, among others, such distinguished writers as Wundt, Durkheim, Freud, Mead and McDougall. Comte is claimed as a common ancestor both for sociology (Rosenberg and Turner, 1981) and for social psychology (Allport,

1954). There were many collaborative research projects between sociologists and psychologists during our period. Three of the four volumes of *The American Soldier* series, for example, were edited by sociologists (see chapters 1 and 9). These volumes were concerned, primarily, with social surveys and with the measurement of attitudes and the prediction of behaviour. The volume edited by psychologists (Hovland et al., 1949) was on experimental studies of persuasion. Also, at the start of the modern era, there were doctoral programmes in social psychology at Harvard, Yale and Michigan which were the joint responsibility of sociologists and psychologists. A joint programme was to emerge, somewhat later, at Columbia University in New York (Klineberg and Christie, 1965).

Sociologists and psychologists often shared the same theoretical notions, e.g. social attitudes. Thomas, the Chicago sociologist, defined social psychology in the 1920s as being the scientific study of social attitudes. In his classic study with Znaniecki on *The Polish Peasant in Europe and America* (1918–20), Thomas used the notion of social attitudes to differentiate between groups; for example, between immigrants and the host community. Psychologists came to use the term to differentiate between individuals (Jaspars and Fraser, 1984). This is a further instance of the individualization of social psychology in America (see chapter 6). While sociologists at Chicago regarded attitudes as the subjective side of culture, psychologists there, like Thurstone, showed how these collective values could be scaled. Sociologists provided nearly as many definitions of attitudes as psychologists in the list considered by G. W. Allport (1935) in his classic article on attitudes in the Murchison *Handbook* (see chapter 5). This is the chapter in which Allport edited out the collective and social components of other people's definitions and ended by offering his own purely psychological definition (Jaspars and Fraser, 1984). When, also in 1935, Gallup introduced opinion polling in America (appendix 1) it proved to be a useful research tool for social scientists in general, including psychologists. Much of the early research on inconsistencies between attitudes and actions – for example, the research of La Piere (1934) – was carried out by sociologists.

While Durkheim (1898) was the most hostile to psychology of all the major sociologists, the psychology to which he was so strongly opposed was the psychology of the individual. He was not at all opposed to the development of social psychology nor, at one stage, was he particularly proprietorial about sociology as a title: 'We see no objection to calling sociology a variety of psychology, if we carefully add that social psychology has its own laws which are not those of individual psychology.' The contrast, in the modern era, between sociological and psychological forms of social psychology, occurred at an even earlier stage within a wholly sociological context; for example, the debate between Durkheim and Tarde in 1903–4 (appendix 1) at the École des Hautes Études en Sciences Sociales on the relations between sociology and psychology (for a full account of this debate see Lukes, 1973, pp. 302–14).

We must be careful not to read back into the past what, today, differentiates psychology from sociology. For one thing psychology was more explicitly social in the past than it is today (chapter 6). The less social it is, the greater the gulf between it and sociology. Even today it is more explicitly social in some cultures than it is in others – in Russia, say, in comparison to America (Joravsky, 1989). I can think of two plausible reasons for this latter difference. Individualism is not as strong a cultural value in Russia as it is in America. Language, in the history of Russian psychology, is an explicitly social phenomenon. It goes back from Vygotsky through Wundt to Humboldt, Herder and Hegel (Marková, 1983). If psychologists in America had accepted the social psychology of Mead then the gap between psychology and sociology would not have been so great as it is in the modern era. The psycholinguistic tradition in the study of language and thought derives from Descartes rather than from Hegel (Marková, 1982). It is not only the psycholinguists and the behaviourists in psychology who destroyed the social nature of language – so, too, did the logical positivists in philosophy. Where Hegel is an ancestor in the study of language, as in Russia for example, then psychology itself is more social than if Descartes were the ancestor.

The progressive separation between psychology and sociology is a recurrent theme throughout this book. Manicas (1987) helps us to set this process in some sort of historical perspective:

> if, as social scientists, we were to imagine ourselves transported to Oxford, the Sorbonne, or Harvard in, say, 1870, we would find almost nothing familiar. There would be no 'departments' of 'sociology' or 'psychology': the research practices of the faculties and the modes of graduate instruction of those institutions would be for the most part alien. But we would find *very little* which is *not* familiar if we were to make a similar visit to *any* 'department' in *any* American university in 1925. (Manicas, 1987, p. 5)

The separation of the parent disciplines, psychology and sociology, was the prelude to the development of forms of social psychology within each. These developments proceeded apace throughout the modern era in social psychology. I shall argue, below, that the form of social psychology which developed within each of these two contrasting disciplines is influenced by the nature of the parent discipline. Social psychologists in both disciplines act as a countervailing force to the dominant force in the parent discipline. This, necessarily, produces two forms of social psychology that have little or nothing in common with each other since each can be understood only in relation to a different context. In this respect they are like two different species of the same plant.

G. H. Mead and Symbolic Interactionism

I noted, in chapter 4, how it was Morris, the philosopher, who decided on the name 'social behaviourism' to characterize the social psychology of G. H. Mead. It was Mead's critique of Watson that must have been foremost in his mind as he edited the transcript of that 1927 course of lectures in social psychology. Behaviourism was, at the time, the dominant paradigm in psychology and it was a topic of interest also to philosophers. Indeed Morris, himself, had a strong interest in it and he went on to set semiotics on a sound behavioural footing (Morris, 1938). With regard to behaviourism, at the time Morris was editing Mead the action was elsewhere than at Chicago, though it had certainly started there when Watson submitted his doctoral thesis in 1903.

The psychologists at Chicago had separated from the philosophers as far back as 1904 (appendix 1), some three decades before Morris decided to call Mead a social behaviourist. The attempt by Morris to market Mead as a social behaviourist can scarcely be claimed a success. The subtitle of the book he edited (Mead, 1934), 'From the standpoint of a social behaviourist', did little to bring it to the attention of the audience for whom it was primarily intended. There is not a single reference to Mead, for example, in the course of Skinner's book on *Verbal Behavior* (1957), yet both authors are writing about language as a form of expressive behaviour. This, of course, may tell us more about Skinner than it does about Mead. Skinner singularly failed to appreciate that language is also a form of symbolic interaction. This is where the sociologists at Chicago enter the picture.

The sociologists at Chicago, especially since the arrival there of Faris in 1920 (Lewis and Smith, 1980), regarded the course of lectures in social psychology given by Mead as being important to the develop-

ment of sociology at that university. They recommended graduate
students in sociology to take it as their ancillary subject. When Mead
died in 1931, Blumer (figure 7.1) inherited his course of lectures in
social psychology. The sociologists at Chicago regarded themselves as
the legitimate heirs and guardians of Mead's conception of social
psychology. Blumer came to refer to it as 'symbolic interactionism'.
Coser (1977, p. 346) is quite clear that 'the term "symbolic interactionism" was never known at Chicago while Mead lived.' The term at
least has the virtue of accurately reflecting the central significance of
language in the social psychology of Mead. For Mead, the communicative act is the basic unit of analysis in social psychology (Farr and

Figure 7.1 Herbert Blumer, founder of symbolic interactionism

Rommetveit, 1995). This is something that Newcomb (1950), at Michigan, picked up and made central to his sociological form of social psychology within the modern era. Blumer fully appreciated the importance of significant gestures and of symbolic forms of communication to an understanding of social interaction between humans. He probably failed to appreciate what was important to Mead, i.e. the evolutionary significance of this form of symbolic interaction. Without this significance, mind ceases to be a natural phenomenon.

While the sociologists welcomed the publication of *Mind, Self and Society: from the standpoint of a social behaviorist* (Mead, 1934), they quibbled with the way in which the text of Mead's 1927 course of lectures had been edited by Morris (Faris, 1936). The bone of contention this time was the title of the book rather than its subtitle. Faris felt that the order of topics should have been 'society, self and mind'. This would be the logical order for a sociological form of social psychology. It would also be consistent with Mead's own logic, at least in relation to the ontology of the self in humans, i.e. society exists prior to the minds and selves of its individual members. My reasons for thinking that the sociologists at Chicago were mistaken in believing that their preferred order was the historic order in which Mead treated these topics in his course of lectures are set out in chapter 4 and will not be repeated here. The preferred order, as stated by Faris, may reveal how what Morris called the 'social behaviourism' of Mead is transformed into what Blumer calls 'symbolic interactionism'. It would be interesting to have a transcript of the course as taught by Blumer, especially in the early years of the 1930s. The order 'society, self and mind' is followed in a number of the early symbolic interactionist texts (Manis and Meltzer, 1967).

The differences between Mead and Blumer are so great that it is difficult to believe that the latter could have comprehended fully the significance of the work of the former. Mead proposed a complete philosophy of the act; Blumer was more concerned with the interpretation of action than he was with the action *per se*; that is, Blumer was not a social behaviourist. Mead was a completely consistent Darwinian (see chapter 4); Blumer was not. Mead, by profession, was a philosopher and he tackled most, if not quite all, of the problems that philosophers of his generation typically addressed. Blumer, by profession, was a sociologist with a strong interest also in the methodology of the social sciences and in collective behaviour. It is clear from the complete corpus of his writings in the field of methodology that Blumer is strongly opposed to positivism. This is one of my reasons for suspecting that the sociologists at Chicago misunderstood Mead's critique of Watson (see chapter 4). Faris, in his foreword to Lewis and Smith (1980), defends his colleague Blumer's interpretation of Mead. 'Central to the symbolic interactionist social psychology Blumer advanced over these years is the recognition he has given the name and ideas of George Herbert Mead' (p. xvii). Faris clearly believes that Blumer was a faithful expositor of the social psychology of Mead.

Sociologists, generally, fail to appreciate that when Mead reviewed the two textbooks of social psychology published in 1908 he clearly preferred McDougall to Ross (Mead, 1909), i.e. he preferred the psychological over the sociological version of social psychology. This is because for Mead, as well as for McDougall, the basis of life in society is impulsivity. It is the biologism of Mead that is conveniently omitted from the symbolic interactionist tradition of social psychology. Shibutani (1970), in his brief foreword to the set of papers he edited in honour of Herbert Blumer, says of Blumer's distinctive perspective: 'Human beings are neither creatures of impulse nor heedless victims of external stimulation; they are active organisms which guide and construct their line of action while continuously coming to terms with the demands of an ever-changing world as they interpret it' (Shibutani, 1970, p. vi). For Mead, human beings are creatures of impulse. They are, at least initially, the victims of the responses (or non-responses) of others to their actions. It is true, though, that they are not heedless victims. They do learn – primarily to act intentionally. This, then, becomes automatic unless they misinterpret a situation. Swanson (1961), the sociologist, had to warn others (presumably, fellow sociologists) that in comparing Mead and Freud it was necessary to map the 'I' of Mead onto the 'Id' and not onto the 'Ego' of Freud. Blumer was inclined to make the latter equation.

Sociologists, themselves, began to doubt whether Blumer adequately represented the significance of Mead for the whole range of issues that concern the sociologist. Some two years beyond the upper limit of the historical period I have set for this book, Strauss (1956) edited selected papers of Mead that he considered to be relevant to the work of sociologists. These were published under the imprint of the University of Chicago Press some four years after Blumer had left Chicago for Berkeley in California (see appendix 1). In his introduction, Strauss stresses that 'Mead's position was radically different from that of most social psychologists and sociologists who have quoted him or incorporated his thinking into their own systems of thought' (Strauss, 1956, pp. vii, viii). Strauss even suggests that sociologists in the 1920s and 1930s found Mead's views on socialization useful in their fight against biological explanations of behaviour. This is ironic, given Mead's commitment to Darwin's theory of evolution (chapter 4). Strauss adds 'what sociologists . . . selected from Mead's writing was very restricted and pertained mainly to how culture and norms got "internalized" into the person, that is, how self-control was a reflection of social control' (Strauss, 1956, p. xii).

The issue of Blumer's interpretation of Mead became the subject of a controversy within the pages of the *American Sociological Review*. The controversy broke some 12 years after Blumer had officially retired from his post at Berkeley. McPhail and Rexroat (1979) opened the attack with an article entitled 'Mead *v.* Blumer: the divergent methodological perspectives of social behaviorism and symbolic inter-actionism', to which Blumer (1980) replied 'Mead and Blumer: the convergent methodological perspectives of social behaviorism and symbolic interactionism'. The editors allowed the original authors a right of reply to Blumer's response and this appeared in the same issue under the title 'Ex cathedra Blumer or ex libris Mead?' (McPhail and Rexroat, 1980). This exchange of views is primarily about the meth-odology of research and the importance of distinguishing between the perspective of the investigator and the perspective of the investigated – something that Mead does but Blumer fails to do.

Sociological Forms of Social Psychology

Symbolic interactionism

It is best to treat symbolic interactionism as a sociological form of social psychology that was initiated at Chicago by Blumer and based on his interpretation of Mead. He first used the terms 'symbolic interactionism' to characterize this form of social psychology in an article he published in a volume edited by Schmidt (Blumer, 1937). The fullest and most developed elaboration of his position is to be found in his book *Symbolic Interactionism: perspective and method* (Blumer, 1969). This was published after he had left Chicago for Berkeley in 1952. It is still referred to, however, as the Chicago School of symbolic interactionism.

Blumer was also broadly interested in the study of collective beha-viour and he spent a year in Paris studying fashion (see appendix 1). He argued that fashion is to modern society what custom had been to pre-modern society. At the Annual Meeting of the American Sociologi-cal Association in 1947 he presented a paper that was critical of public opinion polling (Blumer, 1948; also included in Blumer, 1969). This involved him in an acrimonious debate on the nature of public opinion. At least one of those whom he criticized (Newcomb) subsequently apologised, after a number of years, for having misunderstood him (see Deutscher, 1973, p. 39). The debate is interesting because the position Blumer attacked is the one with which F. H. Allport is most closely associated (see chapter 6). The technology of sampling ensures that each person's opinion counts equally. This is fine if your objective is to predict the outcome of an election where everyone has only one vote. It is not appropriate in most situations where the formation of public opinion is important. Here the opinions of some people carry more weight than those of others. This is something that a random sample fails to take into account. Blumer's distinction between crowds, masses and the public is really an extension of the work at Chicago of Park (see chapter 3). In the papers published in honour of Blumer and edited by Shibutani (1970), under the title *Human Nature and Collective Behavior*, those relating to human nature refer to Blumer as an expositor of the social psychology of Mead.

At present, symbolic interactionism is still a vital and versatile tradition of social psychology within American sociology. It is quite customary in the modern era to distinguish between at least two schools of symbolic interactionism. There is the Chicago School, associated with Blumer and discussed fairly fully above, and the Iowa School, associated with Manfred Kuhn (Meltzer and Petras, 1970). The latter school is much more positivistic in its methodology and more narrowly focused upon the self as the object of study in social psychology. Since Kuhn is positivistic and also critical of Blumer, this supports my argument (see above) that Blumer, himself, was an anti-positivist. It could even be that Blumer developed his social psychology in opposition to Max Meyer's book *The Psychology of the Other One* (1921), which was an early behaviourist text. Meyer was at Missouri and he published his text two years before Blumer obtained his MA in sociology at the same university.

The first textbook of symbolic interactionism was the volume *Social Psychology* published by Lindesmith and Strauss (1949). There is a continuity of themes and of research interests before and after the Second World War in this sociological form of social psychology that is missing in psychological forms of social psychology. There is no positivistic break between a long past and a short history. Turner and Killian (1957) argue that sociological forms of social psychology are less ethnocentric than psychological forms of social psychology and are not so influenced by positivism and by experimental methodology.

Sociological forms of social psychology are rarely represented in the modern series of *Handbooks* edited by Lindzey (1954) and by Lindzey and Aronson (1968–9, 1985), but when they are it is usually the symbolic interactionist tradition of social psychology that is covered. Since 1981 sociological social psychologists have had their own handbook: *Social Psychology: sociological perspectives*, edited by Rosenberg and Turner. Research within the various traditions of symbolic interactionism is well covered in this handbook.

Social psychology at Chicago

If there is one institution that has featured more prominently than any other in this historical account of the roots of modern social psychology then it is the University of Chicago. Almost certainly this is due to the distinction of its Faculty of Social Sciences. Several different forms of social psychology originated there: the social behaviourism of G. H. Mead; Thomas's scientific study of social attitudes; Thurstone's techniques for measuring social values; Blumer's symbolic interactionism; and, within the modern era, Ichheiser's sociology of interpersonal relations and Goffman's dramaturgical form of social psychology. This is an impressive list by any standards.

The social scientists at Chicago were very much concerned with studying the metropolis in which they lived and worked. They plotted the ecology of crime, juvenile delinquency, mental illness, suicide etc. They were also active in the field of social reform in areas such as education, race relations, the role of women, trade unionism, immigration and journalism. This included philosophers, such as Dewey and Mead, as well as social scientists. We have already noted (chapter 4) how Joas (1985) entitled his brief biographical sketch of Mead 'the development of a radically democratic intellectual'. Many empirical studies in the symbolic interactionist tradition of social psychology at Chicago were participant observational studies in a wide range of milieux within the city. Rock (1979) has shown how participant observation was the generic methodology of symbolic interactionism. After the Second World War, Goffman was able to draw on a veritable storehouse of unpublished masters and doctoral dissertations at the University of Chicago to illustrate the minutiae of his studies of social encounters.

Chicago was the spiritual home of Gustav Ichheiser, one of the Jewish refugees fleeing from his native Vienna after the Anschluss of 1938. He was Director of the Vocational Guidance Centre for the city of Vienna. The details of his tragic life and a fairly comprehensive bibliography can be found in Rudmin et al. (1987). When he fled he had in his possession a manuscript in German which he had originally written for Mannheim's series of publications in the sociology of knowledge. This was translated into English and published at Chicago as a monograph in the *American Journal of Sociology* in 1949 under the title 'Misunderstandings in human relations: a study in false social perception'. Although Ichheiser himself was a psychologist, his monograph was a socio-psychological approach to the study of personality. He is concerned with the images that distinct groups of others form of the self of a particular individual. It was this aspect of personality that Allport (1937) omitted when he individualized the notion of personality, just as he had previously done with the notion of attitude (see chapter 6). Ichheiser suggested it was valuable to distinguish between expression and impression. Goffman, who set out from Chicago to conduct the fieldwork for his doctoral dissertation in the Shetland Islands two years after the publication of this monograph, took up the challenge and produced a theory of expressive behaviour that took into account the impressions forming in the minds of observing others, i.e. the presentation of self in everyday life.

Social representations

French research on social representations is often classified as a sociological form of social psychology. It is certainly distinctly different from the psychological tradition of social psychology that is dominant in the modern era in the United States of America and which is the focus of interest in the first and last chapters of this book. Indeed, it constitutes an important critique of the purely individual nature of much so-called social psychology in the USA and in the UK. In many ways it comprises the antidote to the process of the individualization of social psychology in America which was described in some detail in chapter 6.

In initiating the study of social representations, Moscovici nominated Durkheim as the ancestor of this particular tradition of research. By this single act Moscovici created a tradition of research that, at one and the same time, was both sociological and French. In chapter 8 I argue that one's choice of ancestor reveals a great deal about one's intentions. Allport's choice of Comte as the founder of social psychology (Allport, 1954), for example, reveals his belief that social psychology is now a positive science. The contrast between French research on social representations and American (as well as British) research on attitudes and opinions is a specific instance of the difference between sociological and psychological forms of social psychology. It is one of the few areas of empirical research where serious attempts have been made in the past and continue to be made in the present to establish a *rapprochement* between these two contrasting forms of social psychology (Jaspars and Fraser, 1984). It is a potentially fruitful topic for a transatlantic dialogue between social psychologists from Europe and from America. The problem I am addressing here, however, is predominantly an American problem. It is the absence, *in the American scene*, of any formal links between psychological and sociological forms of social psychology. All of the French research on social representations (Farr, 1987b) was carried out during the modern era of social psychology and so falls outside the time frame of this book.

Context effects

The progressive separation between psychology and sociology is a recurrent theme throughout this book. Manicas (1987) believes that this process was more or less complete, at least in American universities, by 1925. Once formed, however, these parent disciplines come to exert quite contrary pressures on the forms of social psychology that develop within the boundaries of each discipline. The ethos of the parent discipline powerfully shapes the form that any social psychology can assume that is nurtured within it. Social psychology, in both psychology and sociology, acts as a countervailing force to the one that is dominant in the parent discipline.

In psychology, for example, individuals are the most salient objects of study. This makes psychology a rather peculiar social science. Heider (1958) graphically portrays the salience of other individuals within the phenomenal field of the person, considered as a perceiver (P) of others (O). This is why he devised a psychology of interpersonal relations. The skin, here, is a particularly compelling boundary (Farr, 1991a). The distinction between figure and ground is sharp when the figure is another human. The other (O) is highly salient, visually, from the perspective of P, the perceiver. Social psychologists within psychology, however, tend to stress situational determinants of the behaviour of individuals. In doing so they act as a force opposing the tendency to take the individual as the object of study in psychology.

This, I would argue, is necessarily the case if the preferred method of investigation is the experiment. This is because experimenters tend to make situational, rather than personal, attributions. Milgram's experimental studies of obedience to authority can serve as a convenient illustration (Milgram, 1974), even though they fall outside the time frame of the present study. They constitute a salutary corrective to the tendency to perceive individuals as autonomous moral agents. Indeed, his theory of the 'agentic state' declares, quite explicitly, that people often act as the agents of others, i.e. they are not morally autonomous. The dominant tradition within psychological forms of social psychology, especially in the modern era (chapters 1 and 10) is the experimental tradition.

In the context of sociology, on the other hand, social psychologists tend to stress the autonomy of the individual *vis à vis* what Dennis Wrong (1961) called 'an oversocialized conception of man'. The contrast, here, is with deterministic models of the macro-institutions of society produced by most of the major theorists in sociology. Goffman (1959), for example, produces an active model of the individual in the social scene which is both part of and a counter-weight to the Durkheimian tradition in sociology. If psychologists need a social and reflexive model of man, then they should borrow the model devised by Mead (1934). This is widely regarded as a sociological form of social psychology. Psychological social psychologists, since they are trying to correct for too exclusive a focus on the individual on the part of their psychological colleagues, are not well placed to produce adequate models of the human agent. They should borrow their theory from the alternative form of social psychology – the sociological form.

Moscovici (1988) states that if psychologists are unable to produce forms of social psychology that other social scientists find useful then those social scientists will invent their own forms of social psychology. This, historically, is what has happened. The main theorists he discusses are Durkheim, Weber, Marx and Simmel. It is difficult for social psychologists within psychology, however, to gain an adequate appreciation of the distorting effects of the parent discipline. It is prudent, however, to look for other forms of social psychology that are not subject to the same distorting influence. There is no need for psychologists to invent new forms of social psychology. They already exist – but they do so in disciplines other than psychology. One needs, merely, to be literate in those other disciplines. My argument here is essentially an evolutionary one. The varieties of social psychology that continue to flourish are actually quite diverse (Farr, 1978, 1985b). One needs to appreciate, however, how each has evolved to fill a particular niche. This is where it is valuable to have a historical understanding of how these various forms of social psychology evolved.

8

Ancestors and Founders: Reconstructing the Past

There have been occasions, to date, to note some of the hazards involved in choosing ancestors and identifying founders. Samelson (1974), for example, took G. W. Allport (1954, 1968) to task for identifying Comte as the founder of social psychology and, thereby, creating a false origin myth for the discipline. Could Comte have been the founder of social psychology as we know it today? There is a general consensus that Wundt was the founder of experimental psychology (chapter 2). He also founded a form of social psychology, his *Völkerpsychologie*, to which history has not been so kind, to borrow a phrase from Danziger (1983). Why is Wundt, then, not also a founder of social psychology? Mead created a highly original form of social psychology at Chicago at the turn of the century but this remained a purely oral tradition during his lifetime (chapter 4). On his death it then became two quite different forms of social psychology: what Morris, who edited *Mind, Self and Society* (Mead, 1934), called 'social behaviourism' and what Blumer (1937), somewhat later, called 'symbolic interactionism' (chapter 7). Is Mead, then, the founder of two different forms of social psychology, one of which is psychological and the other of which is sociological?

Ancestors and Founders

I wish to distinguish between ancestors and founders. Ancestors are more remote in time than founders. They are also likely to be less embarrassing than founders since they are usually dead by the time

Figure 8.1 Wilhelm Wundt, founder of psychology as an experimental and social science (*archives of the University of Leipzig, Wundt–Nachless*)

they are identified as ancestors. Founders are usually transitional figures. They mark the boundary between the past and the present of a particular field of study. They belong both to the past and to the present of the disciplines they have founded. This is why their followers are often ambivalent about them. Danziger (1979) has graphically depicted this process in his thesis concerning the positivist repudiation of Wundt (see chapter 2). The younger generation of experimentalists were deeply ambivalent in their attitudes towards the founder of the discipline in which they had been trained, many of them by Wundt himself (figure 8.1). They acknowledged him as the founder of that discipline, yet rejected his views concerning the limited nature of the discipline he had established. The ambivalence of the followers about the founder often echoes the ambivalence of the founder about the discipline.

I think a similar thesis could be established with respect to James. If Wundt was the pope of the Old World, then James was the pope of the New World (Danziger, 1980b). His *Principles of Psychology* (James, 1890) was a beautifully constructed masterpiece in terms of both its content and its literary style. It is a landmark publication in the history of psychology. James, like Wundt, established a laboratory. He was, however, by temperament unsuited to being director of such a laboratory. He brought Munsterberg to Harvard from Freiberg in 1897 to take over from himself as Director of the Psychological Laboratory at Harvard. It was in this laboratory, under Munsterberg's supervision, that F. H. Allport obtained his PhD for research on what, today, we would call social facilitation effects. Bjork (1983), in his biographical sketch of James, describes him as a compromised scientist. This was how he was viewed by those whom he influenced. His followers were critical of him for maintaining an interest in psychical research after he had established psychology as a laboratory science. They were also dismayed when he set out for Edinburgh to give the Gifford Lectures on *The Varieties of Religious Experience* in 1901–2. These activities were scarcely compatible with being the founder of a new science. James's own ambivalence concerning the science he helped to found is evident in his switch from being a professor of psychology to being a professor of philosophy. His followers, no doubt, interpreted this move as a return to the metaphysical past of the discipline.

A somewhat similar thesis could be established, at the start of the modern era in social psychology, with respect to Kurt Lewin (see chapter 1). He is widely acknowledged to be the founder of experimental social psychology in America. His American doctoral students at Iowa and at MIT helped to establish social psychology, in the modern era, as a characteristically American phenomenon (Patnoe, 1988). There is a positivist repudiation of Lewin that is not unlike the positivist repudiation of Wundt as described by Danziger (1979). Lewin emigrated to America in 1933 with Hitler's rise to power in Germany (see appendix 1 for relevant dates). Throughout his career in America Lewin sought to establish social psychology as an experimental science and to apply it to solving socially significant problems. These problems included an understanding of the dynamics of anti-Semitism, and proving, in the laboratory, that democracy works better than the autocracy from which he had fled in Germany.

Lewin was able to maintain a creative tension between these two loci of interest during his own lifetime. Lewin is reputed to have said 'There is nothing so practical as a good theory.' For him, research in the field was just as important as experiments in the laboratory. He was able to commute between these two loci with ease. When he died in 1947 his followers were unable to maintain a creative balance between experimental and field research. The former rapidly became more important than the latter. Unlike Wundt and James, Lewin was not repudiated by his followers during his own lifetime. His life was tragically too short for that. It was only in 1947, after his untimely death, that these tensions surfaced among his followers and the Lewinian inheritance split asunder. One of those followers, in a retrospection, described the process in the following terms:

> Post-World War II American social psychology has been largely dominated, until very recently, by Lewin and his students. Lewin himself thoroughly integrated the two orientations of social psychology: the theoretical-research orientation which is imbued with the traditional normative concerns of the scientist – formal elegance, logical rigor, an intersubjective objectivity, and robustness of empirical verification – and the problem-centered orientation of the socially concerned practitioner. He combined this integration with a sense of the necessity to provide knowledge that could be useful in bringing about change and an awareness of the importance of creating the conditions which would encourage the actual use of such knowledge by those in the position to act upon it. Unfortunately, this fusion of orientations was less true of his students. More characteristically, a split developed which widened into a chasm after Lewin's sudden and premature death. Lewin's unifying presence had been able to hold the diverging tendencies together and, in his absence, the bifurcating dispositions became dominant. (Deutsch, 1975, p. 2)

The tradition that became dominant after Lewin's death was the more scientific of the two traditions. Greater prestige attached to running experiments in laboratories than to tackling applied problems in the field. The dominant tradition is reflected in such publications as Festinger (1980) which was entitled *Retrospections on Social Psychology*. The more applied tradition is to be found in such publications as Marrow (1969), Deutsch (1975) and Hirsch (1987).

My account of James and of Lewin as founders of laboratories is brief compared to my account of Wundt (chapter 2). Leipzig served as a model for Harvard and so the achievement of Wundt, in this respect, is more important than that of James. Lewin was able to transport his own model of a laboratory from Berlin, first to Iowa and then to MIT. At the time of his death, he was also working on plans for the establishment of a psychological laboratory at the Hebrew University in Jerusalem. Wundt and James were more ambivalent about what they had established than Lewin. Lewin had joined the laboratory at Berlin rather than established it. It was a good model to follow when he was in a position to establish social psychology as a laboratory science at MIT. The founding of laboratories feature prominently in histories of psychology and of social psychology that are influenced by a positivist philosophy of science. Lewin's laboratory was a collegial enterprise.

The most complete historical account we have to date of the founding of a major laboratory is Mitchell Ash's account of the emergence of Gestalt psychology in Berlin (Ash, 1982). His study covers the period 1890–1920. It finishes in the year in which Lewin joined the Berlin group of Gestalt psychologists. For an account of the experiments of Lewin and his graduate students at Berlin in the 1920s, see De Rivera (1976). For an account of Lewin and his graduate students at MIT immediately after the Second World War, see Patnoe (1988). The important thing about founders, which distinguishes them from ancestors, is that they founded something tangible. They are not just the originators of ideas. Their creativity assumes an institutional form. They are the founders of a laboratory or a journal or a doctoral programme. They may be the editor of a handbook or the author of a textbook but these are more minor forms of innovation.

Danziger (1990), once again, sets a fine example by comparing and contrasting several different forms of laboratory institution. In his book *Constructing the Subject: historical origins of psychological research*, Danziger (1990) compares and contrasts the laboratories of Wundt, Galton and Binet. We need many more such excellent studies. To date the historical study of European laboratories in psychology is more advanced than the study of American laboratories. Morawski (1988), in her edited volume on *The Rise of Experimentation in*

American Psychology, has made a useful start in identifying some of
the salient themes.

The important thing, I believe, is the founding of laboratories and of
doctoral programmes, rather than the devising of isolated experiments.
It is comparatively trivial, in my view, to claim that experimental
social psychology began with Triplett's experiments at Indiana in the
1890s on social facilitation effects. In those days these experiments in
social psychology were merely part of experimental psychology (Farr,
1976). This is why I have maintained, throughout this book, that the
modern era in social psychology did not begin until after the Second
World War. We are still too close to it to see it in a proper historical
perspective. Hovland's experimental studies of mass communication,
within *The American Soldier* series of volumes, did constitute something new and formed the basis of the post-war Yale programme of
research on communication and attitude change (see chapter 1).
Lewin's Research Center for the Study of Group Dynamics at MIT
(1945–7) was also something completely novel that had a dramatic
effect on the development of social psychology in America during the
modern era. Hovland and Lewin, here, were, clearly, founders in the
sense in which I am using that term. They founded, however, two very
different forms of experimental social psychology.

Ancestors are completely different from founders. They are revered
figures from the past who would appear to endorse some project in the
present that the person who nominates them as an ancestor regards as
important. The processes involved in the nomination of ancestors are
closely akin to what Butterfield (1951), the British historian, calls the
Whig interpretation of history. This is 'the tendency in many historians
to write on the side of Protestants and Whigs, to praise revolutions
provided they have been successful, to emphasise certain principles of
progress in the past and to produce a story which is the ratification if
not the glorification of the present' (Butterfield, 1951, p. v).

If the reader accepts my distinction between founders and ancestors,
then Comte would have to be an ancestor of social psychology and not,
as G.W. Allport claims, a founder. Allport was writing a history of
ideas, rather than a history of institutions. The choice of ancestor, of
course, can be very revealing. Comte, plausibly, is the founder of
positivism as a philosophy of science or even of sociology as a discipline but not of social psychology in any institutional sense of the
term.

There are, however, some hazards involved in choosing ancestors.
An inappropriate choice of ancestor could prove embarrassing. Allport, by his particular choice of ancestor, set his seal of approval on

positivistic trends within the social psychology of his own day. Samelson (1974) was, thereby, able to accuse Allport of writing a Whiggish
account of the development of social psychology. He showed how
Allport had depended too heavily on a secondary (English language)
source for his information about Comte.

The choice of a particular ancestor, as in the case of G. W. Allport,
may reveal the chooser's preferred philosophy of science. It may also
reveal the chooser's preferred form of social psychology (see chapter
7). Moscovici's choice of Durkheim (figure 8.2) as an ancestor is a
declaration that his theory of social representations is a sociological

Figure 8.2 Emile Durkheim, a founder of sociology and the ancestor of
Moscovici's theory of social representations

form of social psychology. Deutscher (1984), specifically in relation to the study of social representations, points out some of the hazards involved in the choice of ancestor. Indeed, Deutscher's article provides me with the title for this chapter. The principal danger in choosing ancestors, according to Deutscher, consists in borrowing a single theoretical idea or concept without stating where one stands in relation to the rest of the ancestor's theoretical ideas. This is particularly hazardous when the ancestor is a thinker as complex as Durkheim.

So far in this chapter I have highlighted the role of people (either as ancestors or as founders) in the history of social psychology. History, however, is more than just an account of the exploits of famous people. Carr (1961), among others, has demonstrated the naivety of the common-sense view of history as something written by individuals about other individuals. Social psychologists appreciate, better than most, the impossibility of separating the individual from society. The individual, apart from society, would be both speechless and mindless. This follows from the social psychology of G. H. Mead (chapter 4). Fame, too, like the individual, is a social phenomenon. It resides in the eye of the beholder as much as in the deeds of those deemed to be famous. Reputation is really part of the sociology of knowledge. This should come as no surprise to the social psychologist. History, above all else, is socially constructed.

The work of an ancestor, for example, may appear to be relevant only in retrospect. This is what Butterfield (1951) meant by the Whig interpretation of history. The past is reconstructed from the perspective of the present. Our view of the past is likely to be coloured by the concerns of the present. This is true in science as well as in politics. Our philosophy of science, therefore, may influence our choice of ancestors. It is a moot point as to which comes first – the philosophy of science or the ancestor. In the human and social sciences as they are today Comte is an important historical figure because he justifies our continued use of the word science to describe our activities in these fields. Comte must have appeared to G. W. Allport in this light when, in 1954, he wrote his chapter on the historical background to modern social psychology (see chapters 1 and 10). When we move from the history of ideas to the history of institutions, founders become more important than ancestors.

It would be foolish to believe that we leave our philosophies of science behind us when we write about founders, as distinct from ancestors. I have argued above (chapter 2) that positivism positively promotes the search for origins. It becomes important, in the light of this philosophy of science, to identify precisely when a particular field of study ceases to be metaphysics and becomes a science. Positivism is a potent source of over-sharp distinctions between the past and the present of disciplines once they become sciences. Founders are likely to be controversial figures in terms of the significance of what it is that they have founded. Laboratories and journals of research are more potent symbols of science than, say, textbooks. I would want to argue that handbooks are generally more significant than textbooks in the history of a discipline. This is why I have devoted so much space (chapters 5 and 10) to an analysis of the series of *Handbooks of Social Psychology*.

Is a course of lectures, for example, as important as a textbook? Usually not, but it might be, as it was with Mead's course of lectures on social psychology at Chicago. This was the medium through which, over a period of three decades, he developed his thinking concerning the relationship between philosophy and psychology. At the start he set out to refute Cartesian dualism. By the time he achieved his objective, psychologists, first at Chicago and then elsewhere, had severed their links with philosophy (see appendix 1 for appropriate dates). For them Mead remained, quite literally, a voice from the past. When, posthumously, his lectures assumed a more tangible form (Mead, 1934), they became the key text in a sociological, rather than in a psychological, form of social psychology (chapter 7).

Are textbooks more important than handbooks? Usually not, but they might be. Textbooks usually reflect the popularity of a subject among undergraduates. They are more directly related to teaching than they are to research. Handbooks, on the other hand, are more directly related to the training of successive cohorts of graduate students. Handbooks are multi-authored, while textbooks usually only have a single author. A handbook reflects the views of a community of researchers and scholars; a textbook the view of its author or authors. In the middle to long term, handbooks are probably more significant in the history of a discipline than textbooks.

Yet, a textbook, possibly because it is the work of a single author, might reflect a particular perspective that is important in the historical development of a discipline. The *Social Psychology* of F. H. Allport (1924) was a seminal text in this respect since it helped to establish social psychology as both a behavioural and an experimental science. This, in its turn, contributed significantly, during the inter-war years, to the individualization of social psychology in America (chapter 6). The textbook by Asch (1952), also called *Social Psychology*, reflected a particular perspective: this time a cognitive, rather than a behavioural perspective. It, too, contributed to the individualization of social psychology in America in the modern era. These two textbooks are prototypes, respectively, of behaviourism and of Gestalt psychology. Independently, and cumulatively over time, these two texts have resulted in the individualization of social psychology in America and helped to ensure, in the modern era, that psychological and sociological forms of social psychology would develop quite separately from each other. While the two perspectives of F. H. Allport and of Asch, considered separately, are incompatible with each other, together they are but different manifestations of individualism as a collective representation.

Zeitgeists and Paradigms

The 'great person' and zeitgeist *modes of writing history*

At the start of this chapter the emphasis was upon the role played by categories of individuals, i.e. ancestors and founders, in the development of a discipline. Boring's technique as a historian of science is a naïve amalgam of the 'great person' and *zeitgeist* modes of writing history (Boring, 1929, 1950). Ancestors and founders are prototypes of this first mode of writing history. I hope I have said enough already to show how a historian's philosophy of science might influence his or her choice of ancestor and also shape his or her account of the origins of a discipline.

The contrasting mode of writing history is to stress the *zeitgeist* or spirit of the times. In part this includes philosophies of science such as I have discussed already both in this chapter and elsewhere. Boring (1929, 1950), for example, thought that behaviourism was very much part of the *zeitgeist*, and that the role played by Watson was of only minor importance. If Watson had not invented behaviourism then someone else would have done so. The *zeitgeist* is a handy device that historians can use when they wish to paint someone out of history of whom they disapprove. Watson had been dismissed by his employer in 1920 (see appendix 1) for having an affair with one of his research assistants, Rosalie Raynor (his co-conspirator in the conditioning of Little Albert). The fact that he was no longer an academic did not prevent him from continuing to write about behaviourism in such popular sources as *The New Yorker* and *Harper's Magazine*. Behaviourism, as Boring claimed, was indeed part of the *zeitgeist* and Watson helped to ensure that this was so.

In scientific circles and in academe, positivism was part of the *zeitgeist*. In the history of psychology it assumed the form of behaviourism. It was an important force shaping the development of social psychology in America from as early as 1924 when F. H. Allport published his classic text on *Social Psychology*. It was very much part of the ethos of the social sciences at Chicago throughout the 1920s. Thurstone showed how social values could be measured and he produced his classic attitude scales on divorce, on war and peace, and on the Church and religion. Positivism is to be found in the notion of measurement. In the 1920s at Chicago Thomas defined social psychology as being the scientific study of social attitudes. It was also in the 1920s that the London School of Economics and Political Science adopted as its motto Virgil's words '*rerum cognoscere causas*': to get to know the causes of things (Dahrendorf, 1995). This was a further endorsement of positivism from another distinguished school of the social sciences. The 1930s saw the establishment of public opinion polling in America. This provided an important boost to the scientific aspirations of the social sciences. Gallup founded the American Institute of Public Opinion in 1935. F. H. Allport was an enthusiastic supporter of public opinion polling since it was completely consistent with his own brand of methodological individualism (see chapters 3 and 6).

The *zeitgeist* includes a great deal more than the philosophies of science which are current in academic and research circles. There was also a great deal of popular support for those same philosophies. The popular hope was that the methods of research which had proved so spectacularly successful in the natural sciences would prove equally successful when applied to the problems of the human and social sciences. There was also popular support for particular forms of science. O'Donnell (1985), for example, argues that public interest in America in phrenology helped to prepare the ground for behaviourism and later led to its rapid acceptance. De Tocqueville (1835–40), in his observations on the workings of democracy in America, commented on individualism as an important value in American culture. I hope I have said enough, especially in chapter 6, to convince the reader that this key value in American life has had a detectable effect on the history of social psychology in that country.

Paradigms in science and in philosophy

Paradigm is a key notion in Kuhn's discussion of the structure of scientific revolutions. It is a common set of assumptions concerning theory and methods shared by a community of scientists, usually over a significant period of time, in a particular field of research (Kuhn,

1962). He refers to research carried out within the established paradigm as normal science. The primary objects of concern to Kuhn are the natural sciences. Here he thinks paradigm is a useful explanatory device. He believes, and I would agree with him, that many of the human and social sciences, especially psychology, are still in a pre-paradigm phase of development. This is because there is little or no consensus within these disciplines as to either the object of study or the most appropriate methods for the study of that object. The work of Kuhn is important, in my opinion, because within the field of the philosophy and history of science he helps to redress the balance a little in favour of the historian of science over the philosopher of science.

Social psychology throughout the period under discussion is certainly in a pre-paradigm state. I think this is true also of modern social psychology. In the final chapter I analyse, in some detail, the positivist framework that the editors of the modern series of the *Handbook of Social Psychology* (Lindzey, 1954; Lindzey and Aronson, 1968–9, 1985) provide for the discipline. This relates only to psychological forms of social psychology and not to sociological forms. Within the former are two highly individualistic, yet incompatible, perspectives (see chapter 7) that together fail to make a social science. I believe it is possible, by incorporating the sociological perspective, to create a coherent paradigm for social psychology. This involves treating psychology itself as a social science.

Marková (1982) moves back in time Kuhn's notion of paradigm and applies it to the incommensurability between the philosophies of Descartes and of Hegel. Descartes helped to prepare the ground for the emergence of the natural sciences in the seventeenth and eighteenth centuries. Hegel prepared the ground for the emergence of the human and social sciences in the nineteenth and twentieth centuries. This brings us back to the emergence of the research university in Germany at the start of the nineteenth century (see chapter 2) and to the conflict within the German university system between the *Naturwissenschaften* and the *Geisteswissenschaften*. This was the context within which psychology was born as an experimental and social science (chapter 2). If we bring the distinction between these two rival forms of *wissenschaft* forward to the time of Kuhn, then we have two quite different (and incommensurable) models of science each of which could be paradigmatic for psychology. Marková (1982) has exposed the Cartesian assumptions underlying much modern research on language and thought. I hope, in the course of this book, I have demonstrated why the ghost of Descartes continues to haunt modern social psychology.

The philosophy of the present

Mead, Wundt and Vygotsky would argue that Hegel, rather than Descartes, ought to be paradigmatic for psychology, especially for social psychology. Mead had the advantage over Hegel of being able to base his philosophy on Darwin's theory of evolution. He developed his own philosophy of history which was more than just an extension of Hegel's philosophy of history. It was rooted in the work of both Darwin and Einstein, especially the latter's general theory of relativity, and influenced also by Bergson's philosophy of time. One's conception of time, according to Mead, ought to allow for the emergence in the present of that which is totally novel, e.g. the emergence of a new species. The event could not, by definition, have been predicted on the basis of our knowledge of the past at the time of its emergence – otherwise it would not be novel. Once it has emerged, however, we need a new version of the past in terms of which this event follows naturally. We are always reconstructing the past from the perspective (an objective point in space/time from which events are viewed) of the present *and there is no end to this process*; it does not just happen once and for all as when, for example, a field of study ceases to be metaphysics and becomes science. It is also likely to happen more often than a shift in paradigm in Kuhn's sense of that word. I much prefer the pragmatism of Mead and of Peirce to the positivism of Comte when it comes to the philosophy of history, especially the history of science.

Positivism, in the context of historiography, is most clearly evident in a search for origins (e.g. Allport, 1954) and in charting the progress of a discipline once it becomes a science. Jones (1985) falls into the latter category. History here means the history of a science, and the past of the discipline is written off as metaphysics. This is conducive to the creation of a clear break between past and present. In diachronic perspective this leads to a separation between philosophy and science which is strictly in accord with Comte's vision of progress. Comte, Allport's nominee as the founder of social psychology, envisaged three historical phases in the evolution of a discipline. The first was the theological phase which, in European thought, corresponds roughly to the Middle Ages. The second was the metaphysical phase which, again in Europe, corresponds approximately to the Renaissance and the Enlightenment. The third and final phase is that of positivism or science.

Allport (1954), in his choice of Comte as the founder of social psychology, endorses this particular view of progress. The strict separation this entails between philosophy and science calls for two quite distinct forms of history to cover these different phases in the evolution of social psychology (Allport, 1954; and Jones, 1985, respectively). Since progress is now cumulative the one account (i.e. Jones, 1985) will need to be updated regularly; the other (i.e. Allport, 1954) can be reprinted almost indefinitely since it is an account of the long past of the discipline. A further consequence of the strict separation between the metaphysical and the positive phases in the history of a discipline is that paradigms originating in the former period may be perpetuated, unwittingly, in the latter period (Marková, 1982). This is because scientists (i.e. the positivists) foolishly believe that they have broken decisively with their own metaphysical past. This is also why, as I suggested in chapter 4, Mead failed to influence the historical development of psychology.

There is another curious paradox here. During the positive phase in the evolution of a discipline, history and philosophy become inextricably intertwined. This is because we are dealing here not with history and with philosophy but with the history and philosophy of a science. This is a particular type of history (e.g. Jones, 1985) and a particular type of philosophy (e.g. Smith, 1988). Positivism is the link between the two. History here becomes the history of a science, history is hijacked by the scientists. These same historians of science deeply resent it when their science is described as history rather than as science (Gergen, 1973). Jones (1985) accused Gergen of making statements that are 'intellectually irresponsible invitations to despair'. The frame for the historical account, in the case of both Allport and Jones, is a particular philosophy of science. The accounts, however, are both read as history, and the philosophy that unites them remains largely unexamined. The philosophy of science to which Jones subscribes led him to exclude sociological forms of social psychology as not being part of that science and so they do not feature in his account of the history of modern social psychology.

9

War and the History of Social Psychology

This is a brief, and a seriously incomplete, chapter. It is incomplete because I have not undertaken the detailed research that would be needed to do justice to such a theme. It would warrant a whole library of books rather than just a chapter in one. Indeed, such a library already exists. In my opening chapter I paid tribute to the formative influence on the development of social psychology of the four-volume series on *The American Soldier* published under the general editorship of the sociologist Samuel Stouffer (Hovland et al., 1949; Stouffer, Lumsdaine et al., 1949; Stouffer, Suchman et al., 1949; Stouffer et al., 1950). Volumes I and II were surveys of the opinions of American soldiers on, respectively, adjustment to army life and combat and its aftermath. Volume III, edited by Hovland et al., was concerned with experiments in mass persuasion and was the basis of the programme at Yale, after the war, on communication and attitude change. Volume IV, which appeared a year later, was entitled *Measurement and Prediction* and was concerned with techniques of attitude measurement, including Guttman scaling. This was a landmark publication in the history of social psychology in America at the start of the modern era. To this could be added the publication by Geuter (1993), in the Cambridge Studies in the History of Psychology series, of *The Professionalization of Psychology in Nazi Germany* which reflects the role of psychology in Germany in the lead up to and during the Second World War.

There are three reasons why this chapter, brief and incomplete as it is, is necessary to the structure of my argument. First, I need to be able to take on board the perfectly legitimate claim by Cartwright (1979) that, to date, the single most influential figure in the history of social psychology is Hitler. Since Hitler is neither an ancestor nor a founder (see chapter 8), we need a conception of the discipline that relates it to the wider world within which it develops. Paradigms are important to the coherence of a discipline but even they can be disrupted by events outwith (as the Scots say) the paradigm. There can be few events so disruptive of normal science as war. Secondly, I began this history with an account of the origins of psychology as an experimental and social science in Germany (chapter 2) and I conclude it with an account of modern social psychology as a characteristically American phenomenon. So, what happened in between? Germany became involved not in one, but in two, world wars, both of which completely devastated Europe and its educational institutions. At the beginning of this period Americans (some 10,000 of them, according to Sokal, 1981) flocked to Europe (mainly Germany) for their graduate education; by the end of it it is Europeans who flock to America for their graduate education. Thirdly, the modern era in social psychology began with the end of the Second World War. I have argued in chapter 1 that the Second World War did for social psychology what the Great War of 1914–18 did for psychometrics and the study of individual differences.

The Great War of 1914–1918

Before the war the hegemony of the German universities in the development of psychology and other new subjects of academic study was unchallenged. The rest of the world had to learn German if they were to keep abreast of developments. After the war other nations were quick to copy the Germans. The PhD degree was introduced into British universities after the war in the hope of attracting Americans to study in Britain, as it was assumed they would no longer be flocking to Germany for their graduate studies. This was all to no avail as American universities had developed their own excellent graduate schools by the 1920s. The international emphasis was still there but one did not need to travel abroad in order to find it. It became a requirement in many doctoral programmes in psychology in America and elsewhere to demonstrate a competence (at least at the level of reading) in European languages other than English.

The war interrupted the work of many scholars on both sides of the conflict. Wundt was more than halfway through the ten volumes of his *Völkerpsychologie* when war broke out (see chapter 2). The war forced

McDougall to delay publication of the second of his two volumes of social psychology (*The Group Mind*, which did not appear until 1920). The first volume had only been *An Introduction to Social Psychology* (McDougall, 1908) (see chapter 3). The war also marked the transition in Freud's thinking between his clinical studies of individuals and his development of a psychology of the masses (chapter 3). The war marooned Köhler on Tenerife where he was Director of the Anthropoid Station there. He spent the duration of the war studying the problem-solving abilities of a colony of nine chimpanzees. He was particularly interested in their use of tools. These studies were the basis of his book on *The Mentality of Apes* (1925, English translation; German original, 1917).

The loss of life in the trenches of the First World War was horrendous. Many of the younger generation of Durkheimians were killed (Lukes, 1973). Lewin's first professional paper in psychology was a phenomenological study of the war landscape between the trenches from the perspective of a foot soldier (Lewin, 1917; see appendix 1). Lewin was awarded the Iron Cross for his services in defending the Fatherland in the Great War. He spent the Second World War helping the Americans to defeat his native country. He is widely accepted among Americans as the founder of experimental social psychology in that country. Heider (1983), in his autobiography, recalls his disappointment at not being accepted for service in the Austrian army at the outbreak of war because of the injury he had incurred to his left eye at the age of ten.

The mobilization of a civilian population for war is a mammoth task. How does one predict whether a bank clerk will make a good tank driver or not? Psychologists quickly proved their usefulness in time of war by devising tests that could be used in the allocation of civilians to different types of military task. The Army Alpha and Army Beta tests were devised in America and validated. Psychological tests quickly replaced the interview as the principal means of selecting people for jobs. This gave a tremendous boost, after the war, to applied psychology in a wide range of different civilian settings. Some academic psychologists resented the popularity of applied psychology. This was true of Boring. O'Donnell (1979) has shown how Boring, during the 1920s, used his position within the American Psychological Association to promote the cause of experimental psychology and, systematically, to undermine the cause of applied psychology. His *History of Experimental Psychology* (Boring, 1929, 1950) was part of his strategy to champion the cause of a pure experimental psychology at the expense of the applied fields of psychology.

The war, together with Wundt's increasingly vociferous support for the cause of German nationalism, cut Wundt off from his many former students in America. His lecture tour of America, which previously had been much talked about, never materialized and he died in 1921. It is easy to overestimate the extent to which experimental psychology was well established and resourced in Germany before the outbreak of war and to underestimate the extent to which it was established and resourced in America by the end of the war. Ash (1980) has issued a salutary warning concerning the former tendency. After outlining various aspects of the academic identity problem facing experimental psychologists in Germany before 1914, Ash notes 'experimental psychology remained ambiguously housed within philosophy for the first forty years of its German existence . . . By 1914 . . . the limitation of this situation had become as obvious as the advantages' (Ash, 1980, p. 83). Hilgard (1987, pp. 31–5) lists, in chronological order of their founding, the 42 laboratories that had been established in North American colleges and universities by the year 1900, and cites a survey to the effect that by 1926 there were such laboratories at some 117 colleges and universities. Ash (1980), reviewing the situation in Germany in the period between the wars, notes a deterioration in a situation that had already been critical in 1914 before the outbreak of war:

> German experimental psychology was apparently still more on the defensive at the beginning of the 1930s than it had been in 1914. Further research is clearly needed to obtain a clearer picture of the social and institutional situation of the field in the 1920s and 1930s. For the present, it must suffice to say that psychology's advance to sustained institutional growth in Germany did not occur until the 1950s, and then only within the framework of different social and economic circumstances, primarily a reformed university organization granted to it the relative independence enjoyed by the field in the United States for decades. (Ash, 1980, p. 84)

The Great War of 1914–18 is important to the overall theme of this book for yet another reason. Two quite different forms of psychology began to develop on separate sides of the Atlantic just before the outbreak of war. I refer to behaviourism in America and to Gestalt psychology in Germany (see appendix 1 for relevant dates). The war and its aftermath helped to ensure that these two contrasting forms of psychology developed quite independently of each other on separate continents throughout the inter-war years.

The contrast between these two forms of psychology stems from the fact that behaviourism represents the perspective of an observer, while

Gestalt psychology represents the perspective of an actor. According to Jones and Nisbett (1972), these are two quite divergent perspectives. We are talking, here, about an incompatibility between two perspectives rather than about an incommensurability between two paradigms (see chapter 8). A perspective is much more limited than a paradigm. According to Mead (1927), it is an objective point in space/time from which events are viewed (see chapter 4). It is, as Watson (1919) quite properly claimed it to be, a standpoint. What is visible from that standpoint is behaviour. This is why, according to Watson, psychology is the science of behaviour.

The perspective of an actor is quite different from that of an observer (Jones and Nisbett, 1972). Actors tend to see their actions as being appropriate to the situations in which they find themselves. Observers of those same actions tend to make inferences concerning the traits of the actor that would account for why he or she acts in the way that he or she does. Actors, according to Jones and Nisbett, do not make dispositional attributions when accounting for their own actions. The coexistence of these two individual, yet incompatible, perspectives in modern American social psychology does not constitute a paradigm in any sense that Kuhn (1962) would recognize.

The coexistence of the two perspectives is due, almost entirely, to a sequence of political events in Germany starting with Hitler's rise to power in 1933. This led directly to the migration of the Gestalt psychologists from Austria and Germany to America (see chapter 6). Until their arrival in the New World they had not previously encountered behaviourism. When they did encounter it, they were opposed to it because it was incompatible with their own perspective. It is only in the context of American behaviourism that they became social psychologists (chapter 1). This injection of a divergent perspective from the Old World into the New World gave rise, in the modern era, to a form of cognitive social psychology that is characteristically American. The person who indirectly brought about this transformation was Adolf Hitler. In this respect Cartwright (1979) is correct in his account of the history of modern social psychology.

The Years between the Wars (1919–1939)

In the inter-war years it was Europeans who migrated to American universities, thus reversing the flow across the Atlantic that had characterized the earlier era. At first it was only a few isolated individuals but, as the clouds of war began, once again, to amass over Europe with

Hitler's rise to power in Germany, the trickle became a virtual torrent with whole 'schools' of researchers fleeing to the comparative safety of America. Lazarsfeld, together with some of his co-workers, emigrated from Vienna and settled in New York at Columbia where he helped to establish the Bureau of Applied Social Research. Lazarsfeld became a dominant influence with regard to the methodology of social research in America in the post-war years. He was a co-author, for example, of volume IV of *The American Soldier* series. He was particularly interested in the mass media of communication and in the role played by people in the flow of such communication (Katz and Lazarsfeld, 1955). The famous Frankfurt School of social scientists (Adorno, Horkheimer, Marcuse, Fromm et al.) also emigrated, wholesale, to America after Hitler had closed down their research institute. Immediately after the war they produced their monumental study of *The Authoritarian Personality* (Adorno et al., 1950), which was to become such an important landmark in American social psychology of the post-war era (chapter 1). It was a sophisticated study of the origins of anti-Semitism.

Other important refugees of this period were Heider, Brunswik and Ichheiser from Austria and the Berlin group of Gestalt psychologists – Koffka, Wertheimer, Lewin and Köhler. It is also worthy of note that it was refugees from continental Europe who contributed so significantly to the development of social psychology in Britain, e.g. Tajfel at Bristol, Himmelweit at the London School of Economics, Gustav Jahoda at Manchester, Glasgow and Strathclyde and, later, Marie Jahoda at Brunel and then at Sussex. This exemplifies a point I made earlier (chapter 1) that, in the history of social psychology, the movement of people between cultures is at least as important as what is happening within any one culture.

The Second World War

I have already indicated in chapter 1, as well as in the introduction to this chapter, some of the classic work carried out by social psychologists during the Second World War that laid the basis for the modern era in social psychology in America after the war. This is best exemplified in the four-volume series, *The American Soldier*. The wartime uses of social psychology included, among other things, surveys of the morale of the troops, attitude scaling, experimental studies of persuasion (i.e. the briefing of military personnel for involvement in war) and the waging of psychological warfare (Linebarger, 1948). Immediately after the war and during the post-war reconstruction of Germany and of Japan, there were retrospective surveys (Janis, 1951) of the effects of aerial bombardment on civilian populations in both countries (including interviews with survivors of the atomic bombs dropped on Hiroshima and Nagasaki).

Just as the Great War led to the loss of a whole generation of young French sociologists, the Second World War led, on the German side, to the great loss of many young Gestalt psychologists. Though the leaders of the movement emigrated to America, they took up academic positions mainly at élite East Coast colleges like Swarthmore or Smith College which lacked graduate schools. With the notable exception of Lewin (and he for too brief a period), they did not produce new cohorts of doctoral students. This is how Mary Henle (1986a) assessed the situation: 'the Gestalt immigrants found themselves in an intellectual atmosphere dominated by behaviorism and its relatives; they were mainly without graduate students: and several of them died too soon to have much influence on the psychology of their new country. It is scarcely surprising that a new generation of Gestalt psychologists did not grow up in America' (Henle, 1986a, p. 120). I have argued in chapter 6 that they did contribute very significantly to the development of a cognitive social psychology in America in the modern era. This was no mean achievement.

There was considerable interest both during and after the war in understanding the dynamics of small groups. This was not an exclusively American interest. There was at least one joint Anglo-American endeavour in the field of social psychology immediately following the end of the war. This was the founding of the journal *Human Relations* which was published jointly by the Tavistock Institute of Human Relations in London and the Group Dynamics Research Center, first of all at MIT and then at the University of Michigan when it moved there after Lewin's death in 1947. The common interest was in studying the dynamics of small groups. Due to the chronic shortage of psychiatrists in the British army during the war, soldiers requiring psychotherapy were treated in groups rather than on a more traditional one-to-one basis. The psychiatrists involved quickly came to appreciate that the dynamics of a small group were quite different from those of a therapeutic dyad. Group psychotherapy, therefore, originated in Britain under these wartime conditions. A number of the psychiatrists involved in this innovation continued their collaboration at the Tavistock Clinic when the war ended. For a British account of some of these developments, see Foulkes and Anthony (1957).

Several classic papers by Lewin, Festinger, Schachter and others, including Festinger's theory of social comparison processes (Festinger, 1954), were published in *Human Relations* at the beginning of the modern period in social psychology. The combination of group dynamics with a psychoanalytic interpretation of social phenomena, however, was unique to the Tavistock. It did not feature in the American tradition of research in group dynamics. There is a quite sharp theoretical divide between the purely a-historical approach of Lewin to the study of both personality and small groups and the much more historical approach of Freud to the same topics. With the exception of the work of Jaques at Brunel, the psychoanalytic study of organizations developed in Britain outside the universities in the context of the Tavistock Institute.

In America, Lewin's ideas concerning the dynamics of small groups were developed and applied in the work of the National Training Laboratories at Bethel, Maine, which he had helped to establish (Hirsch, 1987). Indeed the whole t-group (i.e. training-group) movement, as it developed in America after Lewin's death, was more like a social crusade than a scientific enterprise. Unlike its British counterpart, it developed completely unencumbered by the complexities of a psychoanalytic interpretation of what was happening in the group.

There was considerable funding in America, following the end of the war, for research relating to the dynamics of small groups. This was funded mainly through the Office of Naval Research and provided a boost for many teams of social psychological researchers. The main interest was in small autonomous groups of persons who were highly task interdependent and who might be isolated from the world for considerable periods of time. Most of this research was unclassified, though it clearly related to possible future military missions. It was not clear at the time whether these small groups would be in midget submarines or space craft or just wintering over in Antarctica during the International Geophysical Year. So, even during peacetime, research in social psychology continued to have possible military application.

Coming to terms with the Holocaust set the research agenda in social psychology for decades following the end of the war. It was difficult for many to understand, never mind to come to terms with, what had taken place in the death camps. G. W. Allport had accepted for publication in the *Journal of Abnormal and Social Psychology* an article by Bettelheim (1943) on what life in a concentration camp was like, while these camps were still in existence. Bettelheim, himself, had been in Dachau and Buchenwald. Eisenhower insisted that his soldiers read this article before they went in to liberate some of these camps.

The principal ethical guidelines on experiments involving humans emerged from the deliberations of the Nuremberg Tribunal on war crimes (Katz, 1972). The principle of informed consent was of particular significance. Milgram's much later attempts to understand the nature of obedience to authority gave rise to similar concerns of an ethical nature, specifically in relation to experiments in social psychology (Milgram, 1974, 1977). While this takes us beyond the time frame I have set for this book, it is illustrative of how the Holocaust did set the agenda for several decades following the end of the war. Milgram was interested in the observations of Hannah Arendt on Eichmann on trial in Jerusalem. It was the banality of evil, rather than the psychopathology of the accused, that struck Arendt. Milgram's own experimental techniques contributed to what others have called the 'crisis in social psychology' (Ring, 1967; Elms, 1975). This latter topic, however, would take me well beyond the bounds of the present volume.

Postscript

I hope I have illustrated some of the diverse effects of war on the historical development of social psychology in the first half of the twentieth century. In the second half of the twentieth century it has been the Cold War that has had the most dramatic effects upon the development of the social sciences in general, and of social psychology in particular. If social psychology is a distinctive discipline, and I believe it is, then it is uniquely concerned with the relationship between the individual and society. When individualism becomes an ideology ranged against collectivism as the counter-ideology, as occurred for the duration of the Cold War, this form of political propaganda distorts the development of social psychology on both sides of the former Iron Curtain. Social psychology, this century, has never been free of the distorting effects of wars, both hot and cold.

10

The Long Past and the Short History of Social Psychology

Positivism as a Source of Distortion in Historiography

Many of the errors and biases in current histories of psychology and of
social psychology (Farr, 1983a, 1985a, 1987a) are a *direct* consequence of subscribing to a positivist philosophy of science. Danziger
(1979) has worked this out in relation to the history of experimental
psychology (see chapters 1 and 2). Here I am applying his thesis to the
history of social psychology during the modern era.

One manifestation of the influence of positivism on historiography
is, as we have seen (chapter 8), an obsession with identifying the
precise origins of a particular field of study (Farr, 1983b). Comte, the
founder of positivism, noted three phases in the development of a
discipline. The first was 'a theological stage, in which the world and
man's destiny within it was explained in terms of gods and spirits,
through a transitional metaphysical stage, in which explanations were
in terms of essences, first causes, and other abstractions, to the modern
positivist stage' (*Encyclopaedia Britannica* entry on Comte). For
Comte, this sequence of changes was evidence of 'progress'. In the light
of such a philosophy of science, it then becomes imperative to identify
when a particular field of study ceases to be metaphysics and becomes
science.

A positive philosophy of science, then, engenders a break with the
past. The positivists were victorious and so it was they who wrote the
histories. Once a field of study has become a science, positivists also
assume that research will be cumulative. There are important implications, here, for the writing of history. According to the positivist credo,

it is the duty of the neophyte historian to celebrate the achievements of the science and to chart its progress. This is often done by contrasting the history of the field (long or short depending upon the particular science) with its 'long past' of metaphysics and theology.

Modern social psychology and its historical background

I wish to demonstrate how Lindzey (1954) and Lindzey and Aronson (1968–9, 1985), in the series of *Handbooks* they have edited, in effect, distinguish between the 'long past' of social psychology as part of the Western, mainly European, tradition of thought and its 'short history' since it became an experimental science, mainly in America. The point of inflection between the 'long past' and the 'short history' of the discipline is the Murchison *Handbook* (1935) (see chapter 5). The modern series of *Handbooks* is important in training successive generations of graduate students in social psychology as a subdiscipline of psychology. I am concerned, in this final chapter, with the editing of *Handbooks* and the writing of historical accounts over some three decades of modern social psychology *beyond* the upper limit of the historical period covered by my book as a whole. I feel my incursion into the modern era is justified on two main counts. First, I wish to demonstrate why the currently available histories of social psychology are inadequate. This is principally because they are informed by a particular philosophy of science, namely, positivism. They are also partial accounts in that they rarely cover sociological as well as psychological forms of social psychology (see chapter 7). I need to justify why another account of the history of social psychology – namely, my own – is necessary. Secondly, I hope that my critical examination of the past will lead to a better understanding of the present.

The reader should be warned that the analysis contained in this final chapter is likely to be controversial, at least in certain quarters. The original version of this chapter was a paper I wrote specifically for publication in the *Journal of Personality and Social Psychology*. I chose to submit my article to this journal because it is the premier journal in the field of social psychology and because I wished to influence the views of the community of researchers who publish in and read the journal. Following C. S. Peirce, I believe that science is a collective enterprise which, in the long run, is self-correcting. It depends heavily upon the expression of divergent points of view. The article, however, was resoundingly rejected by the reviewers, sometimes in quite vituperative terms. It was subsequently published with only minor amendments in the *European Journal of Social Psychology*

(Farr, 1991b). It is possible that social psychologists in America will read the article as a European attack upon the American establishment. I wished, quite specifically, to avoid such a possible construction; hence my decision to submit it, originally, to an American journal.

One anonymous review of my article comprised the following:

> The simplest thing I can say about this essay is that it is inappropriate for *JPSP*: there are no data, no theory, no nothing. It *is*, however, very interesting.
>
> But I will say a bit more. The author is so committed to historiography, as a method, that he uses it in preference to the simplest kind of empiricism. For example, he speculates about what was going on in the minds of Allport, Lindzey, Aronson, Jones and others. That is a very reasonable approach as a last resort – and certainly makes sense in the case of Allport.* But I think he might have come up with a more accurate assessment if he had pretended that Lindzey, Aronson and Jones were still alive – and had asked them why they had made the decisions that they did. Empiricism may have its limitations (as the author is quick to point out – at great length), but one would think that this is carrying his contempt for it a bit far.
>
> It *is* an interesting piece; but rather silly.

Readers will, of course, be able to judge for themselves the extent to which they agree with the reviewer's comments. The article is, in fact, highly empirical in content but I am being empirical about the text rather than about the world. The editorial process is transparent *across* the three editions of the *Handbook*. The evidence is behavioural. Inferences about what might have been going on in the minds of the editors are, at least, constrained by the behavioural facts. Attribution theory, in the classic Heiderian sense, is all about these rules of inference. Gathering the subjective recollections of editors and writers, today, of what they might have had in mind, say, some 40 years ago, is unlikely either to strengthen or to weaken my case. I have confined my commentary to what is in the public domain.

The Lindzey *Handbook of Social Psychology* of 1954

The editor's preface

Lindzey observes in his preface that 'Murchison's Handbook of Social Psychology . . . is out of date and out of print' (1954, p. ix). After

---

* The reason why speculation is justified in the case of Allport but not in the other three cases is that Allport is dead. Now, sadly, Jones, too, is dead.

explaining how he had set about the task of devising a handbook 'that would represent the major areas of social psychology at a level of difficulty appropriate for graduate students' (p. ix), Lindzey then details his rationale for its layout in two volumes. Volume I comprises theoretical positions and methods of research; volume II focuses on the substantive findings and applications of social psychology. Volume I is 'a necessary preparation for good investigation', while volume II reflects 'the empirical fruits stemming from the theories and methods summarized in the first volume' (p. x). Lindzey concedes, however, that this ordering of the material does not reflect current realities: 'the precedence we give to theoretical positions reflects our conviction of the importance of theories as spurs to research, but may also represent a program for the future rather than a reflection of the past' (p. x).

After reviewing, from the vantage point of the editor's desk, some of the weaknesses of the two-volume work, Lindzey, with good reason, could claim that 'the volumes . . . provide the most comprehensive picture of social psychology that exists in one place today' (p. x). In essence, then, the position, as of 1954, is this: Murchison is 'out of date' as well as being out of print, i.e. it is old-fashioned; here is a summary of the present and a blueprint for the future. The provision of a blueprint for the future entails a break with the past. The 1954 *Handbook* is, thus, the beginning of the modern era in social psychology.

Allport's chapter on the historical background to modern social psychology

This was the opening chapter of the *Handbook*. It was also my point of departure in the opening chapter of this book. It was an account of the 'long past' of the discipline. It was an *introduction* to modern social psychology. It was not, itself, modern social psychology. The rest of the *Handbook*, presumably, is modern social psychology. Allport's chapter has the status, within the *Handbook*, of the book of Genesis in the Bible and perhaps contains as many myths. G. W. Allport was well qualified, as a scholarly and revered figure, to lead the reader through the wilderness of past metaphysics to within sight of 'the promised land' – the modern era in social psychology. He lacked, however, the necessary experimental credentials to lead the tribes in settling the promised land. He was a positivist of an older generation – who looked to Comte rather than to Mach and Avenarius. It was the experimentalists in psychology who looked to Mach and Avenarius. In this sense G. W. Allport, himself, is more of an ancestor than a founder of modern social psychology (see chapter 8).

In his chapter on the historical background to modern social psychology, as we noted in chapter 8, Allport nominates Comte as the 'founding father' of social psychology. The influence of Comte is not confined to the section in which Allport discusses him as a historical figure. The chapter opens with a rhetorical question concerning the wisdom of studying the past. 'Why bother with the "metaphysical stage" of speculation, as Comte called it, when a new era of positivism and progress has dawned?' (G. W. Allport, 1954, p. 3). In his discussion of objective methods of research, Allport concludes:

> Since most of these signal strides in method are of recent date, they do not form a part of our historical story. The fact is that empiricism and positivism did not enter social psychology to any appreciable extent until the decade of the 1920s. The ideals of objectivity and precision then rapidly assumed a dominant position. (G. W. Allport, 1954, p. 48)

Allport also quotes, with evident approval, *both* at the beginning *and* at the end of his chapter, the work of Hornell Hart (1949) who 'has plotted convincingly the recent upswing in the productions of social science, and argues that the recent acceleration marks the delayed entrance of social science into the era of positivism' (G. W. Allport, 1954, p. 4).

Allport himself explains this upsurge in research

> in terms of Comte's theory of three stages (1830, Vol. I, Ch. 1). Comte would say that only recently have the social sciences left the constraints of the first two stages, the *theological* and *metaphysical* respectively, and entered fully into the third stage of *positivism*. While Comte himself endeavored to inaugurate the third stage, it is clear that the fruit of his effort was delayed for nearly a century until the positivistic tools of experiment, statistics, survey methods, and like instruments were more adequately developed. (G. W. Allport, 1954, p. 4)

Clearly, Allport's indebtedness to Comte could not be removed merely by excising the section specifically dealing with Comte's 'discovery' of social psychology. It is also clear that Allport conceives of social psychology as a social science, rather than as a purely experimental science.

Allport covers, fairly extensively, Western traditions of thought with major sections on the search for what he calls 'simple and sovereign theories' (pp. 9–29) and an outline of various attempts to analyse 'the group mind' (pp. 31–40). The history, here, is very much the history of ideas. He distinguishes between the roots of social psychology and its flower. This is the distinction that gives me the title for my own book:

'While the roots of social psychology lie in the intellectual soil of the whole Western tradition its present flowering is recognized to be characteristically an American phenomenon' (G. W. Allport, 1954, pp. 3–4). The distinction, here, is between a European past and an American present. I am returning now, in this final chapter, to my point of departure in chapter 1.

The Lindzey and Aronson *Handbook of Social Psychology* of 1968–9

The editors' preface

The second edition of the *Handbook* (Lindzey and Aronson, 1968–9) appeared, in five volumes, between 1968 and 1969. Aronson, a noted experimental social psychologist, who had contributed significantly to the development of cognitive dissonance theory, joins Lindzey as co-editor. Aronson, since becoming editor, has also contributed an excellent chapter on experimentation in social psychology to each successive edition of the *Handbook*.

In their preface the editors note that 'this *Handbook* is very different from its predecessor. It is substantially larger' (Lindzey and Aronson, 1968, p. vii). They then discuss the turnover in both authors and chapters from the previous *Handbook*. Clearly, it is a story of significant progress. There are two and a half million words instead of one million; five volumes instead of two; and 45 chapters instead of 30. Here, indeed, is tangible evidence of *positive* progress based on the blueprint outlined in the previous *Handbook*.

Allport, mark 2

Over 95 per cent of the text is *identical* to the 1954 chapter, 89 per cent of the references in the 1954 version reappear in the 1968 version; only 9 per cent of the references in the 1968 version are new. One could hardly claim, as the editors do in general terms, that this is a *thorough* revision. The editors may have thought that there was no need for Allport to revise his account of the past. Perhaps they believed that there is a difference between history and science and that only the latter needs to be revised and updated. Here, history is not the history of science.

The textual amendments are fairly minimal. A new heading is occasionally inserted but without any change of text. Usually the more up-to-date references are tacked on to paragraphs taken from the previous edition. Very occasionally new paragraphs are added. There is one such significant addition at the end of the section on 'The beginnings of objective method': 'Today the outstanding mark of social psychology as a discipline is its sophistication in method and in experimental design. It has come a long way from the days of "simple and sovereign" speculation ... Comte would say that now, at long last, social psychology has entered the "positive stage" with a vengeance' (G. W. Allport, 1968, pp. 67, 68). Allport here invokes, once again (i.e. in 1968, rather than in 1954), a positivist philosophy of science. His own chapter is an account of the search in the past for simple and sovereign remedies. Here, in Mark 2 of his chapter, he is noting the progress that has occurred since he wrote the original chapter. He thus endorses the views of the editors as discussed above.

The section on 'Textbooks' was very much abridged as it was clearly out of date. In his 1954 analysis of textbooks Allport was able to estimate that 'two-thirds of the texts are written by psychologists and one-third by sociologists' (Allport, 1954, p. 50). Rather remarkably, this same ratio is cited again in 1968, though somewhat more tentatively. '*Perhaps* two-thirds of the texts are written by authors who consider themselves to be psychologists, about one-third by sociologists' (Allport, 1968, p. 69, emphasis added). The data presented by Jones (1985, p. 48) (see figure 10.1), however, show that, by the time the second edition of the *Handbook* was published (i.e. 1968), the ratio of psychologists to sociologists publishing textbooks of social psychology was 10 : 1. This is quite a long way from the probable ratio of 2 : 1 cited by Allport!

Reprinting an article, virtually unchanged, some 14 years after it was first published is bound to lead to some anachronisms; for example, a team of five *contemporary* authors who provide a *modern* example of 'the group mind' completed their work some 18 years previously; the tide of collaboration between psychologists and social anthropologists, which was described in 1954 as still rising and as not yet reaching its crest, is so described again in 1968 and, *yet again*, in 1985. Surely, by now, we should be flooded with such studies!

The Lindzey and Aronson *Handbook of Social Psychology* of 1985

The editors' preface

The editors, Lindzey and Aronson (1985), write a lengthy preface to the third edition in which they explain why they are reverting to a

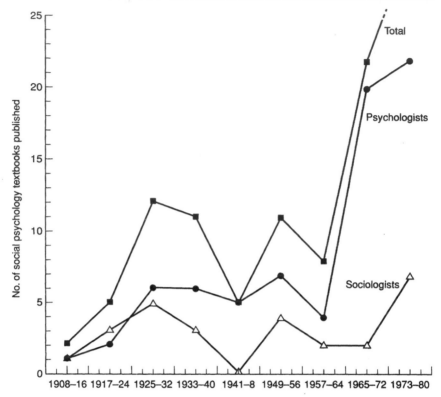

Figure 10.1 Introductory social psychology textbooks published in the
United States, 1908–80, written by psychologists and sociologists. Figures for
'total' include collaborations by psychologists and sociologists, as well as
texts authored by neither group (from Lindzey and Aronson, *Handbook of
Social Psychology*, 1985, p. 48, *reproduced with permission of
The McGraw-Hill Companies*)

two-volume work after the five volumes of the previous edition. They
create as much distance as possible between the series of *Handbooks*
(1954, 1968–9, 1985) edited by themselves and the Murchison (1935)
Handbook of Social Psychology which had been published half a
century earlier (see chapter 5). After quoting *in extenso* from Murchison's introduction, they continue:

A mere decade later this paragraph already seemed to many observers
archaic and poorly informed. Even more remarkable is the fact that more
than one-third [of] the chapters in the 1935 Handbook dealt with the
social psychology of bacteria, plants, and lower animals. Moreover, four
chapters dealt with the social history of the negro, the red man, the white
man, and the yellow man – labels that if used today would create a wave

of revulsion. These chapters and others not mentioned, strike no note of resonance with contemporary social psychology. (Lindzey and Aronson, 1985, p. iii)

They then indulge in their own piece of Whiggish history by singling out a few chapters from the Murchison *Handbook* that seem, to them, to anticipate future trends. There are echoes, here, of a distinction between 'the long past' of the discipline, reflected in the contents of the Murchison *Handbook*, and its short history since it became an experimental science. They are also able to operate with the benefit of 20 : 20 hindsight. They single out for special mention Dashiell, who wrote the only chapter in the Murchison *Handbook* concerned with the analysis of experimental data on humans gathered under laboratory conditions. They also mention G. W. Allport's classic chapter on attitudes. Allport, interestingly enough, is the only author contributing both to the Murchison *Handbook* and to the modern series of *Handbooks* edited by Lindzey and by Lindzey and Aronson.

Allport, mark 3

The footnote to Allport's chapter indicates that 'This chapter has been lightly abridged by Gardner Lindzey but otherwise is unchanged from the version published in the Second Edition of the Handbook of Social Psychology' (G. W. Allport, 1985, p. 1). It is now 'The historical background of social psychology', and no longer 'The historical background of *modern* social psychology' (emphasis added). It is clearly part of the 'long past' rather than of the 'short history' of social psychology. Its appearance for the third time and in the same form as before strongly suggests that the editors believed that there was no need to revise the account of the 'long past' they already possessed. Revision is inappropriate since the past is now long past. It is part of the prehistory of social psychology. It is metaphysics rather than science. Only the latter needs to be revised. Science is cumulative and progressive and so is in constant need of updating. The same cannot be said for history.

The most significant of the four omissions is the offending section on 'Comte's discovery of social psychology' (1968, pp. 6–10). So much for the 'light abridgement' by the senior editor! Social psychology is now an orphan discipline. Its 'founding father' has been laid to rest. An embarrassing ancestor is no longer mentioned. The positivistic framework of the whole account, however, is left unchanged. It is very much like Hamlet without the Prince in its present version!

The anachronisms are, by now, even more noticeable than before. The 'modern example' of research on 'the group mind' is 35 years old. The concept of 'personality in culture' still continues to be as productive as it had been in 1954; the 'recent literature' referred to in the section on attitudes is now 20 years old; the ratio of psychologists to sociologists writing textbooks of social psychology is still 2 : 1 as it had been in 1954 and then again in 1968!

Jones, mark 1

The 'short history' of social psychology appears now for the first time. This is the chapter by Jones on 'Major developments in social psychology during the past five decades' (Jones, 1985). The 'past five decades' from 1985 take us back to 1935, the year in which Murchison published his *Handbook* (see chapter 5). This provides me with my point of inflection in the transition from 'the long past' to 'the short history' of social psychology. It is only in retrospect that the Murchison *Handbook* is seen to belong to a different era. It stands as a milestone in the evolution of social psychology as a discipline. We now have a history of *modern* social psychology (written by Jones) together with a historical background to social psychology in general (Allport, mark 3). There was no need for Jones to be concerned with either the origins of the discipline or its long past since both were adequately covered by Allport in the neighbouring chapter. 'Chapter 1 by G.W. Allport sets the stage for the following review of the past five decades of social psychology. We need not recapitulate, then . . .' (Jones, 1985 p. 47).

Jones was thus free to celebrate the achievements of the new science and to chart its progress. The separation between past and present is now complete. This neat separation is the culmination of a process that started with the editing of the 1954 *Handbook*. It is now clear, in retrospect, that Lindzey and Aronson see the Murchison *Handbook* of 1935 as the watershed between the long past of social psychology as part of the Western tradition of intellectual thought and its short history (since 1935) as an experimental, and a predominantly American, science. I shall now show that this editorial vision of the historical development of social psychology is shared by Jones (1985).

Jones treats social psychology as a subdiscipline of psychology. He thus fails to appreciate the significance of sociological forms of social psychology (chapter 7). While he discusses various attempts (at Harvard, Michigan, Columbia and Yale) to break down barriers between social disciplines (pp. 48, 49), he fails to include Chicago as one of his models. Yet Chicago did produce its own distinctive forms of social psychology; for example, Mead's social behaviourism (chapter 4); the symbolic interactionism of Blumer (chapter 7); Thomas's study of social attitudes; Ichheiser's sociology of interpersonal relations; and Goffman's dramaturgical model of social interaction. The history of social psychology should include sociological as well as psychological traditions of research (Farr, 1978, 1983b,c, 1985b). None of the sociological forms of social psychology, however, is experimental in the strict sense in which this term is used in psychology.

Jones is quite explicit in his attitude towards the Murchison *Handbook*. He describes it as comprising, essentially, a series of essays in comparative psychology. The implicit contrast, here, is between essays and experiments. He must have failed to note that the five chapters in part VI of Murchison were all concerned with the experimental reconstruction of social phenomena. Admittedly, three of these five chapters were concerned with the study of animal behaviour. In his own contribution to a Whig interpretation of the history of social psychology Jones singles out Dashiell's chapter as reflecting the antiquity of experimental research in social psychology: 'If Murchison's Handbook can be cited to affirm the antiquity of experimental research in the one area of social facilitation effects, it may also be cited as a clear indication of the status of social psychology as a non-experimental discipline in the mid 1930s' (Jones, 1985, p. 63). There is no doubt that for Jones, as well as for Lindzey and Aronson, the Murchison *Handbook* marks the end of an era: 'Murchison's Handbook of Social Psychology marked the end of the pre-experimental era in social psychology' (Jones, 1985, p. 63).

Now we have the 'long past' of social psychology (Allport, 1985) and its 'short history' (Jones, 1985) conveniently available as adjacent chapters in the most recent edition of the *Handbook*. This represents the working out, with respect to the history of social psychology, of the positivist psychology of science that Danziger (1979) first identified at work with regard to the history of experimental psychology.

Two Rival Forms of Positivism

The positivism that informs the chapter by Allport is that of Comte. This is the positivism of psychology as a social science. The positivism that informs the chapter by Jones, however, is that of Mach and of Avenarius. This is the positivism of social psychology as an experimental science. These are two quite distinct forms of positivism. The positivism of Comte is much older than that of Mach and of Avenarius. It was the positivism of the latter that led to what Danziger (1979) described as the repudiation of Wundt (see chapter 2). In many ways they are rival versions of the same broad philosophy of science. The proponents of the two views are not necessarily in agreement with each other; for example, G. W. Allport had some reservations about the virtues of a purely experimental social psychology:

> Noteworthy scientific gains result from this 'hard-nosed' approach. There is however, one serious disadvantage: neat and elegant experiments often lack generalizing power . . . some current investigations seem to end up in elegantly polished triviality – snippets of empiricism, but nothing more. (Allport, 1968, p. 68)

Jones is much less likely than Allport to have reservations about the value of experimentation in social psychology. For Jones, experiments are a hallmark of science. In commenting on the rapid expansion of social psychology in American universities in the period following the Second World War, he refers to 'an additional impetus stemming from a new perception of social psychology as constructively linked to the experimental method and therefore entitled to a place in the psychological mainstream' (Jones, 1985, p. 54).

We now have rival forms of the same philosophy of science, i.e. positivism, underpinning the claims of social psychology to be (a) a social science and (b) an experimental science. Allport makes out the former case by nominating Comte as 'the founder' of the discipline (see chapter 8); Jones makes out the latter case by treating social psychology as a subdiscipline of psychology and by focusing on major developments during the past half-century.

First of all, psychology became an experimental science (chapter 2). This was over a century ago. Then, half a century later, social psychology became one, at least in America. Two separate waves of positivism have thus helped to shape the structure of the Lindzey and Aronson series of *Handbooks*. The 1954 volume established as plausible the claim of social psychology to be considered a social science. The contrast then was with the multi-disciplinary nature of the Murchison *Handbook* of 1935. The 1954 edition also held out the promise of social psychology becoming a science of a different sort – it was a blueprint for the future. This promise was fulfilled in large measure by the second and third editions with the co-option, as editor, of Aronson – a noted experimentalist – and the inclusion of chapters on experimentation in social psychology. The process is now complete in the third edition with two chapters of a historical nature – one covering the long past of the discipline and the other its short history. The problem with this is that the history is now the history of a science and what went before is treated as a form of prehistory.

Postscript

'The history of social psychology, as a critical examination of the past leading to a better understanding of the present, still remains to be written' (Samelson, 1974, p. 229). The rejection of over-simplistic distinctions between the 'long past' and the 'short history' of the discipline may be a good point of departure. It should be possible to write a history of social psychology that is both international and interdisciplinary. It would be neither a history of ideas (such as Allport wrote) nor an ethnocentric account of the achievements of experimental social psychologists in America (such as Jones wrote). There is nothing wrong, in my opinion, with making distinctions between the past and the present of a discipline so long as the distinction is not too closely tied to a particular philosophy of science. 'Internal' historians are more likely than 'external' historians to subscribe to such a philosophy since, as well as being historians of a science, they are also practitioners of that science.

One of the other reviewers, who negatively reviewed the original article on which this chapter is based, wondered what a non-positivistic history of social psychology would look like. I hope the reader of this volume will now have some idea of what such an account might be like.

Appendix 1: Some dates and their significance in the emergence of psychology as an experimental and social science 1872–1954

1872	**Darwin** (1809–82) publishes *The Expression of the Emotions in Man and Animals*.
1874	**Wundt** (1832–1920) publishes the first edition of his *Grundzüge der physiologischen Psychologie*.
1875	**Wundt** appointed to the Chair of Philosophy at Leipzig.
1876	**Bain** becomes the founding editor of the journal *Mind*.
1879	**Wundt** establishes the Institut für Psychologie at Leipzig.
1881	**Wundt** establishes a journal *Philosophische Studien* in which to publish the research of his laboratory.
1885	**Freud** (1856–1939) visits **Charcot** (1825–93) in Paris in order to observe his use of hypnosis in exploring the origins of hysteria.
1885–6	**Durkheim** (1858–1917) visits various German universities, including Leipzig, and is impressed by what he observes. He is particularly impressed by **Wundt**.
1887	**Mead** (1863–1931) enrols as a graduate student at Harvard. Lives in the household of William James and tutors one of his children. Influenced by the Hegelianism of Royce.

1888–9	Mead and his friend Henry Castle enrol in Wundt's classes at Leipzig. Mead takes Wundt's course on 'The Foundations of Metaphysics'.
1889–91	Mead moves to Berlin on the advice of G. Stanley Hall. Studies experimental and physiological psychology under **Ebbinghaus** (1850–1909), psychology, anthropology, philosophy and education under **Paulsen** and philosophy under **Dilthey** (1833–1911). He began a doctoral dissertation with the latter on a critique of the rationalist conception of space, but left in 1891 with this incomplete.
1890	**James** (1842–1910) publishes his *Principles of Psychology*.
	Tarde (1843–1904) publishes *Les Lois de l'Imitation*.
	Von Ehrensfels (1859–1932) publishes his article 'Über Gestaltequalitäten'. This is the basis of the Austrian School of Gestalt psychology, as distinct from the later Berlin School. Von Ehrensfels obtained his doctorate with **Meinong** (1853–1920) at Graz.
	Ebbinghaus and **Konig** found the *Zeitschrift für Psychologie und Physiologie der Sinnesorgane*. This was a general journal set up in opposition to the *Philosophische Studien* which was the house organ of the Leipzig Laboratory.
1891–4	Mead at the University of Michigan as an instructor in philosophy and psychology. Here he becomes a colleague and close personal friend of **Dewey** (1859–1952). He also meets and is influenced by **Cooley** (1864–1929) who was completing a PhD in economics.
1892	**Titchener** (1867–1927) emigrates from Germany to America to become Professor of Psychology at Cornell where he remains until his death. He is widely assumed, by Americans, to represent the Wundtian orthodoxy in relation to experimental psychology and to the use of introspection.
1892–3	**Münsterberg** (1893–1916) is a visiting professor at Harvard.
1894	**Dewey** becomes Head of the Department of Philosophy at the newly established University of Chicago. Mead accompanies him as an assistant professor. *Psychological Review* founded.
	Durkheim publishes *Les Règles de la Méthode Sociologique*.

1895	Le Bon (1841–1931) publishes *Psychologie des Foules*. Baldwin (1861–1934) publishes *Mental Development in the Child and in the Race* in which he proposes the theory that the ontogenetic development of the individual recapitulates the history of mankind.
1896	Dewey, 'The reflex arc concept in psychology', *Psychological Review*, 3, 357–70. Warns of the dangers of taking the reflex arc as the basic unit of behaviour. Based on conversations with Mead. Later elaborated and developed by Mead in his *Philosophy of the Act* (1938). Durkheim becomes Professor of Sociology at Bordeaux.
1897	Durkheim establishes the journal *L'Année Sociologique* in which he publishes the work of his School. Münsterberg becomes Director of the Harvard Psychological Laboratory. He remains at Harvard until his death in 1916.
1898	Durkheim, 'Représentations individuelles et représentations collectives', *Revue de Metaphysique et de Morale*, 6, 273–302. He distinguishes between sociology (the study of collective representations) and psychology (the study of individual representations). He claims they are autonomous disciplines.
1898–9	Cambridge Anthropological Expedition to the Torres Strait under the direction of Haddon (1855–1940). This involves the first systematic fieldwork in experimental psychology carried out by Rivers (1864–1922) with assistance from Myers (1873–1946) and McDougall (1871–1938).
1900–20	Wundt publishes *Völkerpsychologie: eine Untersuchung der Entwicklungsgesetze von Sprache, Mythus und Sitte*, 10 vols.
1900–8	Watson (1878–1958) becomes, first, a graduate student, then, an instructor at the University of Chicago. Originally he intended to study under Dewey but, instead, completes his doctorate on animal studies under Angell (1869–1949).
1900	Tarde becomes a professor at Le Collège de France.
1900–1	Mead first gives his annual course of lectures on social psychology in the Department of Philosophy at Chicago. A stenographic record of the 1927 course was published posthumously as *Mind, Self and Society: from the standpoint of a social behaviorist* (1934).

1901	**Tarde** publishes *L'Opinion et la Foule*.
1903	**Watson** obtains his PhD degree in psychology at the University of Chicago for a thesis on the education of rats. **Mead**, 'The definition of the psychical', *Decennial Publications of the University of Chicago*, first series, volume III, pp. 77–112.
1903–4	**Durkheim** and **Tarde** each give a lecture on 'Sociology and the Social Sciences' at the École des Hautes Études en Sciences Sociales, Paris, followed by a third meeting in which they publicly debate their differences 'with much heat'. **Koffka** (1886–1941) in Edinburgh as a student.
1904	**Dewey** leaves Chicago for Columbia University in New York. The psychologists at Chicago under **Angell** form a separate department. **Mead** remains with the philosophers; **Watson** transfers with the psychologists. **Mead**, 'The relations of psychology and philology', *Psychological Bulletin*, 1, 375–91. This was Mead's review of the first two volumes of Wundt's *Völkerpsychologie*. **Park** (1864–1944) submits his thesis 'Masse und Publikum' (1904) at Heidelberg in which he distinguishes between 'crowds' and 'publics'. A journalist by profession, **Park** later joins the Faculty of Social Sciences at the University of Chicago. **Haddon** becomes a reader in ethnology at the University of Cambridge, a post he held until 1925.
1905	**Wundt** gives an invited lecture at The Royal Society of Edinburgh.
1906	**Mead**, 'The imagination in Wundt's treatment of myths and religion', *Psychological Bulletin*, 3, 393–9. This is Mead's review of the second two volumes of Wundt's *Völkerpsychologie*. **Morton Prince** (1854–1928), at Harvard, establishes the *Journal of Abnormal Psychology*.
1907–8	**Thomas** (1863–1947), the distinguished Chicago sociologist (co-author with Znaniecki of *The Polish Peasant in Europe and America*) enrols in Wundt's classes at Leipzig.
1908	**Watson** leaves Chicago and goes to Johns Hopkins as a full professor at the age of 30. **McDougall** publishes *An Introduction to Social Psychology*. He identifies a limited number of instincts that form the basis of life in society. He also stresses the importance of the self-regarding sentiment.

Ross (1866–1951) publishes *Social Psychology: an outline and source book*. Summarizes European, mainly French, traditions of thought with regard to forms of social influence. Strongly influenced by Tarde. Influential in interesting sociologists in social psychology.

Malinowski (1884–1942) at Leipzig. Studies physics and chemistry. While recovering from an illness, reads Frazer's *The Golden Bough* and becomes interested in anthropology. Influenced by Wundt.

1909   Freud, accompanied by Jung (1875–1961), delivers five lectures on psychoanalysis to celebrate the twentieth anniversary of the founding of Clark University, Worcester, Massachusetts.

Lewin (1890–1947) enrols as a student at the University of Berlin where he studies psychology until the outbreak of war in 1914.

Baldwin forced to resign from his post at Johns Hopkins University, leaving Watson as Chairman of the Department and editor of *Psychological Review*.

1910   Malinowski leaves Leipzig for London where, at the London School of Economics, he establishes social anthropology as a discipline.

1912   Watson gives a series of lectures at Columbia in which he begins systematically to develop his ideas on behaviourism.

Wertheimer (1880–1943), Koffka and Köhler (1887–1967) conduct the first experiment, in Frankfurt, that led to the establishment of Gestalt psychology. The experiment was on the phi-phenomenon.

Wundt publishes *Elemente der Völkerpsychologie*. This is the synchronic version of the *Völkerpsychologie* (1900–20) which is diachronic in its format. Freud's reaction to this synchronic version of Wundt's *Völkerpsychologie* appears in his book *Totem and Taboo* (1913). The *Elemente* is translated into English by Schaub and published in 1916 with the title *Elements of Folk Psychology: outlines of a psychological history of the development of mankind*.

1912–13   Major publications on the Australian aborigines appeared from Malinowski, Radcliffe-Brown (1881–1955), Durkheim and Freud. Freud was reacting, quite explicitly, to Wundt's account of the totemic age in *Totem and Taboo* (1913).

1913	**Watson,** 'Psychology as a behaviourist views it', *Psychological Review*, 20, 158–77. This is the behaviourist manifesto in which Watson pledges to rid psychology of all reference to mind or consciousness. It would appear that the ghost of Descartes, finally, has been laid to rest.
1914–18	The Great War.
1914	**Watson** publishes *Behavior: an introduction to comparative psychology.* Watson's ethological studies (with Lashley) of the noddy and sooty terns are evidence of his credentials in the field of comparative psychology. Behaviourism, however, eventually led to the demise of a truly comparative psychology in America. This did not happen in Europe to anything like the same extent.
1915	**Watson** elected President of the American Psychological Association. Presidential address: 'The place of the conditioned reflex in psychology', *Psychological Review*, 23, 89–117. He proposes the adoption of the reflex arc as the basic unit of behaviour. This is what **Dewey** had warned against in his article of 1896 in the same journal (see above).
1917	**Lewin,** 'Kriegslandschaft', *Zeitschrift für Angewandte Psychologie*, 12, 440–7. Lewin's first professional paper. It describes a soldier's view of the war landscape between the trenches in the First World War.
1918–20	**Thomas** and **Znaniecki** publish *The Polish Peasant in Europe and America*, 5 vols. Values are here treated as 'collective representations' and social attitudes become 'the subjective side of culture'. Thomas defines social psychology as the scientific study of social attitudes. Thomas is forced to resign his post at Chicago and is replaced by Ellsworth **Faris** (b. 1874).
1919	**Dunlap,** 'Are there any instincts?', *Journal of Abnormal Psychology*, 14, 307–11. In this article Knight Dunlap questions the value of instincts as an explanatory device. A turning away *within* behaviourism from nativistic explanations.
1920	**Watson's** academic career ends with his divorce. **Thomas,** the Chicago sociologist, helps him financially and obtains a job for him in advertising at the J. Walter Thompson Organization. This is the start of a highly successful career in advertising. Becomes vice-president of the organization (1924–36).

McDougall publishes *The Group Mind*, the second volume of his social psychology. The gap in time between this and the introductory volume (1908) was caused by the Great War and McDougall's service in the medical corps during this war. He is fiercely attacked by **F. H. Allport** (1890–1978) for appearing to assign agency to entities other than individuals. McDougall leaves Britain for Harvard University.

Heider (1896–1988) submits his thesis on *Ding und Medium* to **Meinong** at Graz.

1921   **Freud** publishes *Massenpsychologie und Ich-Analyse*. The first of a series of books in which Freud switches his attention from the analysis of clinical cases to the analysis of cultural phenomena. In *Massenpsychologie* he develops the ideas of **Le Bon** and of **Tarde** on the psychology of crowds.

Psychologische Forschung, the journal of the Gestalt group is established with the following editorial board: **Wertheimer, Köhler, Koffka, Goldstein** (1878–1965) and **Grühle** (1880–1958).

The Journal of Abnormal Psychology and Social Psychology is created with **F. H. Allport** and **Morton Prince** as joint editors. Prince's experiences in the Great War led him to include the field of social psychology. In 1925 the title is shortened to *The Journal of Abnormal and Social Psychology*. This becomes the premier journal of social psychology in the world. The divorce between the abnormal and social halves of the journal did not occur until 1965.

1922   **Levy-Bruhl** (1857–1939) publishes *La Mentalité Primitive*. Believes the mentality of primitive people is essentially mystical and pre-logical and differs in kind from the rational and logical thought of Western civilization.

1923   **Freud** publishes *The Ego and the Id* (London edn, 1927).

Bartlett (1896–1969) publishes *Psychology and Primitive Culture*.

1924   **F. H. Allport** publishes *Social Psychology*. Establishes social psychology as an experimental and behavioural science. He explains social phenomena in purely behavioural terms at the level of the individual. There is no need to change one's model in moving from the psychology of the individual to the psychology of such collective entities as the public, social institutions, culture etc.

Thurstone (1887–1955) publishes *The Nature of Intelligence*. In the preface Thurstone indicates the seminal influence on his work of Mead's lectures on social psychology.

Vygotsky (1896–1934) presents his paper on 'Methodology of reflexological and psychological research' at the Second Psychoneurological Congress in Leningrad. He argues that if reflexology is to become a general theory of behaviour it must first accept the existence of consciousness and must incorporate the methods of psychological investigation. His stance is similar to that of **Dewey** (see 1896 above) and opposed to that of **Watson** (see 1915 above). Watson had taken the work of Pavlov as his model of how psychology could become an objective science.

1925   **Blumer** (b. 1900), with an MA in sociology from Missouri, enrols as a doctoral student in social psychology at the University of Chicago where he takes courses taught by Mead and by Faris.

1927   **Koffka** joins the faculty at Smith College in America where he remains until his death in 1941.

Morton Prince founds the Psychological Clinic at Harvard. His young assistant, Henry **Murray** (b. 1893), assumed the directorship of the Clinic on Prince's death at the age of 75.

1929   **Boring** (1896–1968) publishes his *History of Experimental Psychology* in which he defends 'pure' experimental psychology over against the recently popular brands of applied psychology. The book is also a powerful statement for the separation, at Harvard, of psychology from philosophy.

Thurstone and **Chave** publish *The Measurement of Attitude*. Thurstone's methods for constructing his classic attitude scales at Chicago during the 1920s imply a collective representation of the object of study on the part of the judges who comprise his panel. His pool of opinion items for the construction of a scale is drawn from a trawl of the mass media of communication. We have seen above (see 1924) how he was influenced by the social psychology of Mead.

1930	**Heider** joins **Koffka** at Smith College. Initially intended as a short visit, he marries an American citizen, Grace Moore, and settles in the States where he remains until his death in 1988.
1931	**Mead** dies in Chicago. His lecture course on social psychology is taken over by **Blumer**. This is the origin of the symbolic interactionist tradition of social psychology within American sociology. The name is Blumer's not Mead's. Blumer remained at Chicago between 1925 and 1952 when he moved to Berkeley. **Bartlett** becomes Professor of Experimental Psychology at Cambridge, a post he held until his retirement in 1952.
1932	**Bartlett** publishes *Remembering: an experimental and social study*. The interface between psychology and anthropology is very evident in the work of Bartlett. He was familiar with and drew on the Durkheimian tradition of research in France, especially the work of **Halbwachs** (1877–1945). Expedition to Uzbekistan and Kirghizia in Central Asia 'to study the dependence of the mental functions of a people upon the historico-economic conditions of their country'. Leader of the expedition was **Luria** (1902–77). Other members included **Vygotsky** and **Koffka**. The results of this research were not made public until much later in Luria, *Cognitive Development: its cultural and social foundations* (1976). **Blumer** spends a year in Paris, as a social science research fellow, studying fashion. He contends that fashion is to modern societies what custom is to static societies. **Lewin** is a visiting professor at Stanford.
1933	**Wertheimer** and **Lewin**, with Hitler's rise to power in Nazi Germany, seek asylum elsewhere. The London School of Economics and Political Science considers offering them appointments but decides not to. They emigrate to America. Wertheimer goes to the New School for Social Research in New York and Lewin to the School of Home Economics at Cornell where he remains until 1935. **F. H. Allport** publishes his book *Institutional Behavior* in which he analyses the main social institutions in terms of the behaviour of individuals.

1934	**Adorno** (1903–69) emigrates from Frankfurt to America where he teaches at the New School for Social Research in New York.
1935	**Murchison** publishes his *Handbook of Social Psychology*. The overall scheme of this work is similar to Wundt's, *Völkerpsychologie*, i.e. a comparative approach. Its table of contents is reproduced in chapter 5. **G. W. Allport** (1897–1967), in his classic chapter on attitudes, converts them from being 'collective representations' into being purely individual tendencies to respond. Progress during the modern era in social psychology is measured in terms of its distance from the Murchison *Handbook*.

Koffka publishes *The Principles of Gestalt Psychology* to explain the nature of this German tradition of research to the English-speaking world.

Gallup (1901–84) founds the American Institute of Public Opinion (known as the Gallup Poll) to conduct political and market research by scientific methods.

Lewin leaves Cornell for the Child Welfare Research Center at the University of Iowa where he remains until 1945. **Festinger** (1919–89) obtains his doctorate there under Lewin's supervision with a thesis on the level of aspiration.

1936	The Central Committee of the Communist Party of the USSR issues its decree on 'Pedological Perversions in the System of the People's Commissariat of Education'. This forbids the use of psychological tests in various applied settings, especially in schools. A number of key journals in psychology also ceased publication from this date. The prohibition of the study of individual differences in the USSR contrasts with the individualization of social psychology in the USA.
1937	**G. W. Allport** becomes editor of *The Journal of Abnormal and Social Psychology* for a 12-year period. He also publishes *Personality: a psychological interpretation*. He individualizes the notion of personality in much the same way as he had earlier individualized the notion of attitude (see 1935).

The journal *Public Opinion Quarterly* established.

1939–45	The Second World War.
1943	**Allport**, as editor, publishes an article on the concentration camps while the war is still in progress: **Bettelheim,**

'Individual and mass behavior in extreme situations', *Journal of Abnormal and Social Psychology*, 38, 417–52. **Eisenhower** (1890–1969) required his troops to read this article before they went in to liberate the camps.

Asch (b. 1907) succeeds **Wertheimer** as Chairman of the Psychology Department at the New School for Social Research.

1945–7   The Research Center for Group Dynamics established at MIT under the Directorship of **Lewin**.

1947   **Lewin** dies. The Research Center for Group Dynamics moves from MIT to the University of Michigan where it forms part of the Institute for Social Research. **Cartwright** becomes Director of the Center. **Heider**, at the age of 51, moves from Smith College to the University of Kansas where he remains until his death in 1988.

              Asch joins **Köhler** on the faculty of Swarthmore College and remains there until 1966.

1949   *The American Soldier: adjustment during army life*, volume I, by Stouffer, Suchman et al. published.

              The American Soldier: combat and its aftermath, volume II by Stouffer, Lumsdaine et al. published. These were social surveys of the armed forces during the Second World War carried out under the general direction of the sociologist **Stouffer** (1900–69).

              Experiments in Mass Communication, volume III of *The American Soldier* series, published by Hovland et al. These experimental studies formed the basis of the post-war Yale programme on communication and attitude change, under the direction of **Hovland** (1912–61).

1950   *The Authoritarian Personality*, published by **Adorno** et al. A major study of prejudice, especially of anti-Semitism, inspired by the work of the Institute for Social Research at Frankfurt, which had been shut down on the orders of Hitler. A landmark publication in the fields of social psychology and of personality.

              Measurement and Prediction, volume IV of *The American Soldier* series, published by **Stouffer** et al. This was the final volume in the series. It was concerned with the construction of attitude scales, especially Guttman scales.

1952   Solomon **Asch** publishes his text *Social Psychology*. He was strongly influenced by Wertheimer, whose lectures he attended at the New School for Social Research in New York. The text represents the perspective of Gestalt psychology. As influential, in the modern era, in the development of a cognitive social psychology as F. H. Allport's 1924 text had been in the development of a behavioural social psychology in the inter-war years.

1953   **Festinger** and **Katz** publish *Research Methods in the Behavioral Sciences*, a product of the Institute for Social Research at the University of Michigan. **Cartwright** and **Zander** publish *Group Dynamics: research and theory*, a product of the Research Center for Group Dynamics, part of the ISR at the University of Michigan.
Communication and Persuasion: psychological studies of opinion change published by **Hovland** et al. This is the first volume in the Yale programme of research on communication and attitude change.

1954   **Festinger** publishes his theory of social comparison processes in the journal *Human Relations* which is jointly published by the Tavistock Institute of Human Relations in London and the Research Center for Group Dynamics at the University of Michigan.
Lindzey edits the *Handbook of Social Psychology*, volume I: Theory and method; volume II: Special fields and applications. The first of the modern series of *Handbooks of Social Psychology*. It opens with G. W. **Allport**'s chapter on 'The historical background of modern social psychology' in which he distinguishes between the roots of modern social psychology and its flowering as a characteristically American phenomenon.

Appendix 2: Rubric in the mid-1960s for the University of London Honours Degree in Psychology

The course of study will normally extend over not less than three years.

(For examinations in 1964, 1965 and 1966)

The examination in Psychology will be divided into two Parts, both of which must be taken in the same year.

Part I of the examination will consist of four written papers and a practical examination. The written papers will be:

General Psychology I
Experimental Psychology I
Comparative Psychology I
History of Psychology

The General paper will contain questions on any topic within the scope of a comprehensive general course in psychology, including the relevant experiment work. The paper on Experimental Psychology will deal with those matters usually dealt with in standard textbooks on the subject, including a study of work on conditioned reflexes and its bearing on general psychology. Comparative Psychology I will consist of two sections, (*a*) Animal Psychology and (*b*) Psychology of Child-hood. Both sections will presuppose acquaintance with such parts of the sciences of biology, physiology and statistics as may be relevant to the topics included in the paper. The paper on History of Psychology will consist of two or more sections. The first section, which will be compulsory, will presuppose general acquaintance with the main stages in the history of psychology from the period of ancient Greek thought to the present day. The other sections from which options may be selected, will require more specialized knowledge of some period or movement in the history of psychology or in the development of scientific method in psychology.

The practical examination may include questions on any topic forming part of a general laboratory course in psychology. The candidate may be examined orally or in other ways.

Part II of the examination will consist of four written papers and a practical examination. The written papers will be:

General Psychology II
Experimental Psychology II
Comparative Psychology II
Essay

The papers on General and Experimental Psychology will carry the work of Part I to a more specialized stage. In the paper on Experimental Psychology II questions will be set involving translations of passages in French and German and answers with regard to the subject matter thereof. Candidates are required to answer *one* of these questions. Comparative Psychology II will consist of two sections (*a*) Abnormal Psychology, and (*b*) Social Psychology and the Psychology of Primitive Peoples. The section on Abnormal Psychology will presuppose knowledge not only of the functional disorders in mental processes, but also of those disturbances in function for the organic basis of which there is physiological and anatomical evidence. The section on Social Psychology and the Psychology of Primitive Peoples will presuppose knowledge of the statistical and experimental methods of Social Psychology and of the principles of Anthropology. The Essay paper will require either one or two essays on subjects to be selected from any part of the syllabus for the whole examination.

The Practical examination in Part II will consist of questions which require more specialized experimental and statistical methods than those in Part I, and the candidate may be required to plan and in part carry out an investigation of a research character, requiring the adaptation of laboratory methods to problems not usually included in a laboratory course. He may also be examined orally or in other ways.

Candidates will be allowed to take into the examination room and to consult, during the practical examination, notebooks containing mathematical formulae only.

Candidates must produce their notebooks at the practical examinations for Parts I and II showing normally that the candidates have regularly taken part in courses of work in Experimental Psychology extending over the whole course of study for those Parts of the examination.

Subsidiary Subject

A subsidiary subject must also be taken.

References

Adorno, T. W., Frenkel-Brunswik, E., Levinson, D. J. and Nevitt Sanford, R. (1950). *The Authoritarian Personality*. New York: Harper and Row.
Allee, W. C. (1935). Relatively simple animal aggregations. In C. Murchison (ed.), *Handbook of Social Psychology*, pp. 919–46. Worcester, Mass.: Clark University Press.
Allport, F. H. (1924). *Social Psychology*. Boston: Houghton-Mifflin.
Allport, F. H. (1933). *Institutional Behavior*. Chapel Hill: University of North Carolina Press.
Allport, F. H. (1937). Towards a science of public opinion. *Public Opinion Quarterly*, 1, 7–23.
Allport, F. H. and Prince M. (1921). Editorial. *Journal of Abnormal Psychology and Social Psychology*, 16.
Allport, G. W. (1935). Attitudes. In C. Murchison (ed.), *Handbook of Social Psychology*, pp. 798–844. Worcester, Mass.: Clark University Press.
Allport, G. W. (1937). *Personality: a psychological interpretation*. New York: Holt.
Allport, G. W. (1954). The historical background of modern social psychology. In G. Lindzey (ed.), *Handbook of Social Psychology*, vol. 1, pp. 3–56. Reading, Mass.: Addison-Wesley.
Allport, G. W. (1968). The historical background of modern social psychology. In G. Lindzey and E. Aronson (eds), *Handbook of Social Psychology*, 2nd edn, vol. 1, pp. 1–80. Reading, Mass.: Addison-Wesley.
Allport, G. W. (1985). The historical background of social psychology. In G. Lindzey and E. Aronson (eds), *Handbook of Social Psychology*, 3rd edn, vol. 1, pp. 1–46. New York: Random House.
Alverdes, F. (1935). The behavior of mammalian herds and packs. In C. Murchison (ed.), *Handbook of Social Psychology*, pp. 185–203. Worcester, Mass.: Clark University Press.
Asch, S. E. (1952). *Social Psychology*. Englewood Cliffs, NJ: Prentice-Hall.
Ash, M. G. (1980). Experimental psychology in Germany before 1914: aspects of an academic identity problem. *Psychological Research*, 42, 75–86.

Ash, M. G. (1982). The emergence of Gestalt theory: experimental psychology in Germany 1890–1920. Unpublished doctoral thesis, Department of History, Harvard University.

Badcock, C. (1980). *The Psychoanalysis of Culture*. Oxford: Blackwell.

Badcock, C. (1983). *Madness and Modernity: a study in social psychoanalysis*. Oxford: Blackwell.

Badcock, C. R. (1986). *The Problem of Altruism: Freudian–Darwinian solutions*. Oxford: Blackwell.

Baldwin, J. D. (1986). *George Herbert Mead: a unifying theory for sociology*. London: Sage.

Beach, F. A. (1950). The Snark was a Boojum. *American Psychologist, 5,* 115–24.

Beach, F. A. (1960). Experimental investigations of species-specific behavior. *American Psychologist, 15,* 1–18.

Bell, D. (1960). *The End of Ideology: on the exhaustion of political ideas in the fifties*. Glencoe, Ill.: The Free Press.

Bem, D. J. (1967). Self perception: an alternative interpretation of cognitive dissonance phenomena. *Psychological Review, 74,* 183–200.

Bem, D. J. (1972). Self-perception theory. In L. Berkowitz (ed.), *Advances in Experimental Social Psychology*, vol. 6, New York: Academic Press.

Bettelheim, B. (1943). Individual and mass behavior in extreme situations. *Journal of Abnormal and Social Psychology, 38,* 417–52.

Billig, M. (1987). *Arguing and Thinking: a rhetorical approach to social psychology*. Cambridge: Cambridge University Press.

Bjork, D. W. (1983). *The Compromised Scientist: William James in the development of American psychology*. New York: Columbia University Press.

Blumenthal, A. L. (1973). Introduction. In Wundt, W., *The Language of Gestures*. The Hague: Mouton.

Blumenthal, A. L. (1975). A re-appraisal of Wilhelm Wundt. *American Psychologist, 30,* 1081–8.

Blumer, H. (1937). Social psychology. In E. P. Schmidt (ed.), *Man and Society*, pp. 144–98. New York: Prentice-Hall.

Blumer, H. (1948). Public opinion and public opinion polling. *American Sociological Review, 13,* 542–54.

Blumer, H. (1969). *Symbolic Interactionism: perspective and method*. Englewood Cliffs, NJ: Prentice-Hall.

Blumer, H. (1980). Mead and Blumer: the convergent methodological perspectives of social behaviorism and symbolic interactionism. *American Sociological Review, 45,* 409–19.

Boakes, R. (1984). *From Darwin to Behaviourism: psychology and the minds of animals*. Cambridge: Cambridge University Press.

Boring, E. G. (1929). *A History of Experimental Psychology*. New York: Century.

Boring, E. G. (1950) *A History of Experimental Psychology*, 2nd edn. New York: Appleton-Century-Crofts.

Brown, R. (1965). *Social Psychology*. New York: Free Press.

Brown, R. (1986). *Social Psychology: the second edition.* New York: Macmillan.
Bruner, J. (1983). *In Search of Mind: essays in autobiography.* New York: Harper and Row.
Burckhardt, J. (1860). *The Civilisation of the Renaissance in Italy* (1958 English translation of 1860 German original, New York: Harper).
Butterfield, H. (1951). *The Whig Interpretation of History.* London: Bell.
Campbell, D. T. (1963). Social attitudes and other acquired behavioral dispositions. In S. Koch (ed.), *Psychology: a study of a science,* pp. 94–172. New York: McGraw-Hill.
Carr, E. H. (1961). *What is History?* London: Macmillan.
Cartwright, D. (1979). Contemporary social psychology in historical perspective. *Social Psychology Quarterly,* 42, 82–93.
Chomsky, N. (1957). *Syntactic Structures.* The Hague: Mouton.
Cohen, D. (1977). *Psychologists on Psychology.* London: Routledge and Kegan Paul.
Collier, G., Minton, H. L. and Reynolds, G. (1991). *Currents of Thought in American Social Psychology.* Oxford: Oxford University Press.
Coser, L. A. (1977). *Masters of Sociological Thought,* 2nd edn. New York: Harcourt Brace Jovanovich.
Coughlan, N. (1975). *Young John Dewey: an essay in American intellectual history.* Chicago: University of Chicago Press.
Craik, K. H. (1993). The 1937 Allport and Stagner texts in personality psychology. In K. H. Craik, R. Hogan and R. N. Wolfe (eds), *Fifty Years of Personality Psychology,* pp. 3–20. New York: Plenum.
Dahrendorf, R. (1995). *LSE: a history of the London School of Economics and Political Science 1895–1995.* Oxford: Oxford University Press.
Danziger, K. (1979). The positivist repudiation of Wundt. *Journal of the History of the Behavioural Sciences,* 15, 205–30.
Danziger, K. (1980a). The history of introspection reconsidered. *Journal of the History of the Behavioural Sciences,* 16, 241–62.
Danziger, K. (1980b). On the threshold of the new psychology: situating Wundt and James. In W. G. Bringmann and R. D. Tweney (eds), *Wundt Studies,* pp. 363–79. Toronto: Hogrefe.
Danziger, K. (1983). Origins and basic principles of Wundt's Völkerpsychologie. *British Journal of Social Psychology,* 22, 303–13.
Danziger, K. (1990). *Constructing the Subject: historical origins of psychological research.* Cambridge Studies in the History of Psychology. Cambridge: University of Cambridge Press.
Dashiell, J. F. (1935). Experimental studies of the influence of social situations on the behavior of individual human adults. In C. A. Murchison (ed.), *Handbook of Social Psychology,* pp. 1097–158. Worcester, Mass.: Clark University Press.
De Rivera, J. (1976). *Field Theory as Human-Science: Contributions of Lewin's Berlin Group* (compiled with commentary by J. De Rivera). New York: Gardner Press.

De Tocqueville, A. (1835–40). *De la Démocratie en Amérique*, 4 vols. Paris: Librarie de Médias.

Degler, C. N. (1991). *In Search of Human Nature: the decline and revival of Darwinism in American social thought.* Oxford: Oxford University Press.

Descartes, R. (1637). *Discourse on the Method of Rightly Conducting the Reason and Seeking Truth in the Sciences.* London: J. M. Dent (1912).

Deutsch, M. (1975). Introduction. In M. Deutsch and H. A. Hornstein (eds), *Applying Social Psychology: implications for research, practice and training*, pp. 1–12. Hillsdale, NJ: Lawrence Erlbaum Associates.

Deutscher, I. (1973). *What We Say / What We Do: sentiments and acts.* Glenview, Ill.: Scott, Foresman.

Deutscher, I. (1984). Choosing ancestors: some consequences of the selection from intellectual traditions. In R. M. Farr and S. Moscovici (eds), *Social Representations*, pp. 71–100. Cambridge: Cambridge University Press.

Dewey, J. (1896). The reflex arc concept in psychology. *Psychological Review*, 3, 357–70.

Dewey, J. (1931) George Herbert Mead. *Journal of Philosophy*, 28, 309–14.

Dewey, J. M. (1951). Biography of John Dewey. In A. P. Schilpp (ed.), *The Philosophy of John Dewey*, pp. 1–45. New York: Tudor.

Dilthey, W. (1883). Einleitung in die Geisteswissenschaften. In W. Dilthey (ed.), *Gesammelte Schriften.* Leipzig: Teubner (1923).

Dunlap, K. (1919). Are there any instincts? *Journal of Abnormal Psychology*, 14, 307–11.

Durkheim, E. (1898). Représentations individuelles et représentations collectives. *Revue de Metaphysique et de Morale*, 6, 273–302.

Ebbinghaus, H. (1908). *Abriss der Psychologie.* Berlin: Veit.

Elms, A.C. (1975) The crisis of confidence in social psychology. *American Psychologist*, 30, 967–76.

Esper, E. A. (1935). Language. In C. Murchison (ed.), *Handbook of Social Psychology*, pp. 417–60. Worcester, Mass.: Clark University Press.

Evans, R. I. (1980). *The Making of Social Psychology: discussions with creative contributors.* New York: Gardner Press.

Fancher, R. (1990). *Pioneers of Psychology.* New York: Norton.

Faris, E. (1936). Review of G. H. Mead: *Mind, Self and Society. American Journal of Sociology*, 41, 809–13.

Farr, R. M. (1975). Social psychology and psychoanalysis: a rejoinder to Professor Jahoda. *Bulletin of the British Psychological Society*, 28, 143–8.

Farr, R. M. (1976). Experimentation: a social psychological perspective. *British Journal of Social and Clinical Psychology*, 15, 225–38.

Farr, R. M. (1978). On the varieties of social psychology: an essay on the relationships between psychology and other social sciences. *Social Science Information*, 17(4/5), 503–25.

Farr, R. M. (1981). On the nature of human nature and the science of behaviour. In P. Heelas and A. Lock (eds), *Indigenous Psychologies: the anthropology of the self*, pp. 303–17. London: Academic Press.

Farr, R. M. (1983a). Editorial. *British Journal of Social Psychology*, 22(4), 273–5.

Farr, R. M. (1983b). The impact of Wundt on the development of social psychology: a critical reappraisal. In G. Eckhardt and L. Sprung (eds), *Advances in the Historiography of Psychology*, pp. 85–91. Berlin: VEB Deutscher Verlag der Wissenschaften.

Farr, R. M. (1983c). Wilhelm Wundt (1832–1920) and the origins of psychology as an experimental and social science. *British Journal of Social Psychology*, 22(4), 289–301.

Farr, R. M. (1985a). *Some Reflections on the Historical Development of Psychology as an Experimental and Social Science* (an inaugural lecture). London: LSE Publications.

Farr, R. M. (1985b). Varietà e diversità nelle correnti della Psicologia Sociale. *Psicologia Italiana*, 7, 60–73.

Farr, R. M. (1986). The social psychology of William McDougall. In C. Graumann and S. Moscovici (eds), *Changing Conceptions of Crowd Mind and Behaviour*, pp. 83–95. New York: Springer-Verlag.

Farr, R. M. (1987a). The science of mental life: a social psychological perspective. *Bulletin of the British Psychological Society*, 40, 2–17.

Farr, R. M. (1987b). Social representations: a French tradition of research. *Journal for the Theory of Social Behaviour*, 17(4), 343–69.

Farr, R. M. (1990). The social psychology of the prefix 'inter': a prologue to the study of dialogue. In I. Marková and K. Foppa (eds), *The Dynamics of Dialogue*, pp. 25–44. London: Harvester/Wheatsheaf.

Farr, R. M. (1991a). Bodies and voices in dialogue. In I. Marková and K. Foppa (eds), *Asymmetries in Dialogue*, pp. 241–58. London: Harvester/Wheatsheaf.

Farr, R. M. (1991b). The long past and the short history of social psychology. *European Journal of Social Psychology*, 21(5), 371–80.

Farr, R. M. (1994). Representações sociais: a teoria e sua história. In P. Guareschi and S. Jovchelovitch (eds), *Textos em Representações Sociais*, pp. 31–59. Petropolis, RJ: Vozes.

Farr, R. M. and Anderson, A. (1983). Beyond actor/observer differences in perspective: extensions and applications. In M. Hewstone (ed.), *Attribution Theory: social and functional extensions*, pp. 45–64. Oxford: Blackwell.

Farr, R. M. and Rommetveit, R. (1995). The communicative act: an epilogue to mutualities in dialogue. In I. Marková, C. Graumann and K. Foppa (eds), *Mutualities in Dialogue*, pp. 264–74. Cambridge: Cambridge University Press.

Festinger, L. (1954). A theory of social comparison processes. *Human Relations*, 7, 117–40.

Festinger, L. (1980). *Retrospections on Social Psychology*. Oxford: Oxford University Press.

Festinger, L. and Katz, D. (eds) (1953). *Research Methods in the Behavioral Sciences*. New York: Holt, Rinehart and Winston.

Festinger, L., Schachter, S. and Back, K. (1950). *Social Pressures in Informal Groups: a study of human factors in housing*. New York: Harper.

Foulkes, S. H. and Anthony, E. J. (1957). *Group Psychotherapy: the psychoanalytic approach*. Harmondsworth: Penguin.

Freud, S. (1921). *Massenpsychologie und Ich-Analyse*. Vienna: Internationaler Psychoanalytischer Verlag.

Freud, S. (1923). The Ego and the Id, in *The Standard Edition*, vol. 19. London: Hogarth Press.

Friedmann, H. (1935). Bird societies. In C. Murchison (ed.), *Handbook of Social Psychology*, pp. 142–84. Worcester, Mass.: Clark University Press.

Gallie, W. B. (1952). *Peirce and Pragmatism*. Harmondsworth: Penguin.

Gardner, H. (1985). *The Mind's New Science: a history of the cognitive revolution*. New York: Basic Books.

Gergen, K. J. (1973). Social psychology as history. *Journal of Personality and Social Psychology*, 26, 309–20.

Geuter, H. (1993). *The Professionalisation of Psychology in Nazi Germany*. Cambridge: Cambridge University Press.

van Ginneken, J. (1992). *Crowds, Psychology and Politics, 1871–1899*. Cambridge: Cambridge University Press.

Goffman, E. (1959). *The Presentation of Self in Everyday Life*. New York: Doubleday Anchor.

Graumann, C. F. (1986). The individualization of the social and the desocialization of the individual: Floyd H. Allport's contribution to social psychology. In C. F. Graumann and S. Moscovici (eds), *Changing Conceptions of Crowd Mind and Behavior*, pp. 97–116. New York: Springer-Verlag.

Harrower, M. (ed.) (1983). *Kurt Koffka: an unwitting self-portrait*. Florida: University of Florida Press.

Hart, H. (1949). The pre-war upsurge in social science. *American Sociological Review*, 14, 599–607.

Harvey, E. D. (1935). Social history of the yellow man. In C. Murchison (ed.), *Handbook of Social Psychology*, pp. 361–414. Worcester, Mass.: Clark University Press.

Hearnshaw, L. S. (1979). The influence of Wundt on British psychology. *Bulletin of the British Psychological Society*, 32, 446–51.

Heider, F. (1958). *The Psychology of Interpersonal Relations*. New York: Wiley.

Heider, F. (1983). *The Autobiography of a Psychologist*. Lawrence, Kansas: University of Kansas Press.

Henle, M. (1986a). The influence of Gestalt psychology in America. In M. Henle (ed.), *1879 and All That: essays in the theory and history of psychology*, pp. 118–32. New York: Columbia University Press.

Henle, M. (1986b). One man against the Nazis-Wolfgang Köhler. In M. Henle (ed.), *1879 and All That: essays in the theory and history of psychology*, pp. 225–37. New York: Columbia University Press.

Herskovits, M. (1935). Social history of the negro. In C. Murchison (ed.), *Handbook of Social Psychology*, pp. 207–67. Worcester, Mass.: Clark University Press.

Hilgard, E. R. (1987). *Psychology in America: a historical survey*. San Diego: Harcourt Brace Jovanovich.

Hirsch, J. L. (1987). *The History of the National Training Laboratories 1947–1986: social equality through education and training*. New York: Peter Larry.

Hovland, C. I., Lumsdaine, A. A. and Sheffield, F. D. (eds) (1949). *Experiments in Mass Communication*. Studies in Social Psychology in World War II, vol. 3. Princeton, NJ: Princeton University Press.

Ichheiser, G. (1949). Misunderstandings in human relations: a study in false social perception. *American Journal of Sociology*, 55 (suppl.), 1–72.

Jackson, J. M. (1988). *Social Psychology, Past and Present: an integrative orientation*. Hillsdale, NJ: Lawrence Erlbaum.

Jahoda, G. (1992). *Crossroads between Culture and Mind: continuities and change in theories of human nature*. London: Harvester/Wheatsheaf.

Jahoda, M. (1972). Social psychology and psychoanalysis: a mutual challenge. *Bulletin of the British Psychological Society*, 25, 269–74.

Jahoda, M. (1977). *Freud and the Dilemmas of Psychology*. London: The Hogarth Press.

Jahoda, M. (1983). The emergence of social psychology in Vienna: an exercise in long-term memory. *British Journal of Social Psychology*, 28, 343–9.

James, W. (1890). *The Principles of Psychology*. New York: Holt.

James, W. (1902). *The Varieties of Religious Experience: a study in human nature*. London: Longman Green and Co.

Janis, I. (1951). *Air War and Emotional Stress: psychological studies of bombing and civilian defence*. New York: McGraw-Hill.

Jaspars, J. M. F. and Fraser, C. (1984). Attitudes and social representations. In R. M. Farr and S. Moscovici (eds), *Social Representations*, pp. 101–23. Cambridge: Cambridge University Press.

Joas, H. (1980). *G. H. Mead*. Frankfurt: Suhrkamp-Verlag (German original).

Joas, H. (1985). *G. H. Mead: a contemporary re-examination of his thought*. Cambridge: Polity Press.

Jones, E. E. (1985). Major developments in social psychology during the past five decades. In G. Lindzey and E. Aronson (eds), *Handbook of Social Psychology*, pp. 47–107. New York: Random House.

Jones, E. E. and Nisbett, R. E. (1972). The actor and the observer: divergent perceptions of the causes of behavior. In E. E. Jones et al. (eds), *Attribution: perceiving the causes of behavior*, pp. 79–94. Morristown, NJ: General Learning Press.

Joravsky, D. (1989). *Russian Psychology: a critical history*. Oxford: Blackwell.

Katz, E. and Lazarsfeld, P. F. (1955). *Personal Influence: the part played by people in the flow of mass communications*. New York: The Free Press.

Katz, J. (1972). *Experimentation with Human Beings*. New York: Russell Sage Foundation.

Keller, H. A. (1902). *The Story of My Life*. London: Hodder and Stoughton, 1970.

Klineberg, O. and Christie, R. (eds) (1965). *Perspectives in Social Psychology*. New York: Holt, Rinehart and Winston.

Koch, S. (1985). Foreword: Wundt's creature at age zero – and as centenarian: some aspects of the institutionalization of the 'new psychology'. In S. Koch and D. E. Leary (eds), *A Century of Psychology as Science*, pp. 7–35. New York: McGraw-Hill.

Koffka, K. (1936). *Principles of Gestalt Psychology*. London: Routledge and Kegan Paul.

Köhler, W. (1925). *The Mentality of Apes*. London: Penguin Books (German original 1917).

Köhler, W. (1947). *Gestalt Psychology: the definitive statement of the Gestalt theory*. New York: Liveright.

Kuhn, T. S. (1962). *The Structure of Scientific Revolutions, The International Encyclopedia of Unified Science*, vol. 2. Chicago: University of Chicago Press.

La Piere, R. T. (1934). Attitudes versus action. *Social Forces*, 13, 230–7.

Leary, D. (1982). Immanuel Kant and the development of modern psychology. In W. R. Woodward and M. G. Ash (eds), *The Problematic Science: psychology in nineteenth century thought*, pp. 17–42. New York: Praeger.

Lewin, K. (1917). Kriegslandschaft. *Zeitschrift für Angewandte Psychologie*, 12, 440–7.

Lewis, J. D. and Smith, R. L. (1980). *American Sociology and Pragmatism: Mead, Chicago sociology and symbolic interactionism*. Chicago: University of Chicago Press.

Lindesmith, A. R. and Strauss, A. L. (1949). *Social Psychology*. New York: Holt, Rinehart and Winston.

Lindzey, G. (ed.) (1954). *Handbook of Social Psychology*, 2 vols. Reading, Mass.: Addison-Wesley.

Lindzey, G. and Aronson, E. (eds) (1968–9). *The Handbook of Social Psychology*, 2nd edn, 5 vols. Reading, Mass.: Addison-Wesley.

Lindzey, G. and Aronson, E. (eds) (1985). *The Handbook of Social Psychology*, 3rd edn, 2 vols. New York: Random House.

Linebarger, P. M. A. (1948). *Psychological Warfare*. New York: Hawthorn Books.

Lorenz, K. (1950). The comparative method in studying innate behaviour patterns, *Physiological Mechanisms of Animal Behaviour: Symposia of the Society of Experimental Biology in Great Britain*, vol. 4. Cambridge: Cambridge University Press.

Lukes, S. (1973). *Emile Durkheim: his life and work. A historical and critical study*. London: Allen Lane.

McDougall, W. (1908). *An Introduction to Social Psychology*. London: Methuen.

McDougall, W. (1920). *The Group Mind: a sketch of the principles of collective psychology with some attempt to apply them to the interpretation of national life and character.* Cambridge: Cambridge University Press.

Mackenzie, B. D. (1977). *Behaviour and the Limits of Scientific Method.* London: Routledge and Kegan Paul.

McPhail, C. and Rexroat, C. (1979). Mead *v.* Blumer: the divergent methodological perspectives of social behaviorism and symbolic interactionism. *American Sociological Review*, 44, 449–67.

McPhail, C. and Rexroat, C. (1980). Ex cathedra Blumer or ex libris Mead? *American Sociological Review*, 45, 420–30.

Manicas, P. T. (1987). *A History and Philosophy of the Social Sciences.* Oxford: Blackwell.

Manis, J. G. and Meltzer, B. N. (1967). *Symbolic Interaction: a reader in social psychology.* Boston: Allyn and Bacon.

Marková, I. (1982). *Paradigms, Thought and Language.* Chichester: Wiley.

Marková, I. (1983). The origin of the social psychology of language in German expressivism. *British Journal of Social Psychology*, 22, 315–25.

Marková, I. (1987). *Human Awareness.* London: Hutchinson Education.

Marrow, A. J. (1969). *The Practical Theorist: the life and work of Kurt Lewin.* New York: Basic Books.

Mead, G. H. (1903). The definition of the psychical. *Decennial Publications of the University of Chicago* 1st series, 3, 77–112.

Mead, G. H. (1904). The relations of psychology and philology. *Psychological Bulletin*, 1, 375–91.

Mead, G. H. (1906). The imagination in Wundt's treatment of myths and religion. *Psychological Bulletin*, 3, 393–9.

Mead, G. H. (1909). Social psychology as counterpart to physiological psychology. *Psychological Bulletin*, 6, 401–8.

Mead, G. H. (1927). The objective reality of perspectives. In E. S. Brightman (ed.), *Proceedings of the Sixth International Congress of Philosophy*, pp. 75–85. New York: Longman, Green and Co.

Mead, G. H. (1932). *The Philosophy of the Present*, edited by E. Murphy. Chicago: Open Court.

Mead, G. H. (1934). *Mind, Self and Society: from the standpoint of a social behaviorist*, edited by C. W. Morris. Chicago: University of Chicago Press.

Mead, G. H. (1982). *The Individual and the Social Self: unpublished work of George Herbert Mead*, edited, with an introduction, by D. L. Miller. Chicago: University of Chicago Press.

Meltzer, B. N. and Petras, J. W. (1970). The Chicago and Iowa schools of symbolic interactionism. In T. Shibutani (ed.), *Human Nature and Collective Behavior: papers in honor of Herbert Blumer*, pp. 3–17. Englewood Cliffs, NJ: Prentice-Hall.

Meyer, M. F. (1921). *The Psychology of the Other One: an introductory textbook.* Columbia, Mo.: Missouri Book Company.

Miles, C. C. (1935). Sex in social psychology. In C. Murchison (ed.), *Handbook of Social Psychology*, pp. 683–797. Worcester, Mass.: Clark University Press.

Miles, W. R. (1935). Age in human society. In C. Murchison (ed.), *Handbook of Social Psychology*, pp. 596–682. Worcester, Mass.: Clark University Press.

Milgram, S. (1974). *Obedience to Authority: an experimental view*. London: Tavistock.

Milgram, S. (1977). *The Individual and the Social World: essays and experiments*. Reading, Mass.: Addison-Wesley.

Miller, D. L. (1973). *George Herbert Mead: self, language and the world*. Austin, Texas: University of Texas Press.

Miller, G. A. (1966). *Psychology: the science of mental life*. Harmondsworth: Penguin.

Miller, G. A. and Buckhout, R. (1973). *Psychology: the science of mental life*, 2nd edn. New York: Harper and Row.

Morawski, J. G. (ed.) (1988). *The Rise of Experimentation in American Psychology*. New Haven: Yale University Press.

Morris, C. W. (1938). *Foundations of the Theory of Signs, International Encyclopedia of Unified Science*, edited by O. Neurath, Vol. 1(ii), pp. 1–59. Chicago: University of Chicago Press.

Moscovici, S. (1961). *La Psychanalyse: son image et son public*. Paris: Presses Universitaires de France.

Moscovici, S. (1981). *L'Age des Foules: un traité historique de psychologie des masses*. Paris: Fayard.

Moscovici, S. (1985). *The Age of the Crowd: a historical treatise on mass psychology*. Cambridge: Cambridge University Press.

Moscovici, S. (1988). *La Machine à Faire des Dieux: sociologie et psychologie*. Paris: Fayard.

Murchison, C. A. (ed.) (1935). *Handbook of Social Psychology*. Worcester, Mass.: Clark University Press.

Murphy, G. and Murphy, L. B. (1931). *Experimental Social Psychology*. New York: Harper.

Murphy, L. B. and Murphy, G. (1935). The influence of social situations upon the behavior of children. In C. Murchison (ed.), *Handbook of Social Psychology*, pp. 1034–96. Worcester, Mass.: Clark University Press.

Newcomb, T. M. (1950). *Social Psychology*. New York: Holt.

Nisbett, R. E. and Wilson, T. D. (1977). Telling more than we can know: verbal reports on mental processes. *Psychological Review*, 84, 231–59.

Nye, R. A. (1975). *The Origins of Crowd Psychology: Gustave Le Bon and the crisis of mass democracy in the Third Republic*. London: Sage.

O'Donnell, J. M. (1979). The crisis of experimentation in the 1920s: E. G. Boring and his uses of history. *American Psychologist*, 34, 289–95.

O'Donnell, J. M. (1985). *The Origins of Behaviorism: American psychology 1870–1920*. New York: Columbia University Press.

O'Neil, W. M. (1982). *The Beginnings of Modern Psychology*. Sussex: Harvester Press.

Park, R. E. (1972). *The Crowd and the Public and Other Essays*. Chicago: University of Chicago Press.

Patnoe, S. (1988). *A Narrative History of Experimental Social Psychology: the Lewin tradition*. New York: Springer-Verlag.

Perry, R. B. (1935). *The Thought and Character of William James*, 2 vols. Boston: Little, Brown.

Plath, O. E. (1935). Insect societies. In C. Murchison (ed.), *Handbook of Social Psychology*, pp. 83–141. Worcester, Mass.: Clark University Press.

Reck, A. J. (ed.) (1964). *Selected Writings: George Herbert Mead*. Chicago: University of Chicago Press.

Riesman, D. (1950). *The Lonely Crowd: a study of the changing American character*. New Haven: Yale University Press.

Ring, K. (1967). Experimental social psychology: some sober questions about some frivolous values. *Journal of Experimental Social Psychology*, 3, 113–23.

Ringer, F. K. (1969). *The Decline of the German Mandarins: the German academic community, 1890–1933*. Cambridge, Mass.: Harvard University Press.

Rock, P. (1979). *The Making of Symbolic Interactionism*. London: Macmillan.

Rommetveit, R. (1974). *On Message Structure*. London: Wiley.

Rosenberg, M. and Turner, R. H. (eds) (1981). *Social Psychology: sociological perspectives*. New York: Basic Books.

Rosenberg, M. J., Hovland, C. I., McGuire, W. J., Abelson, R. P. and Brehm, J. W. (eds) (1960). *Attitude Organization and Change: an analysis of consistency among attitude components*. New Haven: Yale University Press.

Ross, E. A. (1908). *Social Psychology: an outline and source book*. New York: Macmillan.

Rudmin, F., Trimpop, R. M., Kryl, I.-P. and Boski, P. (1987). Gustav Ichheiser in the history of social psychology: an early phenomenology of social attribution. *British Journal of Social Psychology*, 26, 165–80.

Sahakian, W. S. (1974). *Systematic Social Psychology*. New York: Chandler.

Samelson, F. (1974). History, origin myth and ideology: 'discovery of social psychology'. *Journal for the Theory of Social Behaviour*, 4(2), 217–31.

Schank, R. and Abelson, R. (1977). *Scripts, Plans, Goals and Understanding: an inquiry into human knowledge structures*. Hillsdale, NJ: Lawrence Erlbaum.

Schjelderup-Ebbe, T. (1935). Social behaviour of birds. In C. Murchison (ed.), *Handbook of Social Psychology*, pp. 947–72. Worcester, Mass.: Clark University Press.

Shelford, V. E. (1935). The physical environment. In C. Murchison (ed.), *Handbook of Social Psychology*, pp. 567–95. Worcester, Mass.: Clark University Press.

Shibutani, T. (ed.) (1970). *Human Nature and Collective Behavior: papers in honor of Herbert Blumer*. Englewood Cliffs, NJ: Prentice-Hall.

Simpson, R. (1983). *How the PhD Came to Britain: a century of struggle for postgraduate education*. Guildford: The Society for Research into Higher Education.

Skinner, B. F. (1957). *Verbal Behavior*. New York: Appleton-Century-Crofts.

Skinner, B. F. (1964). Behaviorism at fifty. In T. W. Wann (ed.), *Behaviorism and Phenomenology: contrasting bases for modern psychology*. Chicago: University of Chicago Press.

Smith, A. (1759). *The Theory of Moral Sentiments*. London and Edinburgh. Reprinted 1976 by Oxford University Press, edited by D. D. Raphael and A. L. Macfie.

Smith, R. (1988). Does the history of psychology have a subject? *History of the Human Sciences*, 1(2), 147–77.

Sokal, M. M. (1981). *An Education in Psychology: James McKeen Cattell's Journal and Letters from Germany and England: 1880–1888*. Cambridge, Mass.: MIT Press.

Stagner, R. (1937). *Psychology of Personality*. New York: McGraw-Hill.

Stouffer, S. A., Guttman, L., Suchman, E. A., Lazarsfeld, P. F., Star, S. A. and Clausen, J. A. (eds) (1950). *Measurement and Prediction*. Studies in Social Psychology in World War II, vol. 4. Princeton, NJ: Princeton University Press.

Stouffer, S. A., Lumsdaine, A. A., Lumsdaine, M. H., Williams, R. M., Smith, M. B., Janis, I. L., Star, S. A. and Cottrell, I. S. (eds) (1949). *The American Soldier: combat and its aftermath*. Studies in Social Psychology in World War II, vol. 2. Princeton, NJ: Princeton University Press.

Stouffer, S. A., Suchman, E. A., De Vinney, L. C., Star, S. A. and Williams, R. M. (eds) (1949). *The American Soldier: adjustment during army life*. Studies in Social Psychology in World War II, vol. 1. Princeton, NJ: Princeton University Press.

Strauss, A. (ed.) (1956). *George Herbert Mead on Social Psychology*. Selected papers edited with an introduction by Anselm Strauss. Chicago: University of Chicago Press.

Swanson, G. E. (1961). Mead and Freud: their relevance for social psychology. *Sociometry*, 24, 319–39.

Tawney, R. H. (1926). *Religion and the Rise of Capitalism*. London: Penguin.

Thomas, W. I. and Znaniecki, F. (1918–20). *The Polish Peasant in Europe and America*, 5 vols. Boston: Badger.

Turner, R. and Killian, L. (1957). *Collective Behavior*. Englewood Cliffs, NJ: Prentice-Hall.

Vygotsky, L. S. and Luria, A. R. (1930). *Etiudy po istorii povendeniia: Obez'ian, primitiv, rebenok*. Moscow (Russian original). Translated into English as A. R. Luria and L. S. Vygotsky, *Ape, Primitive Man and Child: essays in the history of behaviour*. Sussex: Harvester/Wheatsheaf, 1992.

Wallis, W. D. (1935). Social history of the white man. In C. Murchison (ed.), *Handbook of Social Psychology*, pp. 309–60. Worcester, Mass.: Clark University Press.

Watson, J. B. (1909). The behavior of noddy and sooty terns. *Carnegie Institution Publications*, 103, 187–255.

Watson, J. B. (1913). Psychology as a behaviorist views it. *Psychological Review*, 20, 158–77.

Watson, J. B. (1916). The place of the conditioned reflex in psychology. *Psychological Review*, 23, 89–117.

Watson, J. B. (1919). *Psychology from the Standpoint of a Behaviorist*. Philadelphia: Lippincott.

Watson, J. B. (1936). Watson. In C. Murchison (ed.), *A History of Psychology through Autobiography*. Worcester, Mass.: Clark University Press.

Watson, J. B. and Rayner, R. (1920). Conditional emotional reactions. *Journal of Experimental Psychology*, 3, 1–14.

Weber, M. (1922). *The Protestant Ethic and the Spirit of Capitalism*. London: George Allen and Unwin, English edn, 1930.

Wells, F. L. (1935). Social maladjustments: adaptive regression. In C. Murchison (ed.), *Handbook of Social Psychology*, pp. 845–915. Worcester, Mass.: Clark University Press.

Willoughby, R. R. (1935). Magic and cognate phenomena: an hypothesis. In C. Murchison (ed.), *Handbook of Social Psychology*, pp. 461–519. Worcester, Mass.: Clark University Press.

Wissler, C. (1935a). Material culture. In C. Murchison (ed.), *Handbook of Social Psychology*, pp. 520–64. Worcester, Mass.: Clark University Press.

Wissler, C. (1935b). Social history of the red man. In C. Murchison (ed.), *Handbook of Social Psychology*, pp. 268–308. Worcester, Mass.: Clark University Press.

Wrong, D. (1961). The oversocialized conception of man in modern sociology. *American Sociological Review*, 26, 183–93.

Wundt, W. (1862). *Beiträge sur Theorie der Sinneswahrnehmung*. Leipzig: Winter.

Wundt, W. (1873–4). *Grundzüge der physiologischen Psychologie*, 2 vols. Leipzig: Englemann.

Wundt, W. (1900–20). *Völkerpsychologie: eine Untersuchung der Entwicklungsgesetze von Sprache, Mythus and Sitte*, 10 vols. Leipzig: Englemann.

Wundt, W. (1916). *Elements of Folk Psychology: outlines of a psychological history of the development of mankind*. London: George Allen and Unwin (German original 1912).

Wundt, W. (1920). *Erlebtes und Erkanntes*. Stuttgart: Kröner.

Wundt, W. (1973). *The Language of Gestures*. The Hague: Mouton.

Yerkes, R. M. and Yerkes, A. W. (1935). Social behavior in infrahuman primates. In C. Murchison (ed.), *Handbook of Social Psychology*, pp. 973–1033. Worcester, Mass.: Clark University Press.

Name Index

Subject Index

Printed in the United Kingdom
by Lightning Source UK Ltd.
134565UK00003B/34/A